P

PERSONAL SYNTHESIS

A complete guide to personal knowledge

Nash Popovic, Ph.D.

PWBC, London

Published in 2005 by PWBC

Personal Well-Being Centre,
28 Hans Place, London SW1X 0JY
tel. 020 75844209   e-mail: info@personalsynthesis.org

ISBN 0-9548387-6-9

Cover Design: Richard Owen
Proofreading: Andy Streat

Printed in Great Britain by Stephen Austin, Hertford

CONTENTS

ACKNOWLEDGEMENTS

The author and the publisher gratefully acknowledge permission to reprint the following poems in this book:

Anvil Press Ltd for '6 A.M. Thoughts' taken from *Devices and Desires: New and Selected Poems 1967-1987* by Dick Davis (Anvil Press Poetry, 1989)

The author for 'The Promised Garden', by Theo Dorgan from *The Ordinary House of Love*

Carcanet publishers, for 'Don't Be Literary, Darling' by Sasha Moorsom, from *Your Head in Mine* (1994)

INTRODUCTION

What is Personal Synthesis?

The amount of knowledge we possess is amazing. You may know about evolution and creation, who invented the light bulb or won at Waterloo, what the capital of Norway is, how to use a computer and drive a car... but how much do you know about yourself and those areas of life that constitute your everyday experience? This personal knowledge is the subject of Personal Synthesis. It is not about the world out there, but about us. It involves understanding and skills related to issues such as handling emotions, developing creativity, making decisions (and putting them into practice), dealing with anxiety, coping with problems, communicating effectively, developing constructive relationships and many more. This book provides, in one place, essential (practical and theoretical) knowledge of all the basic areas of human life. They are also organised in a two-dimensional map that shows the relations and connections between them, hence synthesis.

Why Personal Synthesis?

We are all aware that we live in a time of rapid and dramatic changes. As one historian put it, this is a period that 'breaks the old cycles and the traditional customs of man'[1]. In the past, society played a much greater role in the lives of individuals. Almost every aspect of daily existence was determined by political and social systems, the church, extended family, even neighbours. Life then was more restrictive, less tolerant towards digressions and differences, and often wrong and unfair (at least towards some of its members). Yet, such a situation created a sense of security and predictability. Nowadays, the complex nature of our society, the greater cultural diversity and pluralism of values have increased choice and allowed more freedom, but it has also increased personal responsibility, insecurity, anxiety and confusion.

A recent survey[2] over decades shows that although we have never had it better, we seem to be less happy. According to the World Health Organization, depression is set to become the world's most pervasive serious illness by the year 2020 (more widespread than heart disease and cancer). One in four visits to GPs in Britain is already due to some psychologically related problem (the most frequent reason, after flu and cold). Nearly a quarter of a million people try to kill themselves every year in the UK[3] alone. Alcohol and drug abuse, delinquency and violence are also on the increase.

This is not to say that we should try to go back and embrace outdated ideologies and social systems. But, if we wish to move forward, personal knowledge may help us avoid some of the pitfalls on that journey. And this is not the only reason why it can be valuable. Attributes like class, gender, nationality, cultural or religious backgrounds, affluence and status that used to be decisive regarding employment, relationships and other aspects of life, are now losing their significance (rightly so), while personal qualities are becoming more important. We have to rely on ourselves more than ever, so paying attention to our personal development is not a luxury any more, but a necessity.

Despite all that, it is still hard to know where and how to go about it. Probably the most frequent sentence that I have heard working as a counsellor is "If I'd only known". Our civilisation, focused mainly on the external world, has substantially increased its control and power over the environment (for better or for worse). Much less is done regarding self-knowledge and self-power. Let me try to clarify what I mean.

Numerous pieces of research[4] conclude that personal and psychological development is much more important to successful life than academic achievement, for example. Yet, in mainstream education there are plenty of opportunities to learn about mathematics, literature, geography, science, history, art and other subjects, but little chance to learn about those things that really matter in life – about ourselves and the ways we can experience and relate to the world around us.

Social institutions (media, political or religious organisations etc.) often seem to have their own agenda, so it is not surprising that their attempts to 'educate' us about how to lead our lives are usually met with suspicion.

Speaking to friends or relatives about personal matters, although good in its own right, can be sometimes more confusing than helpful. We often find in these situations that some of them are not interested and are content to follow what the majority do without much reflection, while others come out with very different, sometimes contradictory suggestions or claims.

It is not surprising that counselling is becoming more and more popular, but the majority of counsellors nowadays are committed to being non-committal, 'passive' listeners, which is of limited value. A lot of people find that this is simply not enough.

This is why there are an ever increasing number of self-help books around. However, wading through innumerable titles to find good ones can be wearisome indeed. Even when we find them, they often contain only a few original and useful sentences. No doubt, many of these books can make us feel temporarily better, but that feeling usually quickly wears off and we are back to square one. Even materials that have a real practical value usually deal with one area of life, so it is like patching up one hole, while others are opening up. And who has time to read a book or two for every important area of life?

This book is an attempt to overcome this problem and have it all in one place. To achieve that, all the materials are written in a 'no frills' way. No stories, anecdotes, counselling practice examples, and other gimmicks. Admittedly, it may be easier to read through a book garnished with such additives, but this is not very helpful. How many times did you enjoy reading a self-help book, but when you tried to apply its wisdom you couldn't remember much or didn't know what to do? The materials that really help us learn something practical – those that make a real difference – are usually clear and straightforward (computer or car manuals that are full of stories may be a nice read, but wouldn't be taken seriously by those who really want to learn about cars or computers). Thus, each area in this book is presented in a concise and clear way, so that you can go through, remember its content and return to it without wasting much time. In other words, only essence is given. Such a style also makes the materials more universal, which means that they can be a valuable tool irrespective of one's circumstances and personality.

The aim of the book

The main purpose of this book is to help you be more in charge of your life. Knowledge is power, and personal knowledge leads to personal empowerment. This book does not preach nor does it try to sell a particular formula (such as 'all you need to do is exercise more, or slow down, or cry (laugh, love) more, or recognise that your partner is from a different planet...'). No book can tell you what is good and what is bad for you. There is not a simple magic formula that works for everybody in every situation. What a book like this can do, though, is to assist you in making informed choices for yourself and putting them into practice. So, the aim is not to solve your potential or existing problems, but to empower you to face and deal with life challenges on your own. I do not claim that it can automatically make you eternally happy, successful, rich, or a great lover. You will still be facing ups and downs, frustrations and challenges. However, you will be able to take the place at the helm of your boat and direct it. Personal knowledge can be considered a solid platform that can give you confidence to enter stormy waters.

Moreover, embarking on this journey can make life more interesting – exploring that very complex web of human life has many surprises. It is like having a town map, which makes it easier to get where you want to go and see what you would otherwise miss. This does not mean that a map is always necessary. Sometimes it is more fun just to wander around. But knowing that you won't get lost can give you the confidence to do so.

How to use the book

The book can be used in several ways. The recommended way is to go systematically through each area in the suggested order. The reason for this is that all of the areas are interrelated (they affect each other), and also some of them rely on others. This does not imply just reading through the book from cover to cover. It is important to remain with one area as long as it is necessary, before moving to another. Such a systematic approach would enable a fully rounded development.

However, if you don't have time or patience to go through it systematically, or if you have a burning issue that needs to be attended to immediately, you can also start from an area that you are particularly interested in or that is closely related to your problem, and then perhaps expand your reading to surrounding and cross-referenced areas.

You may wonder for how long to remain with one area. Of course, perfecting your knowledge and skills related to any of them can take an entire lifetime; the materials here should be taken only as a foundation, a starting point. I suggest focusing on an area until you develop some confidence and mastery so that you can continue on your own. It is like learning to swim or drive: at one point you need to decide when you can do it without an external support. On average, it should not take more than a week, in many cases less, depending on how much time you can dedicate to your personal development. What is important to remember is that these materials are only a means to an end. And the end is to be fully in charge of your life.

A MAP OF HUMAN LIFE

Human life is very complicated and diverse. So, how can a model that may be of practical use to everyone be created? Obviously, this complexity needs to be somehow simplified without losing its essential elements. One way of doing so is to locate common denominators of our experience, underlying building blocks that life events are made of (such as feelings, reasoning, confidence, experience, motivation, basic types of relationships etc.). This has several advantages.

First of all, there is a limited number of such basic areas (whereas there is an unlimited number of intricate and unique life situations), so it is manageable. Also, we cannot deal successfully with complex issues if their underlying components are not addressed. Take, for example, smoking. Developing this habit depends on many factors such as relation to pleasure, susceptibility to influence, stability, self-discipline, gratification and so on. If they are not addressed, it is unlikely that you can be in control of smoking. And finally, these basic areas enable endless combinations that can be applied in any situation, so everybody can use them in a way that fits his or her personality and circumstances.

The following criteria are used to locate these basic areas:
• The areas included in the model are irreducible. This means that they cannot be a part of, or be identified with other areas or their combinations (without losing their essential qualities). For example, anger or joy can be reduced to emotions so they are not included as discrete areas (although they are, of course, addressed within other areas). On the other hand, pleasure cannot be, so it is included as a separate one. This criterion is important because it prevents any overlap or repetition.
• All these areas are universal and play a role in our lives regardless of cultural background, beliefs, inclinations or personal qualities, so they are relevant to everybody. This also means that they are 'timeless', therefore pertinent to any future that may come.

- The areas are also transferable, meaning that the relevant knowledge and skills are not specific, but can be applied in a wide range of situations.
- All of them together should cover the totality of human experience. In other words, no gaps are left. This is vital because they are connected and support each other.

The above criteria, however, are not sufficient on their own to demarcate the areas of human life with typically fuzzy boundaries. The 'bottom-up' approach needs to be combined with the 'top-down' approach. This means that each area must also have its place within an overall structure, map of the territory. The following explanation of how such a map can be created may seem in some places a bit complicated, but it is worth persisting with it, because understanding the map will enable you to be more creative in using it and discover connections that are meaningful for you.

The map design starts with the fundamental dimensions of human life. They consist of two modes and two domains. The two basic modes that define us as human beings are *existence* and *agency*: in other words you *are* (you exist) and you *do* (your are able to choose and act). These two modes are applied in the two general domains: *internal* and *external*. Internal domain includes areas that focus around some aspects of yourself, such as thinking, feelings, desires, past experiences and so on, while external domain includes areas directed towards the world and others (expectations, achievements, communicating, relationships etc.) [5]. Although, of course, these domains influence and mould each other, it is of great practical importance to make a distinction between them. For example, if you are afraid, you can respond to the *situation* that has caused the fear (you can run away, fight, freeze, etc.), or you can respond to the *internal state*, fear itself (you can suppress, accept, fight, project, or ignore it). The first type of responses would belong to the external domain, the second to the internal. In fact, many psychological problems arise because the boundary between internal and external is blurred.

These dimensions provide the coordinates for the map:

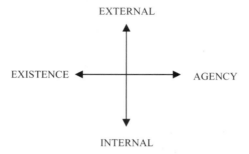

Figure 1

The diagrams below show the space that these dimensions cover:

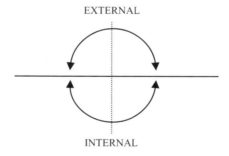

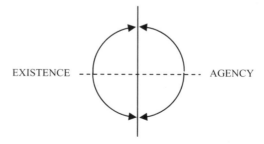

Figure 2

So, we can see that the modes and domains overlap. Put together, they can be presented in the following way:

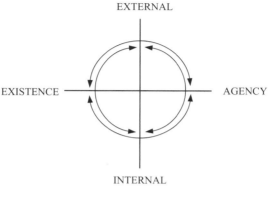

Figure 3

Categories

The areas that are mentioned above cluster around these coordinates and form four categories: *Personal* category, *Being* category, *Doing* category, and *Social* category[6]. They are represented in this diagram:

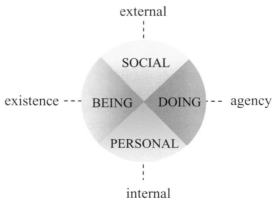

Figure 4

The Personal category, at the bottom of the diagram, is the foundational or root category. This is because the other categories rely to some extent on it. The personal category includes areas that relate to ourselves (such as self-awareness, emotions, reasoning etc.).

The Being and Doing categories are the side categories, and they complement each other. The Being category involves the ways we *are* in the world and the ways we perceive the world. The Doing category is concerned with choice and deliberate actions. The terms *being* and *doing* are close to the more commonly used terms *passive* (or receptive) and *active*. They are preferred, however, because 'active' and 'passive' are value-laden and can be misleading. *Being* here means that the person is affected, while *Doing* means that the person affects. So, the *Being* category can include an activity if it is a re-action (an incentive comes from the outside), and the *Doing* category can include inactivity if it is the result of one's choice (an incentive comes, as it were, from the inside).

The Social category, at the top of the diagram, is mainly concerned with the interaction with others. It depends to some extent on the other categories and also overarches them.

Let's see how these categories relate to the modes and domains. Figure 5 (on the following page) shows that the Internal domain includes the Personal category and one side of the Being and Doing categories; the External domain includes the Social category and the other side of the Being and Doing categories; the Existence mode includes the Being category and one side of the Personal and Social categories; and the Agency mode includes the Doing category and the other side of the Personal and Social categories. So, the modes and domains overlap. The Personal category, for example, belongs to the internal domain, but its one side also belongs to the Existence mode, while the other belongs to the Agency mode.

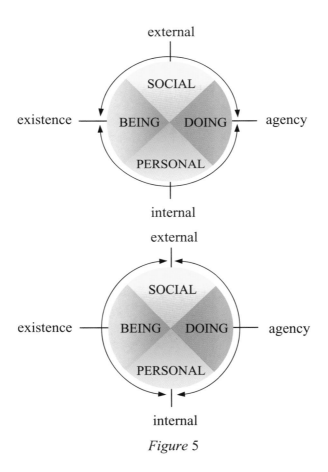

Figure 5

Groups

Each category consists of four groups, which makes sixteen groups (see figure 6). The groups relate to each other in the same way as the categories. The root group of each category is always near the centre of the model. In the Doing category, for example, it is the Choice group. Each category also has two side groups (relative to the root group) that belong to either different modes or different domains. The side groups in our example are the Directive group and Problem group[7]. The former belongs to the Internal domain, while the latter belongs to the External domain. The groups positioned at the corners are called the top groups[8]. In the Doing category, it is the Activity group. They have an overarching role, but rely on certain elements from other groups in the same category.

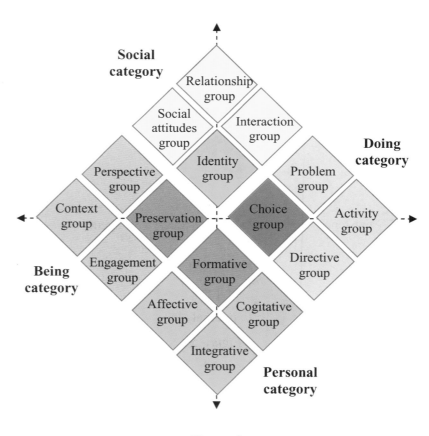

Figure 6

Areas

Each of these groups consists of four areas, which makes 64 areas in total. They are all presented in the final model:

Everything you experience and do is a combination of some of these areas. They relate to each other within a group as the groups relate to each other within a category and as the categories relate within the whole model. The root area of a group is the one nearest to the centre of the model. It usually directly affects the other areas in that group (*Learning, Courage, Strategy, Relationship dynamic* are a few examples of root areas). Two side areas (relative to the root area) are usually counterparts, different poles of the central theme of the group (for example, *Freedom* and *Responsibility* or *Creative thinking* and *Reasoning*). The final area in a group (opposite to the root area) is called the top area. It is usually based on and overarches the other areas in the group (*Self-valuation, Tolerance, Control, Intimate relationship,* are some of them).

The position of each area in the model is determined, however, not only by their place in a group and category, but also by modes and domains they belong to (see figure 1). For example, the area *Relating to oneself* belongs to the internal domain and the existence mode, while *Personal Change* (from the same group) belongs to the same domain, but the agency mode. *Protection* in the Social category belongs to the external domain and existence mode, while *Desires* in the Active category belongs to the internal domain and agency mode. A more detailed description of each group and area is provided in the rest of the book, which should clarify further their positions.

It needs to be pointed out, though, that although each area has its unique position and function, this is not to say that their characteristics are sharply divided. Indeed, the seed of an opposite domain or mode seems to be present in almost every area or group. A model that does not allow for any exceptions would be too mechanical to reflect the true nature of its subject. So, the one here is based on the tendencies with typically fuzzy boundaries rather than on a binary, black and white logic.

You may have noticed that some areas are positioned on the axes of the map. These areas have properties of either both modes or both domains. For example, in the Personal category *Self-awareness*, *Self-valuation*, *Harmonisation* and *Development* are positioned on the Internal axis and encompass both the Existence and Agency mode. Let's look closely why this is the case:

Self-awareness. We are inevitably aware of ourselves to some extent, but to interpret and understand all these processes within our mind, some effort and willingness is needed. Therefore, both the Existence mode and the Agency mode play a role in this area.

Self-valuation (which includes self-respect and self-esteem) depends on both relation to one's existence and relation to one's agency (which will be elaborated within this area).

Harmonisation, which is mainly concerned with resolution of inner conflicts, is first of all about harmonising or balancing two basic modes, existence and agency, in its various forms (security and freedom, feelings and intellect, passivity and activity, etc.)

Development includes a natural process (e.g. puberty) but it also depends on a conscious directing and some effort, which requires one's agency.

The Rings

The map also consists of two rings: the inner and outer (separated by a dotted line and darker shades of colour in the diagram). The four groups in the inner ring are those positioned around the centre of the map, while the areas that comprise the outer ring are those on the periphery of the map. The areas in the inner ring predominantly relate to the self-concept, while the outer ring is predominantly concerned with the interaction with a larger framework within which we are situated – our reality, or the world-concept. The psychologist Rogers defines a self-concept as 'an organised configuration of perceptions of the self which are admissible to awareness. It is composed of such elements as the perception of one's characteristics and abilities; the precepts and concepts of the self in relation to others and to the environment; the value qualities which are perceived as associated with experiences and objects; and goals and ideals which are perceived as having positive or negative valence.'[9] We can see that each element mentioned by Rogers corresponds to qualities associated with the Personal category, Social category, Being category and Doing category, respectively[10]. All of these categories are, of course, represented in the inner ring. The number of groups in the inner ring is smaller, but they underlie the ones in the outer ring. Each of them (as already mentioned) is also the foundational groups for their respective categories.

This is all that is necessary to know about the map (however, it contains many surprises, I am still learning from it). There are several ways that the map can be used. First of all, it provides an overall view and indicates the relationships and dynamics between the areas (which can be as important as the areas themselves). It may help in detecting the cause of one's problem, which can usually be traced by going back towards the centre of the model. Say you lack energy (let's assume that you have a check-up and you are physically O.K.). Of course, it makes sense to look first at the area *Energy*. However, if this doesn't help, you can move to the root area of that group, which is *Motivation,* and further down the line consider the areas *Decisions* and *Meaning* (on which your motivation may depend). The other way of utilising the map is by paying attention to the other areas in the group, and how the area of your concern is connected to them. In the above example, perhaps the balance is what is needed, so it may be worthwhile considering the area *Organisation* (which includes topics such as planning and time use) that is the counterpart to *Energy.* The map can also be used in a creative way – play with it, let intuition take over and see where you will end up. Every person and every situation is to some extent unique, so you can be your best guide.

Before we move on, I would like to address one possible concern. The map may look suspiciously orderly. After all, human life seems much more messy and irregular. Although this is true, it is conceivable that behind the seeming disorderliness there is a certain order on a basic level (as the complexity and variety of the whole biological world is based on 64 combinations of gene sequences[11]). Of course, genes are 'solid' while these areas are not, but as the psychologist Shotter points out, 'just because, in dealing with entities such as "intentions", "beliefs", and "motives", we are dealing with quality without substance, it does not mean to say that great orderliness is not possible.'[12]

Saying that, we still need to recognise that human life is indeed multidimensional and appears much more complex, fuzzy, and disorderly than the map presents it. The model, in any way, is not an attempt to describe reality as it is, but is a representation, a chart – created for a practical, rather than a descriptive purpose. And, like any other map (that is necessarily a simplification of what it represents) it can still have great value as a tool that expresses the totality of human experience in a form convenient for its purpose.

The four main dimensions can be considered the axes of a coordinate system or cardinal points that provide orientation in this field. The equal 'size' of each category (the same number of areas in each) reflects the equal importance and value that they have. The complexity of life derives from combinations of many of these areas in real situations.

The areas in the linear order

A two dimensional map can be very useful, but if we want to approach personal development systematically, it is important to organise the areas in successive order (one after another). Let's see how such an order can be attained from the map (this part does not have a bearing on the rest of the book, so if you are not interested in the explanation, you can skip it).

The first category in the model to be addressed is the Personal category. This is because the areas that belong to this category, such as self-awareness, reasoning, emotions, or self-discipline, are the basis for the rest of the model. The Being category comes before the Doing category because it involves the ways we perceive the world, which is normally prior to agency and deliberate action. The last category to be addressed is the Social category, because it is the most complex, and relies to some extent on other categories.

The first group to be addressed within each category is the foundational group (in the centre of the model). In regard to side groups, a group that belongs to the Internal domain precedes a group that belongs to the External domain, and a group that belongs to the Existence mode precede a group that belongs to the Agency mode. The last groups to be addressed in each category are the top groups (placed in the corners of the model).

The first area addressed within each group is the root or foundational area of that group (always the one nearest to the centre of the map). It is followed by side areas. As above, if they belong to different modes or domains, the one belonging to the Internal domain precedes the one belonging to the External domain, and the one belonging to the Existence mode precedes the one that belongs to the Agency mode. This leaves the order within the eight pairs of side areas that are part of the same mode or domain undetermined. Which area comes first within these pairs is based on common sense (e.g. *Awareness of others* that includes listening and empathy seems natural to precede *Communicating*). The last area to be presented within a group is the top area (positioned opposite to the root area).

This order does not imply that an area is more important than any other. It only indicates that some of them should be approached prior to the others from the same group or category. For example, *Self-valuation* depends to some extent on *Self-awareness,* and for that reason it makes sense to deal with it after.

The list below has all the categories, groups and areas presented in a linear form.

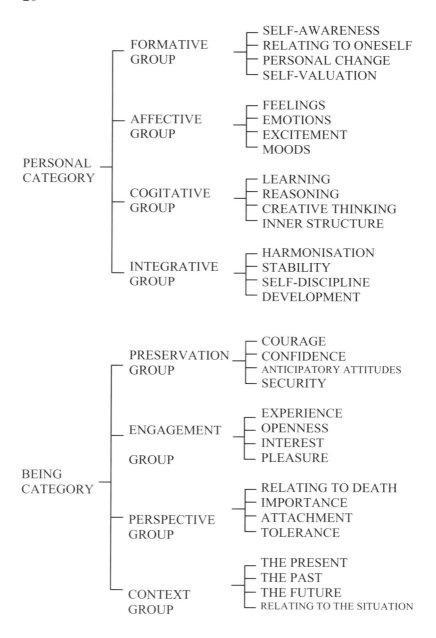

PERSONAL CATEGORY

FORMATIVE GROUP
- SELF-AWARENESS
- RELATING TO ONESELF
- PERSONAL CHANGE
- SELF-VALUATION

AFFECTIVE GROUP
- FEELINGS
- EMOTIONS
- EXCITEMENT
- MOODS

COGITATIVE GROUP
- LEARNING
- REASONING
- CREATIVE THINKING
- INNER STRUCTURE

INTEGRATIVE GROUP
- HARMONISATION
- STABILITY
- SELF-DISCIPLINE
- DEVELOPMENT

BEING CATEGORY

PRESERVATION GROUP
- COURAGE
- CONFIDENCE
- ANTICIPATORY ATTITUDES
- SECURITY

ENGAGEMENT GROUP
- EXPERIENCE
- OPENNESS
- INTEREST
- PLEASURE

PERSPECTIVE GROUP
- RELATING TO DEATH
- IMPORTANCE
- ATTACHMENT
- TOLERANCE

CONTEXT GROUP
- THE PRESENT
- THE PAST
- THE FUTURE
- RELATING TO THE SITUATION

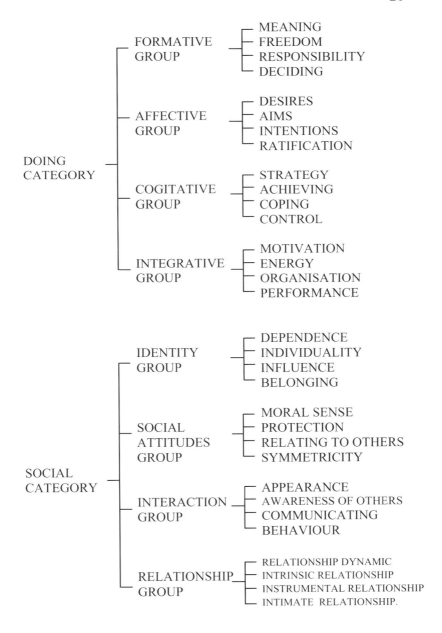

THE MATERIALS

Let's now look at how the materials for these areas are structured. Each of them is approached on the three levels: theoretical, practical and reflective (they reflect the modes of learning as described in the *Learning* area[13]).

The theoretical level consists of relevant information drawn from disciplines such as psychology, psychotherapy, philosophy, and (to a lesser extent) sociology and anthropology. The materials are intended to be comprehensive and non-biased as much as possible. They are composed in such a way that you can apply them in everyday life. Information that has mainly academic value is not included. The aim is not to go into theoretical details, but to provide a basis from which you can take it further in a direction of your choice. For example, in the area *Emotions*, rather than focusing on the neuro-physiological basis or psychological models of emotions, various ways of self-regulating emotions are examined (suppression, reinforcement, transformation, discharge, displacement and diffusion). Wherever it is relevant, materials address a variety of possibilities and their short term and long-term consequences. This includes examining some undesirable aspects of an area and drawing attention to possible difficulties in developing desirable aspects or attitudes. This is important because we can easily become disappointed and discouraged when we decide to put some effort into improving ourselves if we are not aware or prepared for some temporary drawbacks that it may bring. Such an approach also enables better understanding and control of our actions and motives and of the motives and actions of others. Moreover, if the whole spectrum of possibilities is presented, everybody will be in a position to find something that will facilitate herself or himself in achieving a right balance (those who lack self-confidence, as well as those who are overconfident, for example).

The reflective level. There are some aspects of human life that do not have universal answers. The choice will always depend to some extent on personal experience. So, we need to engage in our own search and examine our underlying assumptions. Considering issues raised on this level can help you clarify your views and values. Even if you can't be bothered to do so, and are satisfied with existing views without any reflection, you will at least become aware that this is what your choice is.

The practical level consists of exercises that can increase awareness, the quality of experience and mastery of an area. Group exercises are avoided because they are not practical (it is not always easy to find somebody who will be willing to participate). Individual exercises, on the other hand, can be tried in privacy and repeated whenever needed. Interpersonal skills that aim to produce a certain effect on others are also largely avoided. Those skills have a limited value and short life-span, because they are usually used for instrumental reasons (bordering on manipulation) and because, once they are well known, they are no longer effective. For example, one 'manual' suggests 'charm is a legitimate weapon... you don't have to like dogs, to ask kindly after Miss Jones's beastly little teeth-on-legs...'[14] If Miss Jones has also read the book, the technique would not have the desired effect (or would even have the opposite one). This does not of course invalidate the importance of a *genuine* interest in others, but not as a part of some routine or technique. An exercise in this area will intend to help you develop a real interest in others (if you so desire) not just the appearance of an interest.

All the exercises are tested and are safe. I would suggest that you try them all, especially those that trigger some resistance. This is because the resistance usually indicates that you are stuck and rigid in that area, and doing the exercise may help you to get unstuck or achieve a greater flexibility and fluidity. However, whether you will continue practicing them or not should depend on how useful they are for you. Don't bother with those that don't work, but you can modify some exercises to make them more productive or even create different ones. This is about you, not a correct procedure.

Recommended materials include some relevant theoretical and practical texts and also the work of fiction, if you want to explore further any particular area. They do not include technical or professional materials but accessible ones. In order to save space, only authors and titles are indicated. Full references can be found in the bibliography. Of course, these materials are only suggestions, you may find other materials that may be more up to date or resonate with you better.

A final note before we turn to the areas: it does not seem that gender difference affects any of them, so personal pronouns that indicate gender are used alternately from area to area. This is considered the most practical way.

I AM NOT I

I am not I.
            I am this one
Walking beside me whom I do not see,
Whom at times I manage to visit,
And at other times I forget.
The one who remains silent when I talk,
The one who forgives, sweet, when I hate,
The one who takes a walk when I am indoors,
The one who will remain standing when I die.

Juan Ramón Jiménez

FORMATIVE GROUP

This is the first group in the model, and the root group of the Personal category (see the map on p13). It consists of four areas that define the way we perceive and interact with ourselves. Let's first see what their functions are and how they relate to each other.

Self-awareness is the root area of this group because it influences all the other areas. It refers to our ability to perceive directly our inner world: thoughts, feelings, desires, motives and in some instances their connections and causes. Self-awareness is the receptive component, which does not mean that it is passive. Although we are aware of some inner processes automatically, developing self-awareness also requires a willingness, determination and effort. So (as indicated by its position in the map) it encompasses both, the *existence* and *agency* modes.

Relating to oneself is the re-active component of the group and belongs to the *existence mode*. It addresses the two basic attitudes that we can have towards ourselves, *rejection* and *acceptance*, and also the related feelings of guilt and shame.

Personal change is the pro-active component, which is why it belongs to the *agency mode*. Personal change is the counterpart to the above area. It refers to our ability to deliberately alter or modify some aspects of our own personality, such as behaviour, attitudes, habits and so forth.

Self-valuation[15] represents the valuative component. It is the final area in this group because it relies to some extent on the other areas. Its position in the model indicates that, as *Self-awareness*, it includes both modes. The aspect related to the *existence mode* is identified with self-respect and refers to recognition of the innate value and worth of being a person. The one related to the *agency mode* is identified with self-esteem that depends on our assessments or judgments (of our competence, abilities, achievements, etc). Self-esteem can also be considered contextual, because it is formed to a large extent through interaction with the environment, especially others.

01. SELF-AWARENESS

Turn inward for your voyage! For all your arts you will not find the Stone in foreign parts.

Angelus Silesius

The reason why we often don't fully understand ourselves is several obstacles to self-awareness. What they are, and some methods to overcome them are suggested below.

THEORETICAL LEVEL

Self-ignorance. By ignoring our inner processes we may temporarily avoid unpleasant feelings or postpone facing some difficult issues, but the ignored will not disappear; in fact, in the long run its influence may increase. Self-awareness may require an effort, but it can be beneficial in many ways. The better you know yourself, the more you will be in charge. Knowing yourself can also help you form realistic expectations, which, among other benefits, minimises disappointments. Finally, an inner world can be as rich and complex as the external one, so a life without self-awareness is impoverished.

This is not to say, however, that you should focus only on yourself and neglect the world around. Perception of the external reality reflects the inner one, and the other way around. So, looking outside may help you learn about yourself, and looking inside can contribute to better understanding of the outside world. For example, the way you perceive and describe a scene, event or person is always to some extent unique, so it can reveal something about yourself. Conversely, self-knowledge can help you understand others better, recognise if your perception is distorted and judge a situation more accurately.

Self-deceit often includes self-ignorance, but adds to it a false or unrealistic self-image. It is usually employed to avoid awareness of those aspects of oneself that are not acceptable or desirable in order to preserve or enhance self-esteem. Self-deceit can make you feel temporarily better, but in time, discrepancies between the real person and a created image accumulate, which eventually leads either to rejecting reality, or to being forced to renounce the idealised self and face the real one. Both outcomes can have unpleasant consequences. To avoid self-deceit it is necessary to be sincere with oneself even if it is uncomfortable. Consider, for example, a person who believes that he wants to study medicine to help others, but is in fact driven by social insecurity and desire for prestige. Although admitting this may be hard, it would enable him to deal adequately with underlying drives and make a right career move.

Obscurity refers to those mental processes and motives that we are not fully aware of (they may be suppressed, but also they simply may not yet be clearly formulated in our consciousness). They can be manifested in dreams, daydreams and fantasies, so dream analysis can be an example of how to throw more light on such processes.

There is much disagreement about the purpose and meaning of dreams. The extreme views maintain that dreams are random and meaningless sensations, or that they are messages from a hidden part of the mind, with universal symbols and language. A midway position considers dreams expressions of our states of mind. While in reality experiences affect our state of mind, in dreams the state of mind creates an experience. So, dreams can be taken as manifestations of our emotions, desires, thoughts and other drives. They can be meaningful, but their meaning is specific to the dreamer rather than universal. However, dreams do not follow logic but a chain of associations, which is why they can be confusing and difficult to interpret. Several techniques to analyse dreams are suggested below, but remember that dreams are not about a message but learning about yourself.

REFLECTIVE LEVEL
It may be worth considering how well you know yourself (e.g. why you have certain preferences or react in a certain way) and to what extent you value self-awareness.

PRACTICAL LEVEL

There are several methods that can help you overcome the above obstacles.

Self-disclosure. Talking about yourself to an accepting listener (e.g. a trustworthy friend or a counsellor) is one of the oldest and best methods of getting to know yourself.

Keeping a diary can help us recognise certain patterns that would otherwise be forgotten. For this purpose, the diary should be a candid description of events and your reactions, thoughts and feelings. It is better to leave interpretations and analyses for later, because they can take you away from the experience or distort its accurate recollection.

Self-representation. Visualise or draw a picture of an image that symbolises your personality. It may be a house, for example. Is it big or small, detached or attached, dark or light? What is in the cellar or the loft? What does this image tell you about yourself?[16].

Dream analysis. One method to analyse dreams is to write down everything you can remember from the dream and then extract several elements (e.g. an object, person or event from the dream). On the basis of whatever first comes to mind, make a short story about each of them (this will eliminate the form of the dream that may an obstacle to understanding). The themes that are common, that repeat, should reveal a dream trigger.

Gestalt psychologists[17] suggest taking one or more elements from the dream and engage in a dialogue with them by alternating the roles of a dream element and yourself.

Another option is to focus directly on the feelings and sensations rather than dream images, and consider how they relate to your present situation, aspirations or concerns.

RECOMMENDED MATERIALS

Chapters one, four, five and six in Rainwater, J. *You're in Charge: A guide to Becoming Your Own Therapist* focus on this area. In fiction, Hesse's *Demian* is an engaging example of self-exploration. A darker and more cynical self-account can be found in *Memoirs from the Underground* by Dostoyevsky.

02. RELATING TO ONESELF

Paradoxically, change seems to happen when you have abandoned the chase after what you want to be (or think you should be) and have accepted – and fully experienced – what you are.

Janette Rainwater

This area considers the two basic attitudes towards oneself: acceptance and rejection. Shame and guilt are closely related to these attitudes, so they are addressed too.

THEORETICAL LEVEL

Acceptance and rejection. We can't get away from ourselves, so accepting yourself is better than rejecting. Rejection doesn't make the rejected disappear, its influence only shifts to the unconscious level and in that way often grows. It also creates an inner conflict, which decreases the amount of energy that can be used constructively. Not only is the initial act of repressing effortful, but continuous energy is needed to keep the rejected suppressed. On the other hand, acceptance enables the person to stop inner fights and build security and confidence. It is the basis of personal integrity. Moreover, those who accept themselves are more likely to be accepted by others too.

Acceptance, however, doesn't mean pampering yourself, but not hating, ignoring, being ashamed or being afraid of yourself. Being imperfect is not a reason for embarrassment. This applies to what you do too. Accepting your limitations will release you from the pressure of unrealistic expectations and minimise disappointment. It is also worth remembering that your weaknesses and mistakes may be hidden intentions, manifestations of (perhaps inadequate) responses to the environment or your needs. Only if you allow them to emerge to the surface, can you learn about them and find the reason for their occurrence. All this doesn't imply complacency – it can be the first step towards a constructive change. It is easier to make an improvement if you first accept your shortcomings. If ignored or denied, they are more likely to grow.

Rejection rarely leads to a constructive change, but it may result in an attempted shortcut, appearance of a change – creating a false personality[18]. Acceptance, on the other hand, requires abolishing self-idealisation. It may temporarily make you feel worse, but it is beneficial in long run. This is not to say that your imperfections should become a focus of your concerns, which may be paralysing. They need to be observed in totality, as a part of a whole picture, from which perspective you can consider what can be improved.

Guilt and shame are not the result of self-rejection, but they may lead to it. They are reactions to a perceived digression from personal and social norms respectively. They indicate that we now know better, that we are ready to change, which can help us stop repeating the same mistakes. Therefore, these feelings are adequate only regarding the actions and their consequences that we are responsible for. Feeling ashamed or shaming others for something that is beyond your or their power (e.g. height, age, race) is misplaced. However, ignoring guilt and shame if they are a response to your actions means also rejecting a part of yourself. If not accepted, they may compel you to repeat an act in order to diminish its importance, which can become a vicious circle. This doesn't mean being stuck with these feelings, which can be debilitating, make you insecure and arouse suspicion among others. The first step of reconciliation with yourself is taking full responsibility and accepting the consequences of your actions. Self-punishment rarely helps and is in fact not necessary. Guilt and shame can be used as a motivational force instead. As one author puts it, 'if [guilt and shame] can instigate us to consideration of the future, [they] can be replaced by a purpose, a resolution'[19]. This means understanding the motives and developing strategies for similar situations. In the case of shame, this doesn't necessarily mean changing your behaviour. The resolution could be to withstand the pressure of others if the related social norms are deemed inadequate.

REFLECTIVE LEVEL

It may be worthwhile to consider the consequences of rejecting and accepting yourself. For example, you can pick an aspect of yourself that you fully accept and see how it reflects on your life, and then choose an aspect that you reject and again see what effects it has (or had in the past). Observing others may give you an insight into what effect self-acceptance and self-rejection have on relationships.

PRACTICAL LEVEL

Developing self-acceptance. This exercise can help you find out how you relate to various aspects of yourself and develop a more accepting attitude (if you wish to do so).

Scan (mentally) various aspects of yourself: body (weight, height, shape, size), mind (thoughts, feelings, fantasies, desires), attitudes and behaviour. This should also include those features that you may be afraid of (e.g. 'a dark side' of the unconscious) and positive sides too (they also may be difficult to accept if you are, for example, shy). Elements that are not fully accepted are those that provoke negative feelings or tension, or are skipped over. Come back to them, observe what you feel and whether it is justifiable. Imagine how it would feel to accept them. One way of doing this is to think that you are your own best friend – treat, talk and behave towards yourself in this way, and see what difference it makes. After that you can clarify which features cannot be changed (or are not worth changing) and which ones can be[20].

RECOMMENDED MATERIALS

Rogers, C. *On Becoming a Person* and Taubman, S. *Ending the Struggle Against Yourself* deal with the subject in some depth. Both books are written in the tradition of humanistic psychology. The latter one is, however, more practically orientated.

03. PERSONAL CHANGE

The Master said, it is only the wisest and the very stupidest who cannot change.

Confucius

A change can happen due to influences of the environment and other factors, but this area focuses on self-induced changes. People often don't believe that they can change and continue to follow the same patterns even when these become self-defeating. Yet, deliberate change is possible – how it can be achieved is the focus of this area.

THEORETICAL LEVEL

The basis of successful personal change is trust that you *can* change and that it is never too late. This is not to say that everything can be changed, but many affective, behavioural or thought patterns are adopted and habituated, and they can be. To build confidence, start from small changes that are more likely to be successful. Bear in mind that the earlier a habit is instilled, the more difficult it is to change it.

Before attempting to make a change it is a good idea to examine the old pattern first. Changing manifestations without finding and dealing with their causes may increase an inner conflict, create resistance and lead to suppression. What is built on bad foundations can easily collapse.

Anxiety or the feeling of deprivation that a change may provoke can be minimised if you dis-identify with that which needs to be changed and take a position from which advantages of the change can be recognised (e.g. if you wish to be more outgoing, look at your shyness from a distance rather than being attached to it). To avoid insecurity that may lead to regression, it is also important to be clear what your goal is. Defining it in positive terms increases motivation (e.g. rather than aiming to lose weight, you can aim to be fit and healthy).

Attempt to make a change only when you are sure that the new way is preferable. Change is possible only if the invested energy is greater than the resistance. So, to avoid disappointment, wait until the pattern to be changed is weak and your determination is strong. A rational decision is rarely sufficient, resolution needs to come from the inside. The stronger and deeper the feelings associated with the change are, the more profound the change.

A pattern to be changed is sometimes a part of a larger system (e.g. staying out late may be a part of one's social life). In this case you may need to deal with the whole system until the new way becomes stronger, otherwise the past habit will be recreated by its other components. You need to be aware that a change may cause some disruptions and decrease predictability. This can provoke a sense of uncertainty in others, so they may refuse to accept the change even if it is for the better.

Persistency is essential in this process because old patterns tend to return out of habit. And despite many possible challenges it is worthwhile persevering: in addition to the specific benefits, every successful change also increases the sense of personal power and control.

REFLECTIVE LEVEL

Before moving to the practical level it may be useful to examine whether you really believe that deliberate change is possible. Consider if you have already made some changes in the past and how you have done it. In what way those experiences can contribute to succeeding this time?

PRACTICAL LEVEL

Making change is a method that consists of several steps. Following them can help you achieve desired change.

Clarify: pick a habit or pattern that you want to alter first. To establish if the change is really desirable and worth the effort, list the advantages and disadvantages of the old way and of the new one. Then consider if you can compensate for the advantages of the old pattern, and the disadvantages of the new one. To come to terms with a loss of the old lifestyle, think about what your life would look like if you continue in the same direction. Then imagine vividly that you have already changed. How would that look like?

Observe: don't initially interfere with your habit (but don't allow it to get worse either). Observe it, locate its triggers, look for possible causes and how they can be redirected (it may be useful to write this down). It sometimes may help (but it is not necessary) to overdo the old pattern (e.g. eating several chocolates in one go). If you decide to do so, take it out of context and focus only on the act (the purpose is to weaken the desire, not to enjoy it for the last time).

Apply: you can make a change gradually, step by step, or in one go. See which way suits you more. Announce your intentions publicly, and minimise, as much as you can, external and internal distractions and influences. This may include, for instance, dissociating with or removing the triggers that support the old habit (e.g. objects, stressful or tempting situations, other people and even your own negative thoughts).

Persevere: rewarding yourself can strengthen determination. In some instances it may also help to mentally identify with an image that has desirable characteristics (this could be another person, an object, or even an animal or phenomenon).

When you make it: enjoy the benefits and appreciate the success fully. It will make the process easier next time.

And if you don't: if you experience a relapse, accept it as a temporary setback – you are defeated only if you give up! Establish why it has happened and develop a strategy for similar situations in the future. For example, if you had a cigarette because you were annoyed, think about what else you can do to deal with annoyance instead of smoking (e.g. a relaxation exercise).

RECOMMENDED MATERIALS

Changing for Good by J. O. Prochaska *at al.* and *I want to change but I don't know how* by T. Rusk and R. Read are self-help resources that can be a valuable support in carrying out desired changes. The former is based on and backed by scientific research.

04. SELF-VALUATION

> Tho' modesty be a virtue,
> bashfulness is a vice.
>
> Proverb

Self-valuation refers to valuative attitudes and judgements of oneself that can encompass a range of categories: self-respect, self-esteem, modesty, conceit, vanity etc. There are two types of self-value: innate and acquired. The former is linked to self-respect, the latter to self-esteem. The emphasis on one or the other plays an important role in developing modesty or conceit, so they are also addressed.

THEORETICAL LEVEL

Self-respect derives from recognising our innate value and it doesn't depend on individual characteristics or merits. You don't even need to think favourably of yourself to maintain self-respect. Innate value is based on two fundamental characteristics of every person: that one is (*existence*), and that one can choose and act (*agency*). The sense of self-respect, therefore, can be lost only if you deny your existence and agency. Existence is denied if you ignore or reject yourself[21]. Agency can be denied if you are not 'your own master'[22]. So, although self-respect does not need to be deserved, it is supported by living in accord with your ideals and values, because this is how we confirm ourselves.

Disrespect can be an excuse for giving in to weaknesses, but it has a negative effect on self-identity, confidence, independence and a general sense of well-being. If you don't respect yourself, you are also less likely to be respected and taken seriously by others.

Self-esteem is linked to our acquired value. This means that unlike self-respect, it has much to do with personal achievement and success. However, it cannot simply be identified with achievements. Self-esteem is relative to personal standards, it is the ratio of our realisations to our expectations. The implication of this is that higher self-esteem can be brought about not only by achieving more, but also by lowering your expectations.

Self-esteem has a strong affective component. That is, it influences how we feel about ourselves. Research indicates that people with high self-esteem are happier and more effective; they are also likely to be more assertive, independent, and creative[23]. However, too high self-esteem may lead to self-satisfaction that can decrease motivation for further development and to an exaggerated sense of self-importance.

Modesty derives from awareness of our place in the world, realisation that we are a part of a greater whole. It is beneficial in many ways: it supports self-control, preserves energy and enables the person to experience the world more fully.

Modesty is different, however, from self-depreciation or submissiveness. Low self-esteem or insecurity don't produce genuine modesty. Giving inflated importance to others (which means in fact to oneself through others) or taking yourself below anybody or anything else can be a form of egotism that indicates false modesty. A modest person simply does not base her value on comparisons with others. This is a more stable attitude because it is less affected by a change of circumstances. Self-assessment based on comparing is relative and often unrealistic. If you have no need to prove your equality, you can maintain dignity even in a humiliating situation. It is possible only if you don't doubt your innate value. Modesty, therefore, requires an emphasis on self-respect rather than self-esteem. People without self-respect can hardly be really modest. This is not to say that modesty indicates low self-esteem, but that the esteemed value is not prioritised (for this reason a modest person appears to have different standards from others). Such an attitude doesn't undermine achievements, but values them for their own sake, rather than as a means to maintain the sense of personal worth. In other words, modesty means taking yourself seriously rather than your image, which is why secondary gains such as praise or fame don't play a major role.

Conceit and **vanity** are the result of a self-centred perspective. Esteemed value, what distinguishes one from others, is emphasised over innate value, what one shares with others. So, self-esteem is more important than self-respect. Such attitudes are in fact often compensation for a lack of self-respect ('I am worthy because of x' implies worthlessness without it). Unlike self-respect, conceit and vanity depend on external factors and need a constant affirmation. Self-image is more valued than the self. Because they are linked to self-esteem, they can make you feel good temporarily, but being driven by conceit and vanity requires a lot of energy and leads to losing touch with yourself and others.

REFLECTIVE LEVEL
To clarify your views about this area, you can compare the value of self-respect and self-esteem, what affects them, and whether they in some instances oppose each other. You can also ask yourself how you can reinforce the sense of self-respect, today.

PRACTICAL LEVEL
Self-characterisation. Write a character sketch of yourself, but in the third person, as it might be written by a friend who knows you well. Besides the content, the tone and style that you use can also indicate the sources of your self-value. For example, if the tone and style change substantially when you write about positive sides and when you write about negative sides, it is likely that your emphasis is on self-esteem. If the tone and style don't change much, your self-respect is probably intact. This is because it indicates a stable sense of self-value below immediate set-backs[24].

RECOMMENDED MATERIALS
Dillon, R. *Dignity, Character and Self-Respect* is a comprehensive collection of essays on this subject. Branden, N. *How to Raise your Self-esteem* provide some practical advice. In fiction, *Pride and Prejudice* by Jane Austen can be inspiring.

SPLEEN

I was not sorrowful, I could not weep,
And all my memories were put to sleep.

I watched the river grow more white and strange,
All day till evening I watched it change.

All day till evening I watched the rain
Beat wearily upon the window pane.

I was not sorrowful, but only tired
Of everything that ever I desired.

Her lips, her eyes, all day became to me
The shadow of a shadow utterly.

All day mine hunger for her heart became
Oblivion, until the evening came,

And left me sorrowful, inclined to weep,
With all my memories that could not sleep.

Ernest Dowson

AFFECTIVE GROUP

There are four aspects of affective experiences: feeling, emotion, excitement and mood. They can easily get confused, so to clarify the difference, some of them are compared.

Feeling and *emotion*: are often used in everyday language as synonyms. However, most experts agree that the experiential (receptive) aspect and expressive (re-active) aspect of an affect can be distinguished. The term *feeling* will refer to the former, *emotion* to the latter.[25] *Feeling* means registering effects the situation has on you, while *emotion* is a response to that situation (which, of course, can be triggered by what you feel). For example, feeling fear includes the experience of some psychological and physiological sensations (e.g. tension, confusion, etc.), while emotional reaction of fear could include screaming, freezing, running away, curling up and so on. Although they often appear together (you may feel rage and react with rage at the same time), feelings and emotions should not be identified. Feelings do not always accompany emotions[26], and also the same feeling can cause different emotional reactions or no reaction at all.

Excitement and *emotion*: the qualitative component of an affect can be identified with *emotion* (which is why there are many emotions), while the quantitative one with excitement (that differs only in intensity). Although emotions and excitement usually appear together, some emotions can be experienced without excitement (e.g. sadness, content), and excitement can be experienced without a specific emotion (e.g. sexual excitement is not always accompanied by an emotion).

Mood and *emotion*: emotion can be described as a process (analogous a river, for example), while mood is better described as a state (analogous to a lake). This means that emotion is directed, has its flow and peak, and is usually more intense than mood. On the other hand, mood is diffuse or global, more muted but last longer. For example, an angry reaction may subside after a while, but it can initiate a less intense but lasting bad mood, not related to anything specific.

05. FEELINGS

People feel disturbed not by things, but by the views they take of them.

Epictetus

Feeling refers to the experiential (receptive) aspect of an affect (e.g. feeling tense, happy, confused, nervous, etc.). A common view is that feelings are spontaneous and 'irrational', and that we are at their mercy, but in fact we can be, at least to some degree, in charge of our feelings. How to achieve this is the main focus of this area.

THEORETICAL LEVEL

The purpose of feeling is to register and evaluate the effects that external or internal events have on us. Therefore, feelings have an important role, closely related to self-awareness. However, they are not necessarily more reliable than other sources of evaluation. Feelings are not completely independent, they can be associated through learning with an object, situation or thought. With repeated experience affective habits can be constructed that will persist even when its trigger is absent. So, what we feel can be a result of an association rather than a proper evaluation of the situation.

Awareness of feelings. Sometimes attending to the situation is more important than our inner state (e.g. when we need to help somebody), in which case ignoring temporarily what we feel may be right. In the long run however, it is usually counter-productive. Avoidance doesn't make feelings disappear, it only neglects their information. Moreover, deadening unpleasant feelings deadens the experience of pleasant ones, too. It also limits our choice and control. For example, an insult can make you feel hurt and react with anger. If feeling hurt is permanently suppressed, the anger can become an automatic reaction in any situation that is perceived as an insult, over which you have little control.

Relating to feelings. Fighting an already existing feeling can wedge it in even more firmly. As psychologists point out, 'the non-acceptance of internal experience... often causes enduring bad feelings.'[27] It is easier to affect your feelings if you first accept them. This doesn't mean being attached or identified with your feelings, but considering them a valuable part of yourself – learning from your feelings, rather than increasing their influence by denying or emphasising them. Accepting what you feel may temporarily lead to an impression of more intense sensations, but it will bring eventual relief and increase your control over your reactions.

Affecting feelings. Dealing only with manifestations of a feeling may not be sufficient if its causes are not tackled. What we feel in a particular situation depends to a large extent on our interpretations. These interpretations in turn depend on our previous experience, expectations and immediate state of mind, and may not always be correct. So, you can affect what you feel about an event or somebody else by modifying your thoughts and underlying assumptions related to that situation or person.

REFLECTIVE LEVEL
It may be beneficial to consider to what extent you are aware of your feelings and how important and reliable they are (e.g. when making decisions). Paying attention or talking to others about the ways they relate to and deal with their feelings can also be insightful.

PRACTICAL LEVEL
Revealing hidden feelings. Some emotional, behavioural or even physiological reactions may be a cover for feelings that we try to avoid (e.g. an angry reaction may conceal feeling hurt or neglected). To reveal a hidden feeling an inadequate reaction has first to be recognised (i.e. overreacting, under-reacting or reacting inappropriately). The next step is to identify what you briefly felt immediately before the reaction. Recall what happened, and now in the safety where you don't need to react, allow yourself to experience what you really felt. It may also

help to write about it (no longer than ten to twenty minutes). Start with describing the event (without judging or interpreting), and then let the writing take over. When the hidden feeling emerges, a shift may be experienced in the body or in the mind (e.g. mental of physical tension release). The original reaction should disappear, although it may be replaced with another one (e.g. anger can be replaced with crying). It is important this time to relax and accept the feeling. It may be painful and intense, but it should not last long. Pay attention to what it makes you think about, and whether it is connected to some other situations from the past. Experiencing a hidden feeling doesn't guarantee disappearance of the inadequate reaction in the future, but it loosens its grip and enables you to be more in charge and open to other alternatives.

Focusing on feeling: the purpose of this exercise is to increase the awareness of what you feel, which may indirectly also affect your perspective on the related situation. The focus can be on a feeling presently experienced or randomly recalled. Detach a feeling from its trigger (to avoid feeding it further by imagination) and then observe and describe it to yourself. Pay attention to where it feels, what it looks like (a colour, shape, sound, word, phrase, image), weather it moves, any associated physical sensations. Writing or drawing can also be used. This externalises and objictifies a feeling, which can help you to be more in control and less likely to be overwhelmed by the experience.

RECOMMENDED MATERIALS
The first four chapters in Goleman, D. *Emotional Intelligence* and Gendlin, E. *Focusing* deal with some of the above themes in more detail. For those who are interested in the technique 'revealing hidden feelings' *Selftherapy* by M. Schiffman is recommended (but the book has not been re-printed recently, so it may difficult to find it).

06. EMOTIONS

Anyone can become angry – that is easy. But to be angry with the right person, to the right degree, at the right time, for the right purpose, and in the right way – this is not easy.

Aristotle

Emotions are the re-active component of an affect, such as crying, laughing, blushing, trembling, running away, shouting etc. (some re-actions may not be obvious though, but inwardly and protective, as in case of grief or sorrow). 'Re-active' means that emotions cannot be deliberately induced as, for example, thoughts, which is why they are (with all the other areas in this group) in the existence mode. Nevertheless, although they are normally involuntary, most of them can be influenced. In fact, we are generally expected to be in charge of our emotions, although conventions about how to react or what to do in affective situations are often either uncertain or no longer in existence. So, the main focus of this area is various ways of self-regulating emotions.

THEORETICAL LEVEL

Emotional reactions are neither positive nor negative. They can facilitate or disrupt an activity, which depends on the way they are directed. However, they are usually swift, and can be easily mistaken. This is why it is important to be aware and as much as possible in control of the ways emotions can be channelled. Several such ways are suggested below (they apply to both, pleasant and unpleasant emotions):

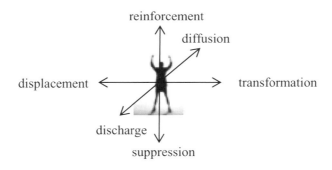

Suppressing or blocking emotional reactions can be useful if a situation or leaving an impression have a priority over your inner state. However, it creates pressure, uses energy, increases chances of involuntary behaviour and may cause some undesirable physiological reactions: tension, indigestion, high blood pressure, etc.[28] Suppressing emotions can also result in being stuck with the underlying feeling. So, this way of dealing with emotions can be facilitative only as a temporary measure.

Reinforcing increases the level of an emotional reaction by making a loop between mutually supportive thoughts, images and emotions. It can be useful when additional energy is needed (e.g. in sport and other demanding activities), but it can be dangerous if the loop is formed between negative thoughts and emotions and spirals downwards.

Discharge is a release of emotional energy when it is neither blocked nor reinforced, but allowed to pass through. It is not always appropriate, but is important for emotional balance. Self-induced discharge in controlled circumstances (*catharsis*) has been practised from ancient times. However, it doesn't always seem productive. For example, research suggests that just giving vent to anger does 'little or nothing to dispel it'[29]. A frequent emotional discharge may also decrease a threshold of tolerance (a reaction is more easily set off). Thus, it should not be indiscriminate, but accompanied with an assessment of the extent to which a situation deserves an emotional reaction.

Transformation means substituting one emotion for another. Basic emotions seem to be mutually exclusive (you can't react with fear and anger at the same time). However, one may be transformed into another. So, to avoid reactions of fear, you can change it into anger or humour, for example. Emotional energy can also be invested in a "cooling off" activity (e.g. a walk) rather than another emotion.

Displacement refers to substituting the *object* of an emotion for another (e.g. an angry reaction triggered by one's boss can be projected on other colleagues, traffic, or even objects). If displacement is uncontrolled, it may cause inadequate reactions such as treating somebody unfairly or developing phobias (when fear is displaced).

Diffusion can be achieved by removing the cause, being distracted, acknowledging the emotional reaction or revaluating the situation (through finding new mitigating information or changing the view). The last one is effective only with moderate arousal, though, research on rage shows that strong arousal leads to 'cognitive incapacitation'[30].

REFLECTIVE LEVEL
There is much debate in psychology about emotions, so try to clarify your own views: what do you think that their purpose is? Are they an asset, burden or irrelevant? Also, are you satisfied how and to what extent you can direct and control your emotional reactions?

PRACTICAL LEVEL
Unblocking emotions. Some emotions can be permanently blocked, which can cause various metal and physical problems. The first step in unblocking them is to recall some situations that could provoke the reaction, starting gradually from the most recent memories. This should be practised in protected circumstances where you feel safe and will not be disturbed. Once the emotion starts "spilling out" it is not necessary to keep recalling memories. The emotion itself may now bring different ones, which only need to be registered. Allow the emotion to pass through freely, with as little interference as possible. However, don't let yourself be carried away or lose control over the emotion. This doesn't require restraining yourself, only that a part of you remains in a position of an observer. After awhile, the emotional reaction should either subside or point to the hidden, underlying feeling. Developing a new, more adequate insight or strategy regarding a trigger situation will prevent the emotion from lingering or coming back out of habit.

RECOMMENDED MATERIALS
Lewis & Havilland (ed.) *Handbook of Emotions*; Ekman, P. and Davison, R. (ed.) *The Nature of Emotion* and Goleman, D. *Emotional Intelligence* (especially chapters five, six and eight); are among many materials on this subject.

07. EXCITEMENT

Most of the evils of life arise from man's being unable to sit still in a room.

Blaise Pascal

Excitement refers to the intensity of affective experience. It is linked to the activation of the sympathetic nervous system and the physiological effects that can be measured (increased heartbeat, pulse, perspiration, adrenalin level, etc.), but it also has a psychological aspect (can be experienced as pleasant or unpleasant).

THEORETICAL LEVEL

Purpose. Excitement is as important for psycho-physical balance as peace. It is a state of arousal, a surge of additional energy primarily developed to enable an organism to act more promptly. However, excitement can be experienced even if an action is not needed or *before* it is needed. This usually happens when excitement is the result of expectations or fantasy (therefore when it is not directly connected to its cause) and it may be counter-productive. If excitement and mental images create a vicious circle, subjective and objective become fused, the internal becomes externalised, and that leads to distorted perception and judgements. Moderate excitement, on the other hand, seems to be desirable, often sought to deal with boredom. However, if it becomes a need or an end in itself, it can be addictive and lead to seeking intensity at the expense of quality of experience, which in fact intensifies boredom in the long run.

Controlling excitement. Excitement affects behaviour and, if not directed, it can cause unpredictable reactions and increase susceptibility to influence. However, its occurrence and intensity in most instances can be modified (providing that there is enough time for conscious interference). There are two basic types of excitement control: inner and outer. The former deals with the causes of excitement and directs it. The latter restrains or prevents expressing excitement. It is a quicker solution, and enables one to leave a 'cool' impression. However, if the surplus energy accumulates, it can create inner pressure, and may cause instability. The more intense suppressed excitement is, the stronger the pressure is (which others can also easily recognise). In the long run, maintaining inner stability may be more important than an impression. The inner control starts with accepting excitement (not being ashamed of being excited). This doesn't mean allowing it to rule your behaviour. The awareness and acceptance of excitement can help you re-evaluate the situation, which makes directing and moderating excitement easier.

Reducing excitement. Moderate excitement can be pleasant and beneficial, but very intense excitement can distort emotional reactions (joy becomes euphoria, fear panic, anger rage, and so on) and reduce control, attention and concentration. A persistent high level of excitement may even produce physiological damage[31]. Predictability, knowledge, familiarity, a good strategy and sense of control can decrease excitement. This can also be achieved by staying out of situations that cause it or evaluating them in a less upsetting manner. However, *excitability* is not reduced by avoiding events that can trigger excitement, but by gradually becoming used to them. Repetitive exposure (in reality or imagination) can be deliberately used to facilitate this process.

Maintaining and increasing excitement. Excitement is proportional to a degree of importance attached to the situation, a novelty (surprise) and a level of expectations. It can also be increased by maximising uncertainty, increasing risk (e.g. choosing an opponent of similar strength or skills in games, or increasing a level of unpredictability in relationships). Repeating an experience decreases excitement, so either a greater intensity or qualitative change (variation) is needed to maintain the same level or enhance excitement. A philosopher Fromm distinguishes between active and passive (self-induced) excitement[32]. The active entails our participation (e.g. playing a game or reading a book – which requires employing imagination or thinking) while passive does not (watching a game or TV). The former can be sustained with less intense and frequent stimulation.

REFLECTIVE LEVEL
Consider how important excitement is for you and what your opinion is about expressing excitement in public. Do you use the same criteria for yourself and others?

PRACTICAL LEVEL
Systematic elimination. To find a cause of excitement (or a feeling) exclude (in imagination) one by one elements of the situation. They can be your expectations, the presence of others, ambience and so on. When excitement or the feeling also subside or disappear, this indicates that they are related to the last excluded element.

Breathing exercises can help when you feel overly excited. Deep abdominal breathing usually has a calming effect[33]. Inhale air by expanding abdomen and hold it for a while. Then exhale slowly accompanied with a gentle, soft sound (it helps control air flow). It is important to empty lungs fully. If repeated several times, the heartbeat will slow and excitement will subside. Alternatively, you can breathe in a rhythm that you find calming (e.g. inhale for the duration of 6 pulse beats, hold air for 3, exhale for 6, and pause for 3).

RECOMMENDED MATERIALS
The entertainment industry thrives on eliciting excitement, yet there are very few sources on this subject. Fromm's essay 'Excitation and Stimulation' is an interesting read.

08. MOODS

If you are feeling low, don't despair, the sun has a sinking spell every night, but it comes back up every morning.

Anon

Moods are states or frames of mind with a global effect on our thoughts, behaviour and emotions (including such states as being enthusiastic, despondent, powerful, etc.) The research has shown that mood affects thinking, self-confidence, memory, problem solving, altruism, perception, evaluation of others and creativity[34]. This area will indicate how you can increase awareness and control over your states of mind. Empirical evidence suggests that 'individuals who believe that negative moods can be relieved through their own actions are more likely to engage in problem-focused coping strategies and less likely to report depression and somatic complaints.'[35]

THEORETICAL LEVEL
Purpose. Moods reflect our general state of being. It is observed that 'although our moods may often escape our attention... they can nonetheless subtly insinuate themselves into our lives...'[36]. Pleasant moods have a positive effect on health, the mind, effectiveness and relationships. Some unpleasant moods have a purpose, too. They can make you re-evaluate your situation and initiate change. They can also bring you closer to yourself and help you discover some personal depths[37]. So, instead of immediately trying to fight or run away from disagreeable moods it may be beneficial to accept them first, find out what has caused them and gain an insight into the related situation. However, when you focus on your moods it is important to avoid identifying or becoming obsessed with them. This could create the sense of being trapped and even increase their intensity. Some moods, pleasant and unpleasant (e.g. despair, frivolity), may not have any purpose and can be unproductive, especially if they become a permanent state.

Mood and situation. Moods are of a diffuse nature, they are not directed towards a particular object as emotions are. They reflect our state of mind, rather than an immediate interaction between us and the world. Nevertheless, moods can be affected by many non-psychological factors: health, weather, nutrition, alcohol, etc. Therefore, situation can affect your mood, but your mood can affect the situation too – i.e. the situation is perceived in such a way as to match a mood[38] (both effects get stronger by repetition). Moods usually attract situations that will confirm them rather than change them, so negative moods tend to attract negative situations. When an inner state corresponds to an external situation, a sort of balance is established that is difficult to change even if it becomes self-destructive. However, the persistent influence of one's surroundings (e.g. support of others, positive developments etc.) can alter even long lasting states of mind.

Affecting moods. Moods can be triggered by generalising one factor only (a feeling, thought, physical state etc.). For example, a relatively brief and localised emotional reaction can be transformed into lasting moods. A person angry with his boss can project that emotion onto other people and situations (friends, traffic, weather, life generally) and in that way create a bad mood. So, an effective way to control the onset of undesirable moods is to prevent generalisation. Generalising is learned, not innate (children can express all sort of emotions, but they are rarely moody), so it can be prevented.

Moods are inert, which means that the longer one resides in one state, the more energy and persistence is needed to alter it. A short-term change of undesirable moods can be induced by thinking about pleasant events or entertainment (films and other programmes, cheerful music, socialising, etc.). Long-term effects can be achieved by giving up beliefs that support your mood, looking at a situation more positively, evaluating yourself more favourably, or setting more attainable goals.

Desired states of mind can be also brought about deliberately. This is not achieved by fantasising about being in such a state, but by consciously creating and maintaining it, and being prepared for possible challenges. This requires not only paying attention to your thoughts and feelings, but also body posture and behaviour (i.e. bringing positive state of mind requires acting positively). When a desired state is achieved, it is more important to remember it than to preserve it, so that you can recall it when needed.

REFLECTIVE LEVEL
It may be useful to pay attention to whether you frequently experience some moods and whether you can recognise any pattern relating to their occurrence. It is also worthwhile considering whether unpleasant moods are always negative, and pleasant ones always positive (one obvious example can be a pleasant mood induced by intoxication).

PRACTICAL LEVEL
These two methods suggest how imagery can be used to affect your mood.

Altering moods. Create a mental image that represents your mood. Then slowly alter the image into one that is desirable. The exercise is more effective if the change is gradual.

Evoking moods. Recall vividly moments when you were in a good mood and allow that state to flood over you again.[39] It is important though to use such memories only as a trigger. Dwelling on them may create different moods (e.g. longing for the past).

RECOMMENDED MATERIALS
The literature on moods is surprisingly sparse compared with the literature on emotions, possibly because of their more elusive nature. David Burns' *Feeling Good: The New Mood Therapy* and Morris, W. *Moods, the Frame of Mind,* are worth looking at.

6 A.M. THOUGHTS

As soon as you wake they come blundering in
    Like puppies or importunate children;
What was a landscape emerging from mist
    Becomes at once a disordered garden.

And the mess they train with them! Embarrassments,
    Anger, lust, fear – in fact the whole pig-pen;
And who'll clean it up? No hope for sleep now –
Just heave yourself out, make the tea, and give in.

Dick Davis

COGNITIVE GROUP

This group is concerned with what is usually referred to as thinking. The term *thinking* is not used, however, because it is too often identified only with conceptualisation or reasoning, while this group has a larger scope. It includes the following areas:

Learning represents the receptive aspect of the mental process, which doesn't imply that it is passive. Learning, considered below, requires the desire to learn, which is why this area belongs to the Agency mode (see the map, p.13). There are some types of learning that are just a response to stimuli (e.g. conditioning), but they are not included here[40].

Two areas are allocated for the pro-active aspect of thinking: ***Practical Reasoning*** (or critical thinking) that is primarily evaluative, and ***Creative thinking*** that is primarily generative. Although the terminology used may sometimes differ, it is largely accepted that they represent two fundamental modes of thinking. Almost half a century ago it was concluded that 'most actual thinking alternates between two poles, which we may call the Realistic and the Imaginative'[41]. Of course, in reality there is no clear-cut distinction between these two modes of thought processes, but rather 'a switching from one pole to the other and much intermediate "mixing"'[42] For practical purposes, however, it makes sense to approach them separately.

The fourth area is named ***Inner Structure*** and it is, to some extent, based on the previous three although it cannot be reduced to them. It refers to the system of our beliefs, concepts, thoughts and ideas that determine the way we perceive reality.

Although decision making and problem solving are often associated with thinking and have a strong cognitive component, they are not included in this group. This is because they cannot be seen only in the light of cognitive processes (a decision, for example, can be based on emotions or intuition). So, rather than here, they are considered within *Choice group* (p.139) and *Problem group* (p.167) respectively.

09. LEARNING

> The purpose of learning is growth, and our minds, unlike our bodies, can continue growing as we continue to live.
>
> Mortimer Adler

Various modes of learning differ significantly, so this area starts with their classification, and then addresses the learning process and also the ability to memorise and recall information.

THEORETICAL LEVEL
Classification. There are four modes of learning (leading to four types of knowledge):

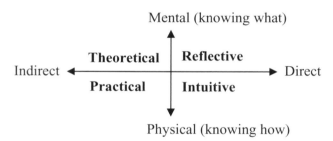

Theoretical learning is indirect mental learning. What distinguishes this mode from simple memorising is understanding. To understand something the process is as important as the final result. Providing the right conditions (a setting and atmosphere) and relevant information, materials and resources is of course, essential, but it also requires active participation (questioning, clarifying, etc.), an enquiring mind and interest in the subject. In addition, understanding is easier if you can relate the new to what you already know.

Practical learning is indirect, physical learning. You learn sequences of a particular operation from others or manuals (learning to drive is one example). It is most useful when you allow so gained knowledge to become mainly unconscious and instinctive. This is achieved through practising.

Reflective learning is direct mental learning that derives from the relation between the subject and the object (therefore it depends to a large extent on personal experience). It can have an important role in forming opinions, judgements, assessments and views. Informed reflective knowledge is a prerequisite for autonomy – an ability to make up your own mind, independent from (although not necessarily opposed to) the opinions of others. This requires not accepting something just because others (e.g. your idols, friends or authorities) say so, but checking it against you own experience and values.

Intuitive learning is direct physical learning (e.g. learning to ride a bike) that is not transmitted through an external medium (which should not be confused with help and encouragement). It often involves the trial and error method and also creativity.

In practice of course, several forms of knowledge are often combined. For example, doctors combine practical and theoretical knowledge, or at a party you may need all four: practical (to be polite), theoretical (to be informative), intuitive (to be spontaneous), and reflective (to be interesting). None of these forms is superior to the others.

Learning process. Knowledge is power that could be dangerous if it is not balanced (e.g. it may be unsafe to learn how to use a gun if you don't know how to control your impulsiveness or are not aware of the possible consequences). Mistakes can be minimised if the unknown is approached carefully, with respect (but not fear). A gradual process, without big leaps, would allow you to develop a solid basis to build on. However, if you become obsessed with a subject (e.g. trying to read everything about it or paying attention to every detail) a knowledge pursuit may become a labyrinth from which it is hard to find a way out. Checking what you have learnt against your experience is also important. This prevents the knowledge from becoming an ideology, enclosed structure that restricts, and allows it to remain open and flexible, to organise what experience brings to the surface.

Retention is an ability to remember, recall and use information or skills. Retention is better if information is related to personal experience and if it is meaningful. The latter involves either understanding an already implied meaning or deliberately connecting various elements in a meaningful way (e.g. creating a story that includes all of them).

Feelings and sensations have the deepest impact on memory, then images, and finally abstractions and symbols (e.g. words). So, abstract information is easier to remember if it is connected to a feeling, sensation or image. For example, a particular scent may assist your memory if it is present during learning and at the time of recalling (using the same sensation in unrelated situations decreases its effectiveness). Research also indicates that recall is easier if the context at recall matches the context at learning[43].

REFLECTIVE LEVEL
Which of the above modes of learning suits you most and which one least? On a more general note, do you think that learning can be an end in itself? In other words, do you sometimes enjoy a learning process regardless of other benefits that it may bring?

PRACTICAL LEVEL
Uplifting learning. This exercise can help you when your motivation to learn is low. Recall a situation when you have enjoyed learning. It could be a skill such as riding a bike or playing a game; a new school subject; something interesting from a book or a TV programme; or insights that you have gained from thinking about or discussing certain issues. Recapture the feeling you had then, and let it flow through you again.

RECOMMENDED MATERIALS
Many books (e.g. Gellatly, A. *The Skilful Mind)* describe various mnemonic techniques. A novel *Nice Work,* by David Lodge, contrasts the values of theoretical and practical knowledge.

10. PRACTICAL REASONING

To treat your facts with imagination is one
thing, but to imagine your facts is another.
John Burroughs

Reasoning is an ability to make assessments, judgements, draw conclusions, and form views and ideas. In this area, aspects of reasoning that are important in everyday life are considered: distorted thinking, objectivity, and realistic thinking.

THEORETICAL LEVEL
Distorted thinking. The reasoning capacity depends on the ability to hold a number of informational elements in awareness and connect them in a way helpful to deal with a new situation. It can be seen as agility, fitness of the mind, so it may be strengthened through practice. However, reasoning can also be distorted, which precludes forming balanced assessments and views. These are some common types of distorted thinking:
Mis-assessment: magnifying or underestimating an issue (which can lead, for example, to phobias on one hand, or recklessness on the other).
Partiality: black and white thinking, taking into account only a negative or only a positive side of an issue or a person (vilifying or glorifying somebody or something, for instance).
Over-generalisation: making general judgements on the basis of limited experience or just one part or aspect of a situation (e.g. using *never, always*, or *all* when making a judgement).

The usual causes of distorted thinking are:
Prejudice: reasoning is not based on facts, but some other indirectly related factors (e.g. adopting the beliefs of a group we belong to without an attempt to verify them).
Impulsiveness: jumping to conclusions, usually by over-simplifying a subject (e.g. 'mind reading' and 'fortune telling': assuming to know what somebody thinks or will do).
Bias: allowing our interest or gains to influence our reasoning.

Selective exposure: exposing ourselves only to information which we know beforehand is likely to support what we already want to believe (e.g. a right-wing person who would read only right-wing papers).

Rigidity: unwillingness to consider alternatives to an initial possibility.

Objectivity is an ability to discriminate between facts and inclinations, which allows a more accurate assessment. Being subjective is not necessarily wrong, but it is beneficial to be able to distinguish between the objective and subjective. This is not always easy. An objective view may coincide with the view of the majority but cannot be identified with it (a group can be biased too). On the other hand, relying on one's own personal experience is also not infallible. Objectivity is more likely to be achieved by stepping outside personal (or collective) interests and preferences. This requires a level of detachment from a subject. Beck, the founder of cognitive therapy, calls the process of regarding thoughts objectively *distancing*.[44] Distancing also increases the scope of information, enables you to see a larger picture – the view expands with the distance (but perhaps at the expense of details and fullness of the experience, so it may not always be appropriate).

Realistic thinking means that assessments are congruent with the facts and that predictions are based on the highest probability. Reality is what it is, not what it could be. Being realistic requires to be honest with yourself and to face reality as it is. This doesn't always come naturally. Research suggests that 'given a compromise between a need for self-enhancement and a need to realistically assimilate the data of experience, it follows that normal individuals can be expected to exhibit modest self-enhancing biases.'[45] However, in the long run being realistic pays off. Distortions can work only temporarily. As one psychologist points out, 'it is through realism that we can most effortlessly reduce our expectations and hence avoid disappointment.'[46]

REFLECTIVE LEVEL
It may be insightful to pay attention how you (and other people) form views and what factors influence that process. For example, do you reason to 'get to the bottom' of an issue, or just to defend or impose already determined conclusions?
You may also consider what being objective really means to you and when it is important to separate objective and subjective thinking.

PRACTICAL LEVEL
Thinking straight. There are several ways to check if your thinking is distorted:
a) Compare your present assessment with other relevant situations (e.g. if you have concluded that somebody is selfish, put it against her attitude in other occasions).
b) Compare your view with the views of others (do they think that she is selfish, too?)
c) Check if you have personal reasons to judge the situation in that light (e.g. seeing somebody as selfish may be a justification for your own actions).
d) Play "devil's advocate", attempt to falsify your own judgement or explanation.
    To form more accurate views, the following methods are suggested[47]:
a) Monitor your automatic thoughts, especially if generalisation is involved, and examine the evidence for their validity.
b) Try to recognise the effect of moods and other states of mind on thinking.
c) Consider alternative interpretations or conclusions. Good thinkers are open to new possibilities and to evidence against possibilities that they favour.

RECOMMENDED MATERIALS
Garnham, A. & Oakhill, J. *Thinking and Reasoning* and Beck, A. T. *Cognitive therapy and the Emotional Disorders* are good introduction into this area.

11. CREATIVE THINKING

> Our imagination is the only companion
> chained to us for the whole of existence.
>
> Charlotte Wolff

Creative thinking is characterised by an element of novelty (at least for the person who is thinking, not necessarily others). It is a universal ability, not exclusive to some people or activities. For example, constructing a sentence that you have not heard or used before inevitably involves some creativity. This area will address two basic modes of creative thinking: a spontaneous one, that will be called *fantasy* and a deliberate one, that will be called *imagination*. Some factors that facilitate creative thinking will also be mentioned.

THEORETICAL LEVEL

Fantasy is a spontaneous creative process often initiated by unfulfilled desires. Fantasy can help alleviate unpleasant feelings and induce pleasant ones. It can also be a partial substitute for the real experience or a temporary respite and in that way may provide some satisfaction. However, fantasy doesn't provide lasting satisfaction and may increase the intensity of a desire, which can lead to bad moods. Moreover, if you are carried away, it may undermine your motivation. Fantasy fulfils your intention in fiction, which can weaken the need for its accomplishment. This is especially the case when we focus in fantasy on the benefits, rather than the process, because it can provide partial gratification without any effort. As the philosopher Ricoeur puts it, 'satisfaction with the image can charm me to such an extent that the imaginary becomes an alibi for the project and absolves me from the charge of carrying it out.'[48] Note, however, that this may be useful with desires that you don't want to put in practice.

Fantasies also may lead to an unrealistic assessment of the situation and easily become a disappointment. This is why it is better not to let your fantasies become expectations and affect your perception of reality. In other words, don't allow yourself to get attached to or start believing in them. This does not mean suppressing fantasising, in which case your desire may come out in a different, perhaps worse way. Fantasies can fly high as long as you stay where you are. Acceptance and awareness of your fantasies can give you an insight into your needs, intentions and ambitions, and why you are not satisfied with the present situation. Moreover, rather than being a substitute or escape, fantasy can be used as a source of creativity.

Imagination is deliberate creative thinking that involves actively searching for new, original possibilities. It can be stimulating and enrich your life (and the lives of others), and also it can help you deal with new situations and find original solutions. On the other hand, imagination can be counterproductive if a situation requires an accurate assessment or thinking that should adhere to pre-determined operations (e.g. driving a car).

Visualisation is one of the most common uses of imagination. It is an ability to deliberately create mental images without corresponding sensory input. Visualisation may be called directed fantasy and it can help you to achieve a desired state of mind and invoke and focus intention. While fantasy can be an impediment, visualisation may help you realise your aim. Research suggests that 'images of desirable future events tend to foster the behaviour most likely to bring about their realisation'[49]. However, imagination is not fruitful if it becomes fantasy. The difference between visualisation and fantasy is in their purpose: visualisation can be used to facilitate satisfying a desire, while fantasy usually facilitates a desire for satisfaction. Imagining yourself and your reactions when the goal is achieved decreases a tension between the present state and desired state that is the motivational force. Therefore, it impedes the realisation rather than assisting it. In order to make visualisation effective, you need to focus on what you aspire, achieving an aim, rather than on the consequences (e.g. a reward or pleasure that may come afterwards).

Factors that affect creativity. Creativity always involves novelty, so it is fostered by breaking habits and rigidity. A creative person is not afraid to leave tradition and established tracks. This enhances the ability to generate a greater number of possibilities. As this always entails some risk, a certain level of self-confidence is also required.

REFLECTIVE LEVEL

Recall some of your fantasies and also situations when you have used imagination. What is the difference between these two activities and what roles they play in your life?

PRACTICAL LEVEL

Analysing fantasies. Any fantasy or daydream can be analysed in the same way as dreams (see the area *Self-awareness*, p.28), which can help you learn more about their causes.

Developing creativity. To practise creativity start from a simple set of elements and generate a number of possible developments. For example, you can finish a simple sketch (e.g. three parallel lines) in several different ways, or create a few stories from a simple situation or sentence. These exercises can be handy whenever you feel bored.

Invocation by image. Find an image that you can associate with a desirable mental state (e.g. tranquillity may be associated with an image of a calm sea, confidence with an image of winning). Bring the image in mind whenever you want to invoke that state. The more you practice, the stronger connection becomes, but save the image only for this purpose. A sound, word (or sentence), and body gesture can have the same effect.

RECOMMENDED MATERIALS

De Bono's *Lateral Thinking* is among a number of books that highlight the importance of creativity and suggest ways of developing it. Chapter 2 in Rainwater, J. *You are in charge* provides many examples of how fantasy and imagination can affect our lives.

12. INNER STRUCTURE

> Man is what he believes.
> Anton Chekhov

A number of philosophers and psychologists[50] point out that we are not aware of reality directly, but through our mental categories. These constructs (of which some have been addressed in this group) don't exist independently. Our thoughts, ideas, attitudes and judgements tend to be organised in meaningful and sensible ways. *Inner structure* refers to this net of mental concepts that creates our belief system. We all, practically from birth, start building (and re-building) our inner structure and continue doing so throughout our lives, so it is the result of an interaction between ourselves and the world. Some elements stem from adopting the common knowledge (science, religion, ideology, cultural assumptions), and some are the result of unique personal experiences (for example, believing that others are (not) trustworthy). However, although our inner structures correspond, to some extent, to reality, they should not be identified with it. In other words, we should not assume that our beliefs are the indisputable truth. If this happens, the inner structure is taken for granted and left unattended, with the consequence that it cannot accommodate new experiences and can easily disintegrate.

THEORETICAL LEVEL

The main purpose of inner structure is to make a meaningful whole of various experiences and also to enable your mind to expand. An inner structure that is fragmented, conflicting, or too rigid can lead to prolonged anxiety, poor adaptability and a number of other personal and interpersonal problems, the causes of which may not be easily identified. In order to avoid this, it is important to consider those characteristics that contribute to better integration and development of inner structure.

Integration of the inner structure is instrumental for its protective and supportive function. The following characteristics lead to better integration:

Congruence requires that your system of beliefs and ideas doesn't conflict with accepted facts or experience. So, you must be ready to replace those elements that can be refuted.

Consistency means that there should not be contradictions among your own beliefs (e.g. holding religious beliefs in some situations and atheist beliefs in others).

Completeness implies that you can account for all the facts and experiences. Therefore, rather than ignoring new experiences, you need to be prepared to expand (or modify) your inner structure in order to incorporate them.

Cohesiveness requires that all the parts of the system are connected, and superfluous ones excluded. The inner structure is your framework of the world, so holes in it may cause insecurity and impulsive reactions. To avoid them, discard a part of your belief system only if it is really unnecessary or if it can be replaced with more adequate concepts.

Development. Psychologists claim that 'because the invalidation of basic beliefs is highly threatening, people have a vested interest in maintaining these beliefs even when they are highly negative, for it prevents disorganisation.'[51] However, it is difficult and often counterproductive to try to maintain a structure unchanged. Reality and ourselves are changing all the time so a rigid inner structure limits your adaptability and prevents development. Adapting your structure to reality, not the other way around, enables mental and emotional stability. The characteristics that enable development are:

Flexibility means modifying your ideas on the basis of a new experience or information, rather than ignoring or misinterpreting your experience to fit the ideas that you already have.

Open-mindedness means considering alternative interpretations. Open-minded people are not without convictions – they are only not overly attached to every bit of their belief system.

REFLECTIVE LEVEL
To what extent the above characteristics relating to the integration and development of the inner structure are present in your own belief system? Is it possible, for example, that you are not good in something simply because you are stuck in believing so?

PRACTICAL LEVEL
Laddering. Our reactions are often the result of unexamined beliefs. Changing the way an event is interpreted can lead to a spontaneous change of the reactions, too. Choose a situation in which you have reacted inadequately. Consider the pre-assumptions your reaction has been based on and whether they are valid. One way to do this is a deceptively simple technique introduced by personal construct therapists, called *laddering*[52]. It is based on the assertion that the inner structure is organised hierarchically. So, there are always deeper, more general constructs behind, but they are often taken for granted. Laddering can enable you to reach those more basic levels. It consists of asking yourself 'Why…?' after an act or statement, and continuing with the question until underlying presumptions are revealed. Virtually any situation or claim can be a starting point.

Mind Mapping can help you clarify relations between various ideas or parts of your inner structure and reveal possible contradictions. Place the main topic of your concern (or a pivotal belief) in the centre of a sheet of paper and circle it. Then, place related ideas in smaller circles and connect them to the central one, and so on[53].

RECOMMENDED MATERIALS
For further exploration see *Beliefs* by Dilts *et al.*, and *A New Guide to Rational Living* by Ellis & Harper. *Don Quixote* and *King Lear* illustrate the effects of rigid beliefs.

IF

If you can keep your head when all about you
  Are losing theirs and blaming it on you,
If you can trust yourself when all men doubt you,
  But make allowance for their doubting too;
If you can wait and not be tired of waiting,
  Or being lied about, don't deal in lies,
Or being hated, don't give way to hating,
  And yet don't look too good, nor talk too wise:

If you can dream – and not make dreams your master;
  If you can think – and not make thoughts your aim;
If you can meet with Triumph and Disaster
  And treat those two impostors just the same;
If you can bear to hear the truth you've spoken
  Twisted by knaves to make a trap for fools,
Or watch the things you gave your life to, broken
  And stoop and build 'em up with worn-out tools:

If you can make one heap of all your winnings
  And risk it on one turn of itch-and-toss,
And lose, and start again at your beginnings
  And never breathe a word about your loss;
If you can force your heart and nerve and sinew
    To serve your turn long after they are gone,
And so hold on when there is nothing in you
  Except the Will which says to them: 'Hold on!'

If you can talk with crowds and keep your virtue,
    Or walk with Kings – nor lose the common touch,
If neither foes nor loving friends can hurt you,
  If all men count with you, but none too much;
If you can fill the unforgiving minute
    With sixty seconds' worth of distance run,
Yours is the Earth and everything that's in it,
    And – which is more – you'll be a Man, my son!

Rudyard Kipling

INTEGRATIVE GROUP

This group consists of the areas that affect or contribute to the integration of the whole person. They are: **Harmonisation**, **Stability**, **Self-discipline** and **Development**. Some of them will be compared to other areas to clarify the difference.

Development is different from *Learning* or *Personal change*, although learning and change may be a part of development. Development affects the whole person, while change and learning usually focus on one aspect (e.g. habits, intellect, skills etc.). Learning needs to be integrated with previous experience and knowledge in order to contribute to development. Psychologist and philosopher Fromm writes: 'if learning means to penetrate from the surface of phenomena to their roots – i.e. to their causes... it is an exhilarating, active process and a condition for human growth.'[54]

Development refers to the process, while change refers to the product (a way to achieve a desirable state). Therefore, change is finite, while development is not. Change does not always imply development (e.g. in some cases of adapting to new circumstances, or changing habits[55]). By the same token, development does not always necessitate a qualitative change (e.g. an improvement or integration of already existing qualities and experiences can contribute to development but doesn't necessitate a change).

Stability refers to a relative equilibrium of the whole person. It should not be identified with the state of low arousal, and this is why it is not a counterpart to *Excitement* (p.48). You can maintain stability even when you are excited, and you can lose it when you are not (e.g. in the case of boredom). The indicators of a low level of stability are nervousness and tension, not the intensity of an affective reaction. Another difference is that excitement is intentional (we are excited *about* something) while stability is not. Although some fluctuations in stability can be triggered by external factors, stability (and nervousness) are in fact dispositions that reflect a relatively enduring inner state.

13. HARMONISATION

> Whether we are happy depends on inner harmony, not on the controls we are able to exert over the great forces of the universe.
>
> M. Csikszentmihalyi

Harmonisation refers to maintaining a dynamic balance between various aspects of oneself. Essential to this is an ability to deal with inner conflicts. There is profound awareness that prolonged inner conflicts can have serious consequences, and some methods to resolve them were developed a while ago[56]. Yet, many people still feel at a loss when experiencing conflicts. This area will address consequences and sources of conflicts, and also point to some basic types of conflicts and the ways of resolving them.

THEORETICAL LEVEL

Consequences. It is practically impossible to avoid conflicts, but if unresolved, inner conflicts make us vulnerable and may lead to some psychological disorders. According to psychologist Erickson without a coherent identity individuals are unable to function. Personal integration and harmony, on the other hand, create a sense of inner contentment: 'people are happier if they have managed to resolve their inner conflicts, and achieve some degree of integration of their personality'[57]. Therefore, happiness reflects our inner state and is different from pleasure (that usually depends on external stimulation) or satisfaction (that depends on comparing with previous situations and achievements or with others). As one author points out, 'to search for happiness betrays a misunderstanding of what it is. It is not something that can be looked for: it is the outcome of you and the world being in a harmonious relationship with one another.'[58] This means that unlike pleasure, happiness cannot be morally indifferent (although being moral does not guarantee happiness). Integration and harmony cannot be achieved if your social aspect (that includes your moral sense) is in conflict or disregarded.

Sources of conflicts can be internal and external. A frequent example of the internal source is a conflict between the present course of an action and decisions or promises to yourself (that may even be forgotten, and yet still influential). The external sources of conflicts are problems that become internalised. For example, a problem with an abusive boss can create an inner conflict between the need for financial security and dignity.

Types of conflicts[59]. Conflicts can occur within the same faculty (e.g. conflicting desires), between different faculties (e.g. thoughts and emotions), and between different dimensions of human life. In line with the work of several authors[60], the following taxonomy of these dimensions is suggested: the physical (instinctual, natural) dimension, the social or public dimension, the personal (private) dimension, and the ideal (abstract, universal, spiritual) dimension.[61] Ideally, all these dimensions should be harmonised, but they may have different aims and require different attitudes and characteristics that can cause a conflict if not appropriate to the situation. For example, you may need a different frame of mind when playing sport, at work, with your close friends, or when being in nature or in church. Every domain has its function and deserves respect, but allowing them to encroach on each other territories can be disruptive.

Dealing with conflicts. Suppressing the awareness of your inner conflicts does not make them disappear, so ignoring, denying or avoiding them is rarely a solution. There are two major tactics to deal with conflicts: distributive and integrative. *Distributive* tactics are mainly concerned with the outcome. Here are some examples:
a) Taking one side of the conflict and ignoring or fighting the other.
b) Separating the sides in the conflict. If they are sufficiently separated so that there is no permeability between them, a conflict may not be experienced.

These tactics can provide a quick respite but prevent integration, limit the experience, can be energy consuming, and need constant reinforcement.

Integrative tactics require more time and effort but they enable you to connect various aspects of yourself in such a way that you can be and act as a whole. They are:

a) Maintaining an accepting attitude and negotiating, looking for common ground, a way that is satisfying (or at least acceptable) for every side in the conflict.

b) Affecting the source of the conflict, by clarifying and reflecting on your beliefs, ideas, and assumptions behind each side, and setting priorities on that basis.

REFLECTIVE LEVEL

Recall some situations in which you have experienced inner conflicts. Have you attempted to avoid or solve them, and if the latter how? How successful have your strategies been, and what would you do now in similar situations (considering the above strategies)?

PRACTICAL LEVEL

Resolving inner conflicts. As with others, acknowledging the needs of different aspects of yourself decreases the conflict even if these needs are not met. So, listening to the demands of the conflicting sides in you may help in resolving an inner conflict. Then, you can negotiate with them. Their immediate strengths should be taken into consideration, but also the long term consequences of possible directions.

RECOMMENDED MATERIALS

Shakespeare's *Hamlet* and Stevenson's *Doctor Jekyll and Mr Hyde* are famous examples in fiction of the consequences of unresolved personal conflicts. In psychology, Horney, K. *Our Inner Conflicts* and Assagioli, R. *Psychosynthesis* can be a stimulating read.

14. STABILITY

Stability is not immobility.
Klemens von Metternich

Stability refers to the state of a relative equilibrium within the person. It is characterised by the sense of calm, inner peace or centeredness on the one side, and restlessness, tension and volatility on the other (on this basis psychologists distinguish A and B types of personality). An accelerating pace of life and competitive atmosphere in the work place are often a challenge for stability. This is reflected in a widely spread use of tranquillising drugs and also an increasing popularity of methods that help achieve and maintain stability. This area will provide some pointers in that direction, too.

THEORETICAL LEVEL

Effects. Although we can have a sense of stability, stability is not an affect – in a way, it is beyond affects. It can be described as an ability to reach and remain in the neutral position. Knowing that such a neutral position exists can release you from the pressure to be all the time in a good mood. Stability benefits mental and physical health, and also assists the process of assessment, decision-making and a variety of other activities. Stability does not decrease excitement or lead to passivity; in fact, it enables a more active life, while passivity is a result of expending energy on internal fights.

Factors that affect stability. Stability can be influenced by external circumstances, but it essentially depends on yourself. It is very much related to personal integration and balance. This means that inner conflicts[62] have an adverse effect on stability and resolving them can contribute to it.

Stability is maintained by controlling the extent to which you are carried away by immediate experiences. This also involves restricting impulsive reactions, another important factor that affects stability.

Tension has the function of protecting, or preparing the body for action. However, the body does not distinguish between the internal and external world. This is why we can become tense even if an action is unnecessary (e.g. when we imagine a danger, as in worrying). The body also does not distinguish between physical and psychological threats, so tension is sometimes inadequate and even counterproductive (e.g. at an exam, or a first date). Prolonged tension is energy consuming and potentially damaging and yet, you may not even be aware that you are permanently tense. Tension release (relaxation) has a positive effect on the body and mind likewise. It is more effective if accompanied with a cognitive component: the message to yourself that tension is not needed.

REFLECTIVE LEVEL
It may be interesting to consider how stability affects various situations and why it is important, and also why people get nervous – what is (if any) the benefit of such a state.

PRACTICAL LEVEL
To achieve lasting stability all aspects of yourself need to be addressed, so this level includes categories that affect physiological, cognitive and behavioural components:

a) *Physiological* consists of relaxation techniques:
Progressive relaxation was developed by Edmund Jacobson at the beginning of the 20th century. It is based on contracting and then relaxing each set of muscles in sequence. You can start from your feet and gradually progresses towards the top of your head.
Autogenic Training was developed by Johannes H. Schultz in 1920. It consists of six steps: Making limbs feel heavy and warm, allowing breathing and the heartbeat to calm, making the solar plexus area warm and making the forehead cool.

More detailed descriptions of these and other relaxation techniques can be found in recommended materials below.

b) *Cognitive* includes guided imagery and meditation:

Peaceful images that are consciously created can have a stabilising effect. For this purpose the memory or imagination can be used to bring up anything associated with calm. Some images suggested in the literature[63] are visiting the 'temple of silence', arriving back to the harbour, or a stroll through the forest.

Meditation usually lasts around 20 minutes. Make yourself comfortable and relaxed and close your eyes. Allow any thoughts, images, feelings and other sensations that enter your mind to pass by without interference or letting yourself be carried away by them (like observing a moving trains from the platform). To anchor yourself, focus on your breathing (but don't attempt to change it in any way). Alternatively you can choose a sound or word to repeat (a word used for this purpose is called *mantra* and does not need to have any meaning). If some pressing or interesting thoughts appear, make a mental note to come back to them later, let them pass and gently focus on breathing (or your mantra) again. It is important not to pressurise yourself in any way, try to block your thoughts forcefully, or compete with yourself (or others). Meditation works only if the process is not forced.

c) *Behavioural* consists of a technique that can be applied in destabilising situations:

Centring. Destabilising effects of external events can be minimised by centring yourself. For this purpose, Japanese tradition suggests to focus on the approximate centre of the body, about two inches below the navel (*hara*). In addition, you can create a sense of heaviness around that point (heavier objects are more difficult to move).

RECOMMENDED MATERIALS

There are many materials that describe various exercises that can help in achieving and maintaining stability (e.g. Wilson, P. *Instant Calm,* Davis, M., *et al. The Relaxation and Stress Reduction Workbook*; Chaitow, L. *Relaxation and Meditation Techniques,* Madders, J. *Stress and Relaxation,* etc.)

15. SELF DISCIPLINE

> When we have done what we need
> to on the inside, the outworking
> will come about automatically.
>
> Goethe

Self-discipline refers to a specific human ability to control and direct one's own faculties[64]. Self-discipline should not be identified only with self-imposed rules. It is a life-long process that enables harmony between inner and outer, adaptation to, and control of one's environment. This area will consider the purpose of self-discipline and the two ways that it can be developed: external and internal.

THEORETICAL LEVEL

The purpose. As many philosophers since Aristotle pointed out, a lack of self-discipline and self-control does not increase freedom and choice nor enable spontaneous development. Quite the opposite, it leads to being enslaved by your urges, affects, instant desires, habits, addictions or obsessions. This creates insecurity and anxiety because you feel that you are not in charge of your life and it can be destructive. On the other hand, self-discipline enables you to act upon long-term goals and outcomes (instead of being compelled to follow immediate impulses) and increases your choice and control.

Types. There are two basic ways of developing self-discipline (and discipline in others).
External discipline is mainly concerned with outcomes. It operates through ordering and imposing, using imperatives such as 'must (not)' or 'should (not)'. External discipline can bring rapid results, but prevents integration and development. An order, even from yourself, is experienced as an alien force. It always comes from above, implies mistrust and often creates an inner conflicts. For this reason external control needs constant monitoring and may have adverse effects (e.g. 'rebelling' against your own orders). Which is why it requires a lot of effort and often appears to be rigid. Checking and controlling,

while in the situation, suppresses spontaneity. The most frequent method of external control is *reinforcement* (punishment and reward). Spontaneous negative experiences can be educative (e.g. an injury may teach you to accept your limits). Moderate negative reinforcement can also achieve some results in preventing, but not in stimulating (e.g. forcing yourself to do something by a threat of punishment is likely to create aversion). Moreover, self-punishment and reproach for existing mistakes or inadequate behaviour lead to pushing them back into yourself, rather than getting rid of them. Rewards also have limited value. Research shows that it is much better to develop intrinsic motivation (enjoying an activity or praise), and use extrinsic rewards (e.g. treats) judiciously[65].

Internal discipline is more concerned with personal improvement than immediate outcomes. It operates with 'I (don't) want' or 'I (don't) need' (taking into account long-term consequences, rather than just short-terms inclinations). This does not mean allowing irresponsibility, but building confidence and trust in yourself. Its function is not to limit freedom, but to use it constructively by making corrections and avoiding excesses. So, its direct influence (and effort) is smaller than in external control. Internal discipline is more flexible, but needs attention and time. Self-mastery is achieved through directing, not imposing, which enables spontaneity and utilising the energy of the controlled part. It is based on the recognition and co-operation of every aspect of the person, so prohibitions and orders are replaced by explanations. *Explanation* answers 'why' questions and creates a dialogue, which implies acknowledgement. It harmonises a part that is directed and one that directs, rather than creating a conflict between them, and in that way enables you to be a whole. This is more humane because it is based on free decision. An action is voluntary rather than forced, and voluntary actions have more substance because, unlike forced ones, they are integrated with the rest of the person.

Developing self-discipline requires an effort, but it enables you to take charge of your life. Its biggest adversary is inertia, following immediate impulses. This does not imply that you need to abide rigidly by a set of rules. Complete rational control can be limiting, prevent spontaneity and decrease enthusiasm and motivation. Self-discipline means being in command of your faculties, not letting one of them (including the will) take over.

REFLECTIVE LEVEL
Consider what type of self-discipline you usually use and how effective it is. You can also examine what sorts of situations are more challenging for you: summoning an effort to do something or refraining from doing something, and whether these situations require different methods to apply self-discipline.

PRACTICAL LEVEL
Developing in this area is a life-long process, so only general pointers can be provided here.
Good discipline. Nobody is born with self-discipline – it is built, so claiming 'I am weak-willed' cannot be a fact, but only an excuse. A famous psychologist Assagioli suggests that envisaging yourself with strong will and the advantages that it would bring would strengthen your determination[66]. The most important factor that supports self-discipline is consistency, not contradicting yourself. It is achieved by making a decision in advance about what you want or don't want to do, and remembering in tempting situations what you have decided or promised to yourself. It helps if your decision and its reasons are clearly and simply formulated (without 'ifs' or 'buts').

RECOMMENDED MATERIALS
'Discipline' in *The Road Less Travelled* by Peck, 'The Nature of the Will' in Assagioli's *The Act of Will* and part two in May, R. *Love and Will* deal with this subject in detail.

16. DEVELOPMENT

> By virtue of being born to humanity, every human being has a right to the development and fulfilment of his potentialities as a human being.
>
> Ashley Montague

Personal development means a cumulative and directed gradual transformation. It should not be identified with aging. Aging is genetically determined, whereas development depends on our situation and intentions. While aging is a natural process, development is a natural potential that requires an effort. Aging cannot be reversed, while development can. The body stops growing at some point and starts deteriorating, but personal development does not need to. Our experience is constantly increasing, so there is always an opportunity for further growth. This area will examine what development involves, factors that contribute to development and challenges in that process.

THEORETICAL LEVEL
Development has two components: quantitative and qualitative.

Quantitative component refers to developing capacities such as awareness, thinking, affect, volition, skills and so on. It is indicated by an increase in the following characteristics:
• Dynamism (e.g. interest, curiosity, a desire to learn)
• Complexity and differentiation (e.g. an ability to recognise the composite elements of a whole or various perspectives)
• Organization and integration (e.g. an ability to connect and keep together various elements of a concept or activity)
• Perspective (e.g. considering long term plans or other people)
• Refinement (e.g. sensitivity to nuances or details)
• Diversity and versatility (e.g. having a variety of interests, knowledge or skills)
• Flexibility (e.g. an ability to incorporate or adapt to a change)
• Creativity (e.g. being able to produce something new)
• Self-control (e.g. an ability to delay immediate gratification)
• Productivity (utilizing your potentials and energy)

Qualitative component refers to the stages of development, considered by a number of psychologists and philosophers[67]. There are many controversies related to this subject (e.g. to what extent these stages are pre-determined). In any case, they do not imply a specific direction or superiority[68] and can't be used to compare individuals (as we can't say that a year three student is necessarily better than a year two student). Different levels only mean different challenges, that's all. The following levels are suggested:

1. *Physical or natural level.* Bodily instincts and urges are dominant. The mind is mainly focused on concrete and immediate events. Physical experiences are most valued.

2. *Social level.* Social norms and customs, and corresponding feelings (acceptance, belonging, shame) are dominant. The long term consequences are also considered.

3. *Individual level* is characterised by developing reflective and abstract thinking, making autonomous choices, and experiences that involve personal depth.

4. *Transcendent level* involves finding meaning, dedication to something beyond oneself (e.g. children, society, an idea, spirituality). Universal values are recognised.

Factors that influence development. Development can be prompted and affected by various external and internal factors. However, because it requires an effort and direction, self-awareness and self-discipline are of pivotal importance. Although you can develop in many ways on your own, it is easier and quicker to do it with some assistance. Nevertheless, help is beneficial only if it facilitates the process, not if it imposes a direction. This is because development involves making autonomous choices, and they are especially relevant for the course your development will take.

Developmental challenges. Development requires opening up, freeing oneself from old patterns, disturbing status quo. This can make you feel temporarily exposed or lost, and may cause anxiety. It is important to recognise that these sensations sometimes indicate progress rather than a psychological problem. In this case, clarifying your direction may help. Development is a natural need and it may cause distress if it is stunted or slowed down. This can be a result of blocking (when development ceases, or finds another outlet), a lack of direction, or insufficient stimulation. However, although fostering development is important, it should not be forced. Development is rarely linear. Periods of advancement are often followed by periods of stagnation or even regression (to allow integration of the new or to accumulate energy). Too fast development can result in weak integration, losing touch with everyday life, which may create confusion, vulnerability, and a decrease in control. It may also cause conflicts with others, loneliness and boredom. Another potential problem is that some parts of you can be developed better than others. So, you can excel in one area of life, and remain immature in others. In this case, the more developed aspects may start to dominate, while others atrophy, which can create conflicts. For this reason it is important to assess how development in a particular area of life affects the other areas and your surroundings.

REFLECTIVE LEVEL
What does development mean to you, what is its value (i.e. is development valuable for its own sake or is it only a means to an end)? You can also examine to what extent that process depends on you, and to what extent on other factors.

PRACTICAL LEVEL
Where do I want to be? To clarify your direction imagine yourself in ten or twenty years and consider what sort of person you would like to be then, and how it can be achieved.

RECOMMENDED MATERIALS
Haaften, W. *et al.* (ed.) *Philosophy of Development* is an excellent introduction to the subject. More practical materials can be found in Peterson, D. B. and Hicks M. D. *Development first*. Personal development is also a popular theme in literature. Hesse, H. *Sidarta* and Bach, R. *Seagull Jonathan Livingston* are some popular examples.

DO YOU FEAR THE WIND?

Do you fear the force of the wind,
The slash of the rain?
Go face them and fight them,
Be savage again.
Go hungry and cold like the wolf.
Go wade like the crane.
The palms of your hands will thicken.
The skin of your cheek will tan.
You'll grow ragged and weary and swarthy.
But you'll walk like a man!

Hamlin Garland

PRESERVATION GROUP

This group relates to the awareness of an inherent physical or psychological vulnerability of our being in the world, and ways of responding to it. It consists of the following areas: ***Courage, Confidence, Anticipatory attitude*** and ***Security***. Each of them relates to some form of apprehension. The way we handle this affective component determines to a large extent the protective mechanisms used and the direction of our response. The two basic directions are either facing or avoiding the situation. In the text below facing is emphasised over avoidance. This is not because the former is considered always better. It is rather an attempt to correct a 'natural' imbalance – most of us would instinctively rather avoid than face situations that make us apprehensive. However, avoidance can sometimes be counterproductive, even for self-protection. So, the aim is not to develop a preference for one response, but to increase the flexibility in choosing a direction in apprehensive situations and the ability to act upon that choice.

Although there might be some overlaps among these areas, they cannot be reduced to each other. This is because it is possible to be at the opposite sides of their spectrums at the same time. For example, a person who lacks self-confidence can still feel secure (if the sense of security relies on external factors); a courageous person can also lack self-confidence (e.g. ready to face a fearful situation as long as it does not depend on her); a person with a positive attitude (believing in a beneficial outcome of the situation) can lack courage, while a courageous one can have a negative attitude about the outcome.

These areas significantly affect the formation of our self-concept (e.g. considering oneself confident or courageous), which is why the group takes a place in the centre of the model. The area *Confidence* belongs to the internal domain because the source of anticipation is the person herself, while *Anticipatory attitude* (worries) belongs to the external domain because the source of anticipation is the outside world.

17. COURAGE

We have nothing to fear but fear itself.

Montaigne

Courage is an ability to maintain self-control or act in spite of fear. So, it is not something objective, but relates to the way you feel, to your experience rather than a situation or action. For example, if you take a long flight despite your flying phobia, you act courageously, although flying as such may not be generally considered so. From this perspective everybody needs some courage (even toddlers to make the first steps).

This area will highlight the meaning and purpose of both, fear and courage, and will suggest some skills that may enhance your control in relevant situations.

THEORETICAL LEVEL

Fear has a valuable role for physical and social survival. It deters us from engaging in potentially damaging situations and actions, and increases our chances to deal with them (by preparing the body for the fight or flight response). The significance of fear for social life is clear considering that one of the characteristics of some antisocial personality disorders is actually a lack of fear[69]. Accepting fear can free you from the fear of fear itself that creates additional problems and is more difficult to deal with because its cause is inside rather than outside you. However, although important, fear is usually experienced as an unpleasant emotion and is often triggered in inappropriate situations. This inadequacy results from the difference between modern life and situations of physical danger for which those 'primitive' responses were developed. So, the ability to separate realistic and unrealistic fears and control fear has become a vital tool in everyday situations. This mastery of fear can be called courage. Courage, therefore, does not mean being fearless, but being able to act upon your decisions despite fear. It is supported by positive motivation and a clear aim or dedication (to an ideal, for example).

Experiencing other strong emotions, such as love, joy or anger can also help because we cannot have two different emotional reactions at the same time. Humour can be facilitative too, since it diminishes the importance of fear. It is worth mentioning that fear and courage can also be affected by some somatic causes (food, alcohol, drugs, tobacco, exhaustion, etc.).

REFLECTIVE LEVEL

Explore your experience of fear and how you react to it. Then, you can consider how important courage is for you. Recall situations in which you have acted courageously (in your own eyes), and what has prompted you to do so. How do you feel now about that? It may be also beneficial to analyse what thoughts and behavioural patterns have supported you in such situations, and which ones have undermined your courage.

PRACTICAL LEVEL

There are several methods that can help you deal with fear:

Uncovering fear. This exercise can help you locate a real trigger of fear. Take something that you are afraid of and ask yourself why. Suppose you are afraid of spiders. The answer could be because they have long and hairy legs. Then ask yourself why you are afraid of long extremities and continue doing so until you get to the root of fear.

Exposure. Confronting fear by exposing yourself to the related situation is the only way to overcome it. Using imagination first seems to be the most convenient and efficient way. Choose the scene that causes fear (it may be a past or anticipated event), divide it in sequences and focus on them one by one. What is important is to imagine the situation, but *not* to engage with associated reactions. This does not mean blocking them. If you start experiencing fear or anxiety let them pass through you, practise systematic relaxation[70] and then rewind the scene again until you can preserve calm and control. It may also help to 'observe' the scene from a distance, as if watching it in a cinema (if this does not help, imagine that you observe yourself sitting in a cinema watching the scene). This will enable you to detach from your habituated emotions. Once you have gone through the whole event until its positive ending you can attempt to do the same in real life. For example, to overcome the fear of heights you may go to the first floor of a building and stand there until you feel comfortable. Try to replace the fear reaction with a more pleasant one (e.g. curiosity, enjoyment, the sense of achievement). Then, you can do the same on the second floor, and so on, until you feel in control at any height. To be effective, the exposure needs to be accompanied, besides relaxation, by serious determination and a positive frame of mind. Avoid imagining possible dangers; a real situation is usually less frightening than what we imagine. Focus instead on gains, something to look forward to (e.g. enjoying a beautiful view from high). The sense of achievement and control are also a support in these situations. And don't get discouraged if you don't succeed immediately. Running away is not cowardly as long as you are determined to come back.

After fear. After going through a fearful situation look back at the experience, see if any residual fear is left, and evaluate how realistic your fear was from an 'outside' perspective. It is also important to remember how it feels to be courageous and defeat fear, so as to be able to recall it when necessary. A decrease in fear is usually manifested as a feeling of expansion (possibly related to expansion of lungs, blood vessels and nerve centres).

RECOMMENDED MATERIALS
There are a large number of materials relating to this subject (including non-fiction and fiction). These are only a few suggestions: Rowe, D. *Beyond Fear*; Fensterheim, and H. and Bear, J. *Stop Running Scared* and Rachman, S. J. *Fear and Courage.*

18. CONFIDENCE

Men can do all things if they will.
Leon Battista Alberti

Confidence means trusting your own abilities. Everybody has some level of confidence, although it is usually taken for granted in routine tasks. This area will examine both, lack of confidence and over-confidence, and how they can be affected.

THEORETICAL LEVEL
Factors that affect confidence. The level of confidence is not innate, it varies from situation to situation and can be changed. Confidence affects your performance, but in turn, the quality of performance affects confidence, and this depends on your knowledge, experience and preparedness. The research suggests that confidence increases if the success is attributed to stable factors (e.g. ability) rather than unstable factors such as effort or luck[71]. Confidence also depends on your sense of personal power (e.g. physical power can give you confidence in dark streets, intellectual at exams, attractiveness in night clubs). Others can affect it too (in a negative and positive direction), to the extent you rely on their support. Confidence based on your own judgment is more stable, but it may be unrealistic. In any case, supporting yourself in critical situations is often crucial. This doesn't mean that upbeat thinking is always better. Psychologists have observed that positive thinking facilitates performance when your thoughts are relevant to the task and when you had positive expectations. However, if this is not the case, negative thoughts can in fact lead to better performance than positive thoughts.[72]

Locus of confidence. Confidence can be related to the action itself or to the end result, the consequences of the action. For example, you may focus on playing well, or on winning, being accepted by an audience, being successful. These two aspects can be related but are not the same. The former depends mostly on yourself, while the latter depends on the circumstances, your opponents, audience etc., so it is less predictable and more likely to cause nervousness and undermine confidence. Therefore, focusing on your performance rather than a final result can have a stabilizing effect and make you feel more at ease and relaxed. Such confidence relies on trust that you will do your best in the circumstances, rather than on the outcomes of your actions.

Level of confidence. Although building confidence is vital, unrealistically high confidence can be even more damaging than the lack of it. The importance of a correct assessment of one's own abilities – how far one can go – has been realised since ancient times[73]. A belief (perpetuated perhaps by previous successes) that one is invincible leads to arrogance and carelessness, which often changes success into failure. This can be avoided if you don't get carried away by success. Modesty in this respect is based on, as one psychologist puts it, 'the recognition of inherent and inevitable limitations'[74]. It can protect you from unrealistic aspirations, from flying too high, and in this way in fact reinforces self-confidence. However, if an action has already been undertaken, doubts and thoughts that there is small chance of success can be counterproductive. In the midst of an action you better believe in yourself rather than the statistics.

REFLECTIVE LEVEL
Consider your level of confidence in various situations and what factors affect it. Feedback from others could be valuable in confirming or correcting the extent to which your confidence realistically reflects the ratio between your abilities and the challenge at hand. However, others may unwittingly or deliberately undermine or overestimate your abilities, so any feedback needs to be taken in conjunction with other means of assessment and with regard to motives of those who have provided feedback.

PRACTICAL LEVEL

Dealing with your 'saboteur'. If you lack self-support try to find what part of yourself is 'the saboteur' and why. This requires recognising first negative messages (such as 'I can't make it' or 'I am not good enough') and finding their origin. It may be an attitude that a significant person from your past had, or an attempt to avoid responsibility. If you still believe that these messages are valid, you may consider giving up the related activity. Otherwise, you need to recognise that they are not helpful and make a promise to stop sabotaging yourself. The next step is to gradually replace negative messages with positive but realistic ones (e.g. 'I trust I will do my best'). Relaxation (see p.74) can reduce tension, which generally improves performance and in that way strengthens confidence.

Visualising confidence. Give your sense of confidence a shape, quality and location (within the body). When you start feeling that you lack confidence, recall and focus on that image. This can bring back or increase confidence itself in critical situations. Dr Claire Weekes suggests: 'lie still and close your eyes and think of something you want very much, something for which you have a deep yearning. It is here, where you feel this yearning, that you will also feel courage and confidence: always the pit of the stomach... If you persevere, with practice it will become courage itself'[75].

RECOMMENDED MATERIALS

Jeffers, S. *Feel the Fear and Do it Anyway* and Hambly, K. *How to Improve Your Confidence* are among many books that aim to enhance confidence. As already mentioned, many Greek myths (e.g. the legend of *Icarus and Deadalus*) deal with arrogance and overconfidence.

19. ANTICIPATORY ATTITUDES

When I look back on all these worries I remember the story of the old man who said on his deathbed that he had had a lot of trouble in his life, most of which never happened.

Winston Churchill

Anticipatory attitudes refer to the specific mental disposition towards an approaching experience. We all have a relatively enduring tendency to react to a coming event in either an accepting or apprehensive way (regardless of whether the situation is assessed in a favourable or unfavourable light) that can be called positive and negative attitudes[76]. A positive attitude is an attitude that has overall a positive affective reaction regarding possible outcomes of the situation, while a negative attitude contains an element of apprehension. These attitudes not only affect our mental state and performance, but they can even have physiological consequences.

THEORETICAL LEVEL

Negative attitudes are often a result of previous experiences and therefore they can be changed. A typical negative attitude is worrying. It is an apprehensive reaction to an undesirable possibility that cannot be eliminated with certainty. It has characteristics of anxiety (because uncertainty is involved) and fear (because it has an object). An object of worries is always at a (space or time) distance, so relief is not possible through an immediate action, which is why they are frustrating. The emotional impact of worrying may help one focus the mind on the problem, though. Goleman (of *Emotional Intelligence* fame) writes that 'worry is, in a sense, a rehearsal of what might go wrong and how to deal with it; the task of worrying is to come up with positive solutions for life's perils by anticipating dangers before they arise.'[77] On the other hand, if we are carried away with worries, they easily become circular, repetitive or a habit: 'instead of coming up with solutions to these potential problems, worriers typically simply ruminate on the danger itself, immersing themselves in a low-key way in the dread associated with it while staying in the same rut of thought.'[78] Worrying can be learnt early (often through identifying with adults in order to increase self-importance and attention). Once learnt, it can become a habit for various reasons: to preserve a sense of self-importance; as a way of sustaining connection with everyday life; or to protect one from facing deeper fears or pains. Worrying is closely related to a desire to maintain control, so it can be motivated by the belief that mental suffering will somehow affect the outcome: 'the worry psychologically gets the credit for preventing the danger it obsesses about.'[79] This belief is superstitiously reinforced simply because most events that worries anticipate never happen anyway. In fact, not only that worrying doesn't help in most cases, but it can exhaust us, make more difficult to assess the situation accurately, and decrease effectiveness. This is because worries occupy our mind, which prevents us from finding a solution.

Positive attitudes. Excessive worries, despair, superstition about predestination of failure, a feeling of futility and bad luck can all sabotage your intentions. Positive attitudes, on the other hand, create enthusiasm, increase energy and strengthen determination. People who are positive also experience less distress and adapt better to negative events. It is not surprising that they tend to be healthier and more productive.

However, if a positive attitude becomes blind optimism or fantasy, it can result in carelessness or unrealistic expectations that can be unproductive in the long run. This can be avoided if you don't allow wishful thinking to influence your assessment of the situation. Having a positive attitude doesn't mean being aware only of positive possibilities but having confidence that negative possibilities can be overcome: 'people who are optimistic see a failure as due to something that can be changed so that they can succeed next time around, while pessimists take the blame for failure, ascribing it to some lasting characteristic they are helpless to change.'[80] So, being realistic is compatible with being positive.

REFLECTIVE LEVEL

Try to find out what anticipatory attitude is dominant when you think about future events. If it is worrying, for example, you can pay attention to what you feel, think or do when you worry and how constructive it is (does it really help?).

PRACTICAL LEVEL

Worry reduction. Providing that you can't do anything about the object of your worries, there is no point in ruining the present by worrying about the future. If what you worry about does not happen, worrying is misplaced, if it does, more reason to enjoy the present while you can. However, trying simply to suppress or inhibit worrying thoughts (following the common advice 'just stop worrying') does not help; in fact, it can even increase worrying[81]. There are some other ways to get around it. Worrying can be reduced if you manage to accept the worst possibility that may happen and make decisions about what to do in that case. Then again, it is easy to exaggerate the probability of an event, so it also helps to determine what the realistic chances are that what you worry about will happen. Habitual worriers may find relief if they 'let go of' and postpone (*not* suppress) worrying to a limited period (e.g. a half hour) that is to occur in the same place at the same time. Letting go of worries can be reinforced by imagery. For example, putting a worry in a box, shelving, burying, tying it to a balloon, dropping it into a lake etc. Distractions (pleasant and unpleasant) can also reduce worrying.

RECOMMENDED MATERIALS

Updated version of one of the first 'self-help' books, Carnegie, D. *How to stop worrying and start living* can still offer some useful advice. Chekhov's short story 'The death of a bureaucrat' depicts, in a comical way, the perils of excessive worrying.

20. SECURITY

> Man's security comes from within himself, and the security of all men is founded upon the security of the individual.
>
> Manly Hall

The sense of security is one of the basic human drives and its importance is well documented. Security is the overarching area of this group because it relates to the other areas, although it cannot be reduced to them. An overall difference is that security is more general, it does not require a specific trigger. For example, you may feel insecure in a certain situation without a specific reason. It could be related to the fear of a particular person, or the worry that you may be assaulted, but it does not need to be. This area will mostly focus on sources of security, and its relation to uncertainty and anxiety.

THEORETICAL LEVEL
Security can have external or internal sources.
External sources of security may be found in a *social network* (a political, economic and legal system), *group* (family, club, class, religion, nation), *personal image* (function, status, wealth) or *individuals* and *objects* associated with the feeling of security (a partner, parent, lucky charm, cross, cigarettes). Although they can be effective, relying only on external sources has some disadvantages: most of them are not entirely in your control, so you are to some extent at the mercy of circumstances; they are often temporary, security lasts whilst you are connected to the source (e.g. security based on professional status is diminished with the loss of one's job); they often limit freedom and prevent personal change; they can be misleading in creating a false sense of certainty. For these reasons external sources, on their own, are not sufficient to provide sustainable security. In fact, although people who rely mostly on external sources may appear to be so, they are not necessarily more secure than people with less external support.

Internal sources are perhaps less tangible, but create a more permanent and stable sense of security and generally do not restrict personal freedom and flexibility. They are:

Acceptance of uncertainty: uncertainty and insecurity are not the same. Uncertainty is an objective characteristic of the world, while (in)security is a subjective feeling that characterises the way we relate to the world. Uncertainty does not necessarily need to cause insecurity. Actually, only if the fundamental uncertainty of life – the fact that anything may change – is fully accepted, will the sense of security not depend on circumstances (like a surfer who glides on waves instead of trying to control them). *Anxiety* is an affective expression of our awareness of uncertainty: 'the cognitive structures which a man creates are never completely secure; anxiety is one manifestation of their impending or actual collapse'[82] Anxiety is different from fear (even on the physiological level[83]). Fear has a clear object, while anxiety does not. Anxiety can both improve and disrupt a performance, so it can have a negative and positive effect. It is unpleasant only when accompanied with insecurity (anxiety induced by the uncertainty of the outcome of a game, book, movie, date or adventure is usually desirable).

Inner Congruence: insecurity is often a consequence of internal conflicts. And the more complex the *inner structure* is, the more likely they are to appear. A simpler world view is usually less conflicting, which is why people with such views appear more secure. However, these views are more limited and susceptible to mistakes because they do not reflect the complexity of reality. For example, one who rigidly adheres to the principle that stealing is wrong may not experience a conflict even if it means stealing a piece of bread to save life. More damaging examples of simplistic views based on over-generalisation that provide a false sense of security are xenophobia or racism.

Self-control developed through self-discipline can be a major source of inner security. It counteracts a lack of external control and powerlessness – a frequent cause of anxiety.

Knowledge: not knowing what is going on and what to do often creates insecurity. Thus, knowing why something happens or how things work, and also anticipating all the possible outcomes (rather than just expecting a desirable one) increases security.

Faith in, for example, science, God, goodness, humankind, progress etc., can also be an inner source of security as long as it does not contradict personal experience.

REFLECTIVE LEVEL
Try to find out what your sources of security are. Also, you may look at the relationship between security and freedom (whether they always oppose each other, for example).

PRACTICAL LEVEL
Anxiety control. In an acute form, negative anxiety usually causes distinct physiological reactions, which can in turn increase it. One way of breaking this vicious circle is deliberately inducing opposite states. So, since anxiety generates tension and fast, shallow breathing, it can be counteracted with relaxing the body and deep, slow breathing with a special attention to exhaling fully (to avoid hyperventilation, often linked to panic attacks). If counteracting the symptoms does not work, try to *increase* the symptoms (e.g. tingling sensations in fingers, heart palpitations etc.). They will indeed increase for a short while, but then they will start decreasing and possibly completely disappear. It doesn't matter what method is used, as long as the sense of control is established. Security will prevail if the state of a passive victim is replaced with an active influence and positive attitude.

RECOMMENDED MATERIALS
Bourne, E. *The Anxiety and Phobia Workbook* offers practical advice, while May, R. *The Meaning of Anxiety* and Tillich, P. *The Courage to Be* provide a good background.

FROM THOUGHTS IN A GARDEN

What wondrous life is this I lead!
Ripe apples drop about my head;
The luscious clusters of the vine
Upon my mouth do crush their wine;
The nectarine and curious peach
Into my hands themselves do reach;
Stumbling on melons, as I pass,
Ensnared with flowers, I fall on grass.

Meanwhile the mind from pleasure less
Withdraws into its happiness;
The mind, that Ocean where each kind
Does straight its own resemblance find;
Yet it creates, transcending these,
Far other worlds, and other seas;
Annihilating all that's made
To a green thought in a green shade.

Andrew Marvell

ENGAGEMENT GROUP

This group consists of the areas that relate to the regulation of engagement with life. They are:

Experience is the root area of this group. Of course, everything in life is an experience, but this area is concerned, more specifically, with the quality of experience, what makes us feel fully alive (which is why it belongs to the existence mode and the internal domain). It is interesting that despite an unprecedented accumulation of material wealth in industrialised countries, this sense of being fully alive seems lost to some extent, and is more often found among less privileged people.

Openness to experience refers to a level of permeability between an individual and the world, the internal and the external. It is the divergent aspect of the group.

Interest deals with the universal drive for stimulation and also *boredom*, subjectively perceived insufficiency in this respect. Unlike openness, interest implies focusing on and connecting with somebody or something. So, it is the convergent aspect of the group.

Pleasure encompasses the way we relate to desirable experiences. Pleasure can be followed by an emotional reaction but it cannot be reduced to an emotion, because it can be expressed in a variety of ways or not be expressed at all. It is also different from *satisfaction* (fulfilment of expectations usually based on comparing with others or different times or situations) *contentment* (a mood), *joy* (an emotional reaction to desirable experience) or *happiness*, which relates to an immediate state of mind. Pleasure always has an object, while happiness does not (they relate to each other like fear and anxiety). These distinctions are important because the other sensations can be situated within other areas, except pleasure, which is irreducible. This has more than theoretical value. For example, we often seek pleasures with an assumption that they will bring happiness. But this is not necessarily the case. We can experience pleasure but not be happy, and we can be happy even if we are not experiencing pleasure.

21. EXPERIENCE

> Life is not a problem to be solved
> but a reality to be experienced.
> Sören Kierkegaard

Feeling alive or the sense of liveliness is nurtured through a fullness and richness of external and internal experiences. They not only affect the quality of life but also sharpen our instincts and perception, which enables a better orientation in the world. However, being exposed to a variety of experiences is not enough. Although circumstances may affect it, how much we get out of life depends more on our attitude. Research shows, for example, that 'money and material wealth has a very small effect on personal feeling of well-being and happiness and it is decreasing even further in rich countries.'[84] The sense of emptiness is not rare among materially privileged people, while some have found fulfilment in extremely deprived situations. So, what is really important is how we *relate* to experience. This area will compare two basic ways of enriching experience and will also address *risk taking*, closely related to this subject.

THEORETICAL LEVEL

Experience can be enhanced *quantitatively* (through diversity and intensity) and *qualitatively* (through the 'variation on the same theme' and depth). Diversifying or intensifying experiences can provide enrichment and excitement because of the element of novelty, but such experiences may be superficial and their benefits short-lived. Variation and deep involvement can often produce fuller experience. Depth is what gives substance to life. An empty and superficial life is never really satisfying. Of course, intensity and depth are not necessarily antagonistic, but intensity is sometimes used to compensate for a lack of depth. If we can't or don't allow ourselves to experience real, deep emotions, excitement can be sought as a substitute. On the other hand, as one author points out, 'when a man has emotional depth, he has a readiness to profound experience which penetrates his total personal being.'[85]

Depth has much in common with 'peak experiences' and 'flow'[86]. Their shared characteristics are:

Absorption and focused attention: experience is richer and more direct if you let go of thinking about it while in the process. Judging and rationalizing may be important before, but they are usually obstructions during the experience.

Profound feelings: depth is achieved by opening up and allowing various pleasant and unpleasant, external and internal sensations to be fully absorbed.

The sense of value and meaning: the process of what you are involved in has to have value in itself, rather than just being a means of achieving a goal. It is observed that 'the key element of an optimal experience is that it is an end in itself.'[87]

Integration and connectedness: an experience can deepen if related to other experiences.

It may be worth mentioning that isolation and sensory and pleasure deprivation are sometimes seen as a way to reach higher experiences. Because of their nature, however, it is difficult to independently verify such claims (which does not mean that they are not real). So, any final conclusion about the validity of this method is hard to reach, but it is spread among most cultures and asserted by a great number of individuals.

Risk taking. Enhancing the quality of life often involves taking a risk and facing anxiety (e.g. a new relationship requires opening up, which makes one vulnerable). Risk taking can always prove to be a mistake, but to miss an opportunity can also be a mistake. However, you can learn from mistakes (providing that you survive them – taking a risk is different from recklessness). Caution in risky or new situations can minimise potential damage. It doesn't mean being tense, but maintaining a state of relaxed alertness.

If you are attracted to a new experience, a reaction on one side of the spectrum would be to stop yourself, stand aside and long, and on the other to allow yourself to be sucked in without any deliberation. The first reaction involves a low level of risk but also low satisfaction, while the second one may be more fulfilling but involves a high risk. It is also possible, however, to allow yourself an experience without necessarily getting stuck in it. This requires assessing first your strength and the consequences of your action. Then making a conscious decision either to 'enter' or leave and, if the former, how far you want to go. In this way you can get through an experience and get out at the other end. The deliberations should not take long though, or you may lose the momentum of spontaneity.

REFLECTIVE LEVEL

What situations and what frames of mind make you feel more alive, and how can you affect it further? For example, you may consider if there is a difference between those experiences that are ends in themselves and those that are the means to an end (e.g. when you are walking for the sake of walking, and when you are walking to get somewhere).

PRACTICAL LEVEL

Enhancing experience. Make a deliberate attempt to try something different. For example, a new sport, game, food, music, groups, etc. (experiencing other cultures can be enriching in this respect, with an additional benefit of understanding cultural differences). You can also try deepening the experience of the familiar. For example, you can read the same book or listen to the same piece of music again, with the intention of discovering new layers of meaning, or enjoy subtlety and details that you might have missed previously.

RECOMMENDED MATERIALS

Moore, T. *Care of the Soul* and Montaigne's essay 'On experience' are recommended. In fiction, Hesse's *Steppenwolf* relates closely to this subject.

22. OPENNESS

Individuals who are open to experience are able to listen to themselves and to others and to experience what is happening without feeling threatened.

Brian Thorne

The term openness is often used to mean either open-mindedness or frankness. These meanings are addressed in the areas *Inner structure* (p.65) and *Intrinsic relationships* (p.117) respectively. Here, the term signifies a human ability to regulate a degree of permeability between oneself and the (internal or external) environment[88]. It includes affective openness too, and does not refer only to openness towards other people, but any experience. Although rarely addressed in literature, this area has a significant effect on the quality of life. Difficulties that can be experienced in connection to this area usually relate to inability to regulate a degree of openness and to determine its direction (i.e. being preoccupied with inner experiences when the situation demands one's attention, or being absorbed with the world and ignoring one's internal processes). So, this area will focus on increasing control over a degree of openness and its direction.

THEORETICAL LEVEL
Openness enables us to internalise the external world and externalise our inner world to some extent. It is different from having 'holes' or 'cracks' in the personality. They are the result of unresolved inner conflicts or unhealed wounds from the past that do not allow the individual to be a harmonious whole. They cause tension, worries, oversensitivity and create barriers. Openness, on the other hand, relates to a level of permeability of a whole person that enables an interchange with the environment. It enriches the quality of experience and enables recognising new possibilities, which contributes to personal development and, as the psychologist Carl Rogers points out[89], also enhances creativity.

Some experiences increase energy and some drain it away, so it is important that openness is selective. There are different degrees of openness, the deeper enable more expansive exchange but also enhance sensitivity. An overly closed, rigid person who allows little interchange, loses the quality and versatility of experience and may feel an emptiness in life. On the other hand, opening too much in some situations can make one exposed, vulnerable and oversensitive, which can result in feeling hurt or overwhelmed. If problems are allowed to be internalised, they become inner conflicts. This is why, especially in new situations, it may be safer to open slowly and gradually. The ability to close yourself can be used as a means of protection. It can be achieved by narrowing the focus (restricting your interests and desires) simplifying the situation in your mind, ignoring something, or lowering expectations. A situation can open you against your will only if it is accompanied by unfulfilled expectations, confusion or surprise.

Direction. You can open towards the inside (introvertive) and the outside (extroversive). The terms in brackets do not imply personality types. Most people are actually capable of both directions (although one may be dominant out of habit). For a fulfilling life it is necessary to be able to open towards both, yourself and the outside world.

Depriving yourself from external stimuli limits your experience. This may increase the intensity of desires and lead to acting inadequately (e.g. being too fast or too slow to engage with a situation). Moreover, turning inside, when with others, can make them feel excluded, which could affect the quality of the relationship.

On the other hand, being closed towards yourself prevents external stimuli from being transformed into an experience. A neglect of the inner life and its depths usually makes people more dependent on external situations and unfulfilled, even if their lives are eventful.

Some situations (e.g. intimacy) require openness in both directions at the same time, which can be enriching, but can also increase one's vulnerability.

REFLECTIVE LEVEL

On this level you can examine whether you find it difficult to be open either towards yourself or the world around and if so, why. You may also consider to what extent and why one should be open to negative situations (e.g. homelessness, wars or famine in remote countries, environmental or ecological disasters, etc.). Relating to this issue is the question to what extent openness should be proportional to one's ability to affect the situation (whether statements like 'It is none of my business', 'I cannot do anything about that' justify closing down or ignoring an issue).

PRACTICAL LEVEL

Openness control. This exercise should increase your ability to deliberately regulate a degree of openness in various situations. First allow a situation to gradually draw you out (without forcing anything), as much as it is comfortable. To achieve this try to suspend any judgements and just absorb the experience in a relaxed state. After that try to close yourself (by implementing one of the above mentioned suggestions). Do it a few times and later compare the effects of both. You can practice this in various situations but, at least at the beginning, avoid situations in which you have to interact with other people (e.g. a party). The exercise, of course, can be used for internal experiences, too.

RECOMMENDED MATERIALS

A number of authors recognize the importance of openness. Rogers, C. *A Way of Being* and Rosenbaum, M. 'Opening versus closing strategies in controlling one's responses to experience' (in Kofta, M. *at al.* (ed.) *Personal Control in Action*) are good examples. However, they often emphasise openness and neglect the importance of the ability to close oneself. Chekhov's short story *Man in a Case* is highly recommended, because it contrasts the two extremes.

23. INTEREST

> Nothing is interesting if you're not
> interested.
>
> Helen MacInnes

There is strong experimental support[90] for the claim that interest - sometimes called the need for stimulation, exploratory drive, stimulus or sensation hunger, or simply escape from boredom – is one of the fundamental and universal drives among animals and humans. The term *interest* is used not only because it is more common than the other terms, but also because it has a wider (not limited only to sensations) and more appropriate meaning in relation to people. Human interest does not depend only on external stimulation. Stimulation can also be internal, or of a different nature (spiritual interest, for example, may even require sensory deprivation). When this drive is not satisfied we experience the sense of boredom. Boredom can be considered the counterpart to interest so it will also be examined in this area. The overall aim of this area is to enable you to increase control over these phenomena.

THEORETICAL LEVEL

The importance. Although stimulation can take very different forms, the lack of stimulation seems generally undesirable. Psychological literature indicates that 'animals, as well as man, possess an innate need for novelty... it has been shown that reducing stimulation to a minimum is noxious if not utterly intolerable for people.'[91] This unpleasant sensation resulting from the unfulfilled need for stimulation can be called *boredom* and it plays a significant role in human lives. Bertrand Russell once stated that 'boredom is a vital problem for the moralist, since half the sins of mankind are caused by fear of it.' It is true that many deeds, and even more often misdeeds, are driven by boredom, so it is important to have some degree of control over that sensation.

Affecting boredom. Interest and boredom do not depend only on circumstances but also on ourselves. The meaning and value that we assign to a situation are not part of the outside world, but us: 'monotony lies not just in the environment, but also in the "eyes of the beholder"'[92]. So, no situation should inevitably cause boredom if you are willing to engage yourself. Philosopher Eric Fromm writes that '...the person who is fully alive does not necessarily need any particular outside stimulus to be activated; in fact, he creates his own stimuli.'[93] However, the fact that these drives can be affected by our perspective does not imply that boring situations and people should be always tolerated. It only means that if there is a reason to remain in a situation that causes boredom, your spirit doesn't need to be deadened by the circumstances. A frequent sense of boredom is usually a sign that there are some barriers within the person or between the person and the world. It can also be a result of ignorance or conceit (when the person considers himself more important than anything else). An appearance of being bored is sometimes even purposefully created to leave an impression of superiority, which can become a trap in itself. Expectations, too, can play a role, because they attach you to the future and distance you from the present. So, non-attachment to expectations and accepting the present decrease boredom. This also refers to prior negative expectations. If you classify situations or persons as boring in advance, the tendency to confirm your expectations will preclude a possibility of finding something interesting. Although boredom is inversely proportional to openness to experience, it can sometimes be overcome more effectively by descending into your own depths rather than remaining on the 'surface' and exposing yourself to external stimuli. Being constantly preoccupied with the need for external stimulation can have a reverse effect and increase the sense of boredom in the long term. Some states do not require stimulation (rest, illness, meditation, sunbathing etc.), so, even if interest is lacking, it does not need to cause boredom.

REFLECTIVE LEVEL

It can be useful to examine what elicits your interest and why, and when and why you are bored (for example, what makes somebody boring in your eyes). You may also recall a situation in which you were bored and consider what it reveals about yourself.

PRACTICAL LEVEL

Combating boredom. To increase your control when feeling bored, try to accept that state first rather than immediately attempting to escape. This may briefly increase the perception of its intensity, but will put you in charge (because you will not be afraid of boredom anymore), which reduces its influence and can even make it disappear. Acceptance, however, does not mean dwelling on the feeling or resignation. Consider boredom a message that needs to be understood before you take an action (either to change your own perspective or to change the situation). Taking a seemingly boring situation or activity as a challenge to make it more interesting can have a rapid effect. There are several strategies that can stimulate interest and minimise the sense of boredom: exploratory attitude (seeking to learn, understand or find something new), engaging with others, being creative, relaxation, or seeing the situation as purposeful or meaningful. The thoughts of one's mortality may also increase the value of even boring moments.

RECOMMENDED MATERIALS

Despite its huge influence on life and human behaviour, interest and boredom have been largely neglected in literature. There are very few writings specifically dedicated to this area. Fromm's 'Chronic depression of boredom' in *The Anatomy of Human Destructiveness* is a worthy exception. Some of Salinger's short stories (e.g. 'Teddy'), exemplify how interest and boredom depend on one's perspective.

24. PLEASURE

> Happiness is not a state to arrive
> at, but a manner of travelling.
> Margaret Lee Runbeck

This area refers to the ways we relate to agreeable or enjoyable experiences and sensations. We will consider the relation between pleasure and happiness, the purpose of pleasure and what can prevent fulfilling experience.

THEORETICAL LEVEL

Pleasure and happiness. Although they can be related, pleasure and happiness are not the same. A psychologist Eysenck writes that 'pleasurable events may enhance happiness at the time of their occurrence, but their effects on the level of happiness tend to be transient.'[94] Pleasure is a sensation, while happiness is an inner state. Pleasure is connected to arousal, happiness to inner harmony[95]. This is why happiness is stable (not time affected), while pleasure is temporary. As Fromm points out, 'continued stimulation requires that the stimulus should either increase in intensity or change in content; a certain element of novelty is required.'[96] Happiness is a natural state of being (originating in love for life), but running after pleasures can make one forget it.

Purpose. Passive, receptive pleasure normally indicates what is beneficial for us. This, however, can be altered through habits (few people enjoy their first cigarette or alcoholic drink). Active pleasure (linked to a process, pleasure in doing something) increases motivation and confidence. It can be followed by passive pleasure (e.g. a reward, winning). However, it is usually better not to expect or link the passive pleasure to the active one (e.g. losing a game does not need to spoil the pleasure of playing the game). Both types of pleasure can be used to avoid facing life challenges. But, using pleasure to forget the rest of life produces a different quality of experience from enjoying fully moments of pleasure when life as a whole is accepted. If pleasure is used as an escape, the rest of life (inevitably a bigger part) becomes grey and dull, and every 'awakening' creates unhappiness. In such a case, pleasure can easily become a habit and create dependency and possessiveness. Also, when pleasure becomes the most important pursuit, it induces nervousness and tension because of its temporary nature.

Experiencing pleasure. Focusing fully on the experience is generally more satisfying and less likely to create dependency or an attachment to the source. Fulfilling pleasure is characterised by a subsequent sense of equilibrium. Obsessiveness, possessiveness and residual excitement are often a result of an incomplete experience. There are several reasons why it may happen:

Tension. Inability to relax during a pleasurable experience can have various causes:
• Fear of losing control allows some people to relax only after an event, in the safety of a distance. However, pleasure can't be fully satisfying if not experienced 'here and how'.
• Pleasure can be spoiled by worrying that something may spoil it.
• Trying forcefully to keep or prolong moments of pleasure can also cause tension.
• Concern for the impression one leaves can lead to suppressing one's reactions. So, it is worth remembering that openly showing pleasure is a sign of a weakness only if it reveals dependency or inferiority towards those who enabled the experience.

Redirected attention. Quality of experience may be spoiled if one focuses on secondary gains, instead of the experience itself. For example, for some people collecting pleasures may be a way to justify their lives. Others may see the purpose of pleasurable experiences to brag about them. Imagining, however, how impressed others are going to be leads to losing the immediacy of that moment. Talking is a different pleasure.

Shame and guilt during an experience can make it less fulfilling, and on some occasions (depending on their intensity) in fact more likely to be repeated. For example, if you are burdened by guilt while having a hearty meal, you will not satisfy your craving fully and therefore you are more likely to succumb to the temptation again.

REFLECTIVE LEVEL
It is worthwhile paying attention to some other sensations while experiencing pleasure. Are you, for example, nervous, relaxed, careless, submissive?
More generally, should pleasures be the means to an end or ends in themselves?

PRACTICAL LEVEL
Mindful eating is an example of how the quality of pleasure may be enhanced, which can also be adapted to other pleasure related experiences. Take a small amount of food in one go (and eat only until you are really enjoying it). Make sure that you are in a relaxed state, focused fully on food, so that you can feel the taste and take pleasure in it. This requires eating slowly and peacefully and chewing properly, so try to avoid other activities while eating (such as watching TV, reading or thinking about something else). This way of eating is not only more pleasurable, but also optimises, without much effort, the amount of food consumed because a full satisfaction is achieved with less.

RECOMMENDED MATERIALS
Many classical philosophers had shown interest in this subject (e.g. Aristotle, Epicures, Mill). However, although pleasure seems more important than ever, contemporary writers have not paid much attention to this area. Eysenck, M. *Happiness,* Fromm's essay 'Pleasure and Happiness', and Huxley, A. *Brave New World* are thought provoking.

BECAUSE I COULD NOT STOP FOR DEATH

Because I could not stop for Death –
He kindly stopped for me –
The Carriage held but just Ourselves –
And Immortality.

We slowly drove – He know no haste
And I had put away
My labor and my leisure too,
For His Civility –

We passed the School, where Children strove
At Recess – in the Ring –
We passed the Fields of Gazing Grain
We passed the Setting Sun –

Or rather – He passed Us –
The Dews drew quivering and chill –
For only Gossamer, my Gown –
My Tippet – only Tulle –

We paused before a House that seemed
A Swelling of the Ground
The Roof was scarcely visible –
The Cornice – in the Ground –

Since then – 'tis Centuries – and yet
Feels shorter than the Day
I first surmised the Horses' Heads
Were towards Eternity –

Emily Dickinson

PERSPECTIVE GROUP

This group consists of the areas that affect or are affected by one's perspective on the human condition and the relation between the individual and the world.

Relating to death is the root area of the group. Many philosophers and psychologists point out that our perspective on life depends on the way we relate to death, or on the extent to which awareness of mortality is included in our outlook. After all, death can be considered the boundary of life. The focus of this area is on two basic ways of relating to death: acceptance and rejection. On the other hand, loss (and accompanied emotions of grief, bereavement etc.) that usually dominate most materials on this subject are not included, because they may be caused by separation that is not necessarily caused by death. These phenomena are considered within some other areas (*Attachment,* p.118; *Coping,* p.174; and *Relationship Dynamic,* p.238).

Importance. What is important for us depends on, and at the same time affects our perspective. It is largely based on the way we construct our experience (see p.65), therefore it has a strong cognitive component.

Attachment is the area that refers to our subjective sense of connectedness between the world and ourselves. Although it cannot be identified with emotions, it usually has a strong affective component and could be considered a counterpart to *Importance.*

Tolerance is the complement to *Pleasure* (p.107) in that it encompasses the relation to undesirable stimuli. Tolerance is included in this group because it depends on one's perspective and is strongly affected by the other areas in this group. It is inversely-proportional to a level of attachment and importance given to stimuli. Although the effect of the *Relating to death* area is not straightforward, it influences tolerance indirectly by affecting the other areas in the group and one's perspective on the experience.

25. RELATING TO DEATH

> Death is the horizon which places the possibilities of life in perspective.
>
> Charles R. Mojock

The subject of this area has some unique characteristics: we may witness death of others and extrapolate that we will also die, but we cannot reflect on our own personal experience; death has special significance also because it is the boundary of physical existence; and finally, death can be considered the only future certainty.

The two basic ways of relating to death and their consequences are examined here: acceptance and denial. A number of philosophers and psychologists (notably of existential orientation) have emphasised the value of accepting death. On the other hand, denial is mainly criticized in literature, although it is common among ordinary people in the Western world. Even Epicurus, a Roman philosopher who is sometimes charged with advocating denial of death, actually only makes a case against worrying about it. While denying the fact that we are going to die is usually an attempt to escape fear of death, Epicures argues that such fears are unfounded.

In any case, the way we relate to death and mortality has a profound effect on our lives, so it is worth paying attention to.

THEORETICAL LEVEL

Acceptance and denial. Denial of death enables us to avoid, at least temporarily, fear and other unpleasant sensations often connected with death. However, death is a part of the life cycle and denying it means denying life as it is. Awareness of death may bring some unpleasant feelings, but it enables us to perceive life in its totality. Sooner or later everybody has to face death (of others and finally his own), which is harder to do if unprepared. Those who don't exclude death from their life concept (accept its possibility), are better prepared and more in control in such situations. Some observations suggest that it also makes us respect life more and value every moment – paradoxically it makes us more alive[97]. Philosopher Heidegger claims that facing up to death, being a solitary act, is a significant factor in developing authenticity. Awareness of death can also contribute to decision-making. The only certainty in life is that we will die, which can provide a firm starting point in conceptualising existence. It puts in perspective misfortunes, possessiveness, attachment, importance, and reminds us that the time to accomplish our projects is not unlimited.

Awareness of death, however, does not imply worrying, expecting, being obsessed or fantasizing about death (e.g. imagining when, where and how one may die). These attitudes may lead to neglecting the consequences of our actions and commitment to long-term goals, resignation, and bad moods in general. Acceptance also does not mean surrendering to death or hastening it by reckless behaviour (which is in fact another way of denial). It is nothing more than accepting the inevitability of death for all, and encompassing life and death as an inseparable unity.

Dealing with fear of death. Some general attitudes (that do not involve denial) may help with anxieties and fears relating to death:

Presence – focusing on *now* and here[98]. Because you *are* now, you cannot die now; you can die at the very next moment, but not now which is the only reality. Therefore, although you are aware of death, by living in the present moment you can minimize anxiety about the moment in which you will meet death.

Meaning of life[99] – people who believe that life has a purpose seem to be more resilient to death anxiety; This is probably because they see themselves as a part of greater whole, which transcends individual death.

Meaning in life (life satisfaction) – research shows that people who are more satisfied with their lives cope better with death anxiety[100].

REFLECTIVE LEVEL

The following questions could help you clarify your assumptions, feelings and attitudes towards death: purpose of death – what would it be like if death did not exist? What is death, and what happens (if anything) after death? The issues of abortion, euthanasia, suicide or killing (in defence, as punishment, etc.) may be worthwhile addressing too.

You can also consider how the awareness of the possibility that you and others can die may affect your present attitude. For example, what would you regret if somebody you know suddenly dies? Can you do something about it now, while that person is still alive?

PRACTICAL LEVEL

Matters of death. It may be useful to separate possible concerns relating to death and deal with them independently: *dying* (pain, sickness, helplessness etc.); *loss* (of at least everything that is a part of physical existence, including the body); *the unknown* (if there is anything after death and what it may be); *unpredictability* (of the moment of death); *those left behind* (children, parents, a partner, friends); *practical issues* (funeral, will, etc.).

Coming to terms with death. Expressing your feelings and thoughts about death and the above mentioned concerns through talking, writing, or other activities can increase self-awareness, relieve emotional pressure, and (if shared) enable others to know how you feel. This, in turn, could lead to developing a more accepting attitude towards death, which can affect your attitude towards life, too.

RECOMMENDED MATERIALS

Literature on death is abundant, but the level of accessibility varies. Chapter 10 in Rainwater, J. in *You're in Charge* is a good place to start. Tolstoy's story *Death of Ivan Ilich* and Coelho's novel *Veronika Decides to Die* can be inspiring.

26. IMPORTANCE

The one serious conviction that a man should have is that nothing is to be taken too seriously.

Nicholas Murray Butler

This area is closely related to values. The term *Importance* rather than, for example, 'value formation' (a more popular term in the literature) is used because it is more encompassing. Values are reducible to importance, but not the other way around: everything valuable is also important, but not everything that is important is valuable (e.g. earthquakes are important but generally not valued). The title also emphasises that this area is not concerned with forming moral, political or cultural values, but with the process of ascribing importance (to an object, person, activity, or idea). The factors that affect this process and its consequences are the main focus here.

THEORETICAL LEVEL

Consequences. Our state of mind depends significantly on what is important to us (and to what extent). One of the consequences of importance is that it increases personal attachment. The more important something is for you, the more you depend on it. This can also affect your emotions. Focusing all emotional capacity in one direction creates an imbalance of importance. It causes possessiveness on one side and detachment on the other (typical examples of this are a person who neglects everybody else when she starts a relationship, or the closedness of those absorbed by hate). Fixation occurs when an object of a need or desire becomes more important than a need or desire itself, which prevents the individual from recognising other options (e.g. infatuation). On the other hand, decreasing importance can reduce worrying and increase personal freedom, but may also cause boredom, isolation, alienation and a lack of motivation. Indifference and cynicism aim to leave an impression of a low level of importance, but this is often false. They are defensive mechanisms that usually disguise insecurity or a feeling of inadequacy. It is impossible to know what may become important, so nothing is so insignificant that it can be ignored (e.g. a little fish bone can suddenly become a matter of life and death). In a complex system like human society, every action may potentially have immense consequences (the so called 'butterfly effect'). Narrowing the gap between what is considered important and unimportant increases the chance of finding a wider range of objects, persons and situations interesting or enjoyable.

Factors that affect importance. Ascribing importance is based on your inner structure (see p.65) but it also depends on needs (the more hungry you are, the more important food becomes), social conditioning and habits (most people, for example, support a club that their parents supported), or personal choice. Generally, giving importance to external objects or events is learnt, but in time it often becomes automatic. However, it is possible to have a conscious re-evaluation, assessment and shift of importance.

Importance is often a projection of self-importance onto the environment, so you can affect it by considering the importance of your own image or desires (e.g. the importance of a new pair of shoes can be re-evaluated if you examine why you really want them).

Changing the perspective (closeness or distance) can also affect importance, while awareness of death and humour can help against taking things too seriously.

Importance is inversely proportional to availability (it is a common tendency to take for granted what is easily available) but it is proportional to an investment. The more you invest (time, thoughts, emotions, effort, money etc.) into something the more important it becomes: 'whenever we make a sacrifice for some goal, our motivation to achieve that goal is strengthened'[101]. The sense of importance is not stable, though. What is important today may be forgotten tomorrow, so investments can be wasted. Giving importance to a process rather than a product, result or aim, enables focusing on what one is doing without excessive pressure or anxiety.

REFLECTIVE LEVEL

Choose an object, person, event, activity or principle and reflect on why it is important for you. Considering the following issues may also be beneficial: do we always attach importance to people, ideas, objects or events, or something has an inherent value? What is more important for you, the process or the end result (e.g. do you prefer a game you can easily win or one in which you can improve)? Do you think that the statement, 'if nothing is important, nothing is unimportant either' makes sense? Is it possible (and desirable) to live without the sense of importance? What is more important, people themselves or what they represent (e.g. is John more important, or his role as a teacher)?

PRACTICAL LEVEL

The pyramid of priorities. Make a list of priorities, so that everything in your life may be situated within one of these categories. Organize them in the shape of a pyramid so that the most important one is on the top. Then, you can decide how much attention each level deserves (of course, categories can change places from time to time).

Importance regulation. If you feel that you are giving more importance to something than it deserves, you may take a larger perspective (for example, awareness of being a part of humankind, or of your mortality) and see if it makes any difference. This re-evaluation should start from less significant phenomena and then be slowly expanded. On the other hand, if you want to increase importance of something, invest more into it. It doesn't matter what, it could be your time, thoughts, emotions, effort, money and so on.

RECOMMENDED MATERIALS

Lewins, H. *A Question of Values* is an interesting read. The short stories 'The door in the wall' by H. G. Wells and 'The Dead' by James Joyce are also highly recommended.

27. ATTACHMENT

As you learn to become more and more detached, you discover that you are then able to love those who are dear to you in a deeper, more constructive way.

Roberto Assagioli

The term *attachment* was first used in psychology in the nineteen sixties to signify the relationship between an infant and its mother (or other carer). Soon after, the use of the term has spread to any other significant relationships. In this model, however, the term has a somewhat different and wider meaning. Attachment is considered to be a subjective sense of connectedness to something or somebody else. This is different from the above-mentioned use in several ways:

Attachment does not refer only to relationships with other human beings. It could include attachment to animals (e.g. pets), objects (e.g. money), ideas (e.g. socialism), places (e.g. one's country), activities (e.g. one's job), pleasures (e.g. addictions), etc.

The sense of attachment cannot be identified with emotions, although it is very often related to them. It is possible to be attached to somebody or something without being emotional (e.g. out of habit), and to be emotional without being attached. By the same token, detachment may be related, but not identified with separation, loss or mourning.

Attachment is not identified with physical proximity or social roles. For example, it is possible to live with one's spouse and not feel attached to her, or not live with somebody (who can even be dead) and still be attached to her. Defined in this way, attachment is an irreducible and yet universal phenomenon.

Attachment plays an important role in life, but misconceptions about its function and relation to other areas are common and often reinforced by popular culture (e.g. an image of a cool, detached hero). So, this area will compare the three related concepts and their consequences: *attachment, non-attachment* and *detachment*.

THEORETICAL LEVEL

Attachment is related to our sense of security, which is why it increases in threatening situations. Attachment may have positive effects on physical and mental health and intimacy, but it may restrict freedom and flexibility, increase dependency and intensify feelings related to loss. When one tries to control an object of attachment, it becomes possessiveness. Possessiveness occurs when emotions originate from the need for attachment, rather than attachment being the result of emotions. It is usually a result of insecurity and is always 'tragic' because nothing can be possessed permanently.

Detachment is a result of a person's inability or unwillingness to connect with the environment, or a lack of response from the environment. It can be a way to protect oneself or an image of oneself by building an armour or barriers against the world. It may decrease intensity of some undesirable feelings (e.g. those related to loss), but it prevents direct experience and intimacy, and impoverishes the quality of life.

Non-attachment means that the subjective sense of connectedness is under your control, so that it does not limit your freedom and can be revoked. It can protect you from getting stuck, enables choice and freedom, and counteracts inertia. Non-attachment does not imply distancing. In fact, it enables you to approach the world, because self-imposed barriers are not necessary any more. It also does not mean denying anything to yourself, but rather freeing yourself from dependency, longing and the need to possess the objects of your desires. Consequences of non-attachment are increased independence, strength (because it decreases vulnerability), flexibility, and a greater variety of experience. On the other hand, in some cases it may lead to a reduced quality and depth of experience, and difficulties in maintaining commitment or persistence.

REFLECTIVE LEVEL

Examine which one of the above three concepts dominates your own attitudes. You may also consider how you deal with the fact that we can only temporarily possess something or be mutually attached. Does it cause anxiety, or you can accept it?

PRACTICAL LEVEL

Dis-identification. It is believed that external attachments are formed through one's attachments to internal states. So, some authors[102] recommend dis-identifying with your emotions, thoughts, body, traits etc., by reminding yourself that they are only elements of your personality. One way of doing this is by repeating to yourself a statement such as 'I am not my emotions, they are a part of myself, I am not by thoughts, they are a part of myself...'. Developing this attitude can put you more in charge of your faculties.

Letting go. If you feel too attached to something or somebody, sensations of letting go, releasing, floating away in relation to the object of your attachment may help. Relaxation and imagery can make it easer to invoke these sensations (you can visualise, for example, allowing a balloon to float away or releasing a bird from a cage).

RECOMMENDED MATERIALS

There are several sources for this area. It takes a prominent place in some Eastern philosophies (especially those related to Buddhism) with an emphasis on non-attachment or detachment. In the West, many popular psychology books also stress the importance of non-attachment, (commonly referred to as an ability 'to let go'). Parkes *at al.* (ed.) *The Place of Attachment in Human Behaviour* provides a balanced and comprehensive overview. Camus' novel *The Outsider* is a potent example of addressing this subject in literature, although most fiction and movies can be analysed from this perspective.

28. TOLERANCE

If you are pained by external things, it is not they that disturb you, but your own judgement of them. And it is in your power to wipe out that judgement now.

Marcus Aurelius

This area focuses on our ability to tolerate experiences such as pain, hardship, noise, etc.[103] A certain level of tolerance is necessary to survive. Common attitudes towards tolerance still reflect some prejudices about what it means, how it is achieved and from whom a high level of tolerance is expected.

THEORETICAL LEVEL

Tolerance essentially refers to power and control over unpleasant or unwanted experiences. Their impact can be intercepted on all three levels: source, experience itself and reaction to it. However, only the third possibility doesn't decrease your sensitivity.

Denial (affects the source or its importance) can be a useful short-term coping strategy, helping you avoid being overwhelmed by a difficult experience where the possibilities for a direct action is limited or of little use. It can alleviate the strength of the first impact that the effects of the situation have, and in that way it can provide a brief respite from distress. However, denial may prevent you from affecting the situation constructively.

Suppression (affects experience) can be physiological (drugs, anaesthetics etc.) or psychological (e.g. hypnosis can have a similar effect as anaesthetics, in reducing *an experience* of pain). It may also be induced from outside (e.g. army drill). Suppression may alleviate unpleasant sensations, but it can have counter-productive long-term consequences. Any experience is information. Physical or emotional pain, for example, signals some disturbance, and suppressing it may prevent you from taking steps to deal with its causes. Suppression also often creates tension. This is not to say that you should dwell on unpleasant sensations in order to avoid suppression. A pain, for instance, has an informative function, but when the information is received and action is taken to deal with a cause, focusing on pain is unnecessary. Empirical evidence shows that '... close monitoring of a stressor or of the physical sensations caused by the stressor results in perceptions of more intense sensations, and slower habituation to the stressor.'[104]

Firmness (affects the reaction): allowing yourself to experience a sensation but not act automatically upon it increases your awareness and makes you stronger and more resilient in the long term. Firmness is not endurance, resignation to suffering, but the ability to control the effects of unpleasant experiences. This means being aware of them, but not giving in, not allowing yourself to be driven by them. Firmness doesn't mean being rigid, it is compatible with being relaxed and open towards the world – though not in an amorphous state, but with a firm core, based on the clarity of your choices. This doesn't imply being insensitive but clear-headed, which enables you to remain in control.

Factors that affect tolerance. Tolerance is decreased by an exaggerated sense of self-importance and especially self-pity (or pity, if it is a result of identification) because it already implies resignation, giving up. Self-pity increases negative feelings and never helps. Avoidance also decreases tolerance, while repeated exposure increases it. Avoiding negative experience (which is different from suppressing) requires avoiding situations related to that experience which limits freedom and choice. A psychologist Kobasa singles out three aspects of the personality which increase tolerance (or *hardiness* as she calls it): *commitment* – believing in truth, importance and value of who you are and what you are doing, an overall sense of purpose; *internal control* – maintaining the sense that you are in charge of the situation; *challenge* – believing that change rather than stability is normal, and interpreting stressful life events as an opportunity for growth[105].

Physical fitness and mental balance contribute to tolerance, too. Personal depth also enhances tolerance because bothersome, superficial experiences lose their importance.

REFLECTIVE LEVEL

It may be interesting to consider the relation between tolerance and social interactions. For example, can we be less considerate if somebody appears tolerant (e.g. does one's ability to tolerate noise gives the right to others to be noisy)? This issue is important, because intolerant reactions are often not related to tolerance itself, but are in fact attempts to make others pay attention or be more respectful.

PRACTICAL LEVEL

Desensitisation is a technique suggested by a number of authors from different backgrounds. It consists of exposing yourself gradually and in a controlled way to the situation that causes inadequate or exaggerated reactions, until you become used to it and manage to regain control. It can be done in real or imagined situations. Allow yourself first to experience your reactions and then (if possible) remove yourself from the situation. Consider possible causes for low tolerance and make an attempt to develop a new, more adaptable insight into the situation. Try to replace negative sensations with more acceptable ones and then return to the situation again. After a while habituation should take place, and the level of unpleasant sensation should start subsiding.

RECOMMENDED MATERIALS

The Resilience Factor by Reivich & Shatte and Argyle, M. *The Psychology of Happiness* can be useful. Some biographies (of Mandela, Gandhi or Marx, for example) exemplify how commitment to ideals and goals may increase tolerance.

HAPPY THE MAN

Happy the man, and happy he alone,
  He who can call today his own:
    He who, secure within, can say,
Tomorrow do thy worst, for I have lived today.
  Be fair or foul or rain or shine
The hoys I have possessed, in spite of fate, are mine.
Not Heaven itself upon the past has power,
But what has been, has been, and I have had my hour.

John Dryden

THE CONTEXT GROUP

One of the universal characteristics of human life is that it is always situated in a particular context. The basic context within which we operate in the world is time-space. This group consists of the areas that relate to the components of this framework: *The present, The past*, and *The future* and *Relating to the situation* (or our 'space').

The present refers to awareness of what is going on at the moment. The position of this area indicates that it encompasses both, the external and internal domains. This is because it includes awareness of our immediate surrounding, but also our internal experiences. 'The present' is the root area of this group, because, it is, as it were, only reality and therefore the basis for other areas.

The past focuses on the various ways we can relate to our past experiences. This relationship is approached here in a general way. More specific influences of the past are addressed in some other areas (for example, the influences of up-bringing, or social conditioning, is addressed in the area *Personal Freedom, p.143*). This area belongs to the internal domain because those experiences are a part of our inner world.

The future examines the abilities that contribute to constructing the fugue, such as expectations, hopes and predictions. It does not, however, deal with the ways we *create* the future (e.g. planning). They are addressed in various areas in the Active Category. This area belongs to the external domain because anticipating forthcoming events is mostly orientated towards external world.

Relating to the situation refers to the perception and evaluation of our situation. It is the final area in this group because our assessments are not only based on the perceived quality of life at the moment, but also on our past experiences and future expectations. Which is also the reason why it encompasses both, the internal and external domain (as its location in the map shows).

29. THE PRESENT

The present which is here and now
Such wise one should aspire to win
What never can be lost nor shaken.

Buddha

This area focuses on the experience of the present (also known as the state of being 'here and now') and *attention* and *concentration* that are usually associated with this state.

THEORETICAL LEVEL

Presence. Although we are inevitably always physically present, we can mentally diverge from the present and focus on the past, future, different places and situations, or fantasize. This ability has some advantages. It can help us tolerate difficult or unpleasant situations and alleviate some sensations and feelings (e.g. boredom, pain etc.). However, if it becomes a habit, it can result in an increase of the intensity and frequency of the very feelings we want to avoid and a reduction in direct experience. Focusing on the present enables us to experience life fully and increases the awareness and control of the situation. It also minimises absentmindedness, forgetfulness and clumsiness, and can reduce stress and anxiety[106]. On the other hand, being too absorbed in the here and now may lead to ignoring a larger perspective, past experiences or long term consequences of present actions (e.g. engaging in a pleasure activity can make us forget other commitments). So, presence should not lead to narrowing yourself, being stuck in the present. It is really productive if it involves focusing the totality of your experience in the present moment including the awareness of the context, previous experiences and future possibilities.

Characteristics of being present:

Attention means focusing awareness. It does not only help us gather information about an object of interest quickly and accurately, but it also releases awareness from other unimportant or undesirable contents (such as worries or a background chatter). However, if the focus remains rigid and narrow, attention can, in fact, contribute to neglecting some information that may be important, so, it needs to be flexible (see the exercises below).

Concentration is an ability to maintain the focus on the object of attention. The factors that contribute to concentration are restfulness, motivation and relative peace. External peace requires minimising distractions (e.g. phone ringing), while internal peace requires minimising inner conflicts (such as a desire to do something else).

REFLECTIVE LEVEL

Consider what the present means to you, how it feels, whether it is more or less important than your past or future. You can also pay attention to when you are present and when you are not, what makes you 'wander off' and if it is helpful. To what extent do you control this ability? Would you like to change anything in this respect (for example, to be more present, or to be less forgetful about the larger perspective)?

PRACTICAL LEVEL

On the top of a mountain. This exercise can help you remember a larger perspective when you are too absorbed in an immediate experience. Try to bring your thoughts about the past, future or other events into the present (so that they become present experiences too). This means letting your thoughts be included without allowing them to consume or exclude the present. To achieve this, it may help to imagine that the present moment is the top of a mountain, from where you can see everything else is below.

Life house. Imagine that your life is a house that has several rooms (work, study, family, leisure, etc.). Although aware of the whole house, try to focus fully on the room you are in. The benefit of this is that while in one section of life you can avoid unwarranted interference and have rest from the other sections.

Mindfulness is a type of meditation that can be applied in many situations (e.g. while cleaning, walking or queuing). It 'embodies techniques for carrying a more tranquil and composed mental state into daily activities...'[107] Mindfulness consists of effortless concentration and full attentiveness to what you are experiencing or doing at that moment. Simply allow yourself to be absorbed in the here and now, rather than being mentally transported somewhere else. This can enhance your sense of presence (and by doing so your sense of liveliness) and usually has a calming and centring effect.

Awareness control can help you develop the elasticity of awareness. Being able to change its focus and scope can be of a significant value. It consists of several stages:
a) Choose a small object. It could be anything, a mug, leaf, part of your body (e.g. a hand), picture etc. Focus on it, observe, touch, hold, smell it. You will probably notice some details that you have not been aware of before (even if it is a very familiar object) relating to shape, colour, structure, texture etc. If your mind wonders off, bring the focus gently back to the object as long as you find that your awareness is enriched. The same exercise can be tried with an imagined object, a sound or a piece of music.
b) This stage is the opposite of the previous one. Try to expand your awareness and become aware of as many sensations as possible at the same time.
c) This step is a combination of the first two. Focus first on one object and then expand awareness as much as possible, then focus awareness again, and so on, until you reach an optimal control over this ability.
Instead of focusing on an object (or other sources of sensations), you can focus only on one sense (e.g. hearing), gradually include the others, and then return to the first one.

RECOMMENDED MATERIALS
Chapter eight in Rainwater, J. *You're in charge,* Kabat-Zinn, J. *Mindfulness Meditation for Everyday Life* and Huxley's novel *Island* are suggested.

30. THE PAST

> Each person who gets stuck in
> time gets stuck alone
>
> Alan Lightman

How important the past is for an individual is a contentious question in psychology. However, there is no doubt that we all have the past and that it affects practically every aspect of our lives, including our thoughts, feelings and behaviour, so it should not be neglected. This area will consider various ways of relating to our past experiences.

THEORETICAL LEVEL

To what extent and how your past will influence your life depends on the way you relate to it. Feelings about the past are coloured by your present state of mind. So, although the past cannot be changed, your perspective on the past can, which in turn can modify its effects on the present. There are several common ways of relating to the past.

Attachment to the past. The memory can be biased and selective, which is sometimes used to idealize the past. This may induce some pleasant feelings and enable a temporary escape from the present. However, if this becomes attachment to what is gone, it can create longing and dissatisfaction, and prevent you from experiencing and assessing the present situation realistically. If you remain bound to the past, you won't be able to live your life fully and freely. It is important to recognize that longing for the past is actually longing for certain feelings or states of mind that are a part of you not the past, so they may be recreated again in new situations.

Blaming the past for the present situation can be a way of avoiding personal responsibility. It can make you feel better in the short term, but it is an impediment to future achievements (leading to 'self-fulfilling prophecy', for example) and restricts your freedom. The past can be dealt with, so it cannot be an excuse.

Avoiding the past. Running away from the past, suppressing unpleasant experiences, can provide a temporary relief. It may be useful if, for example, the present situation requires your full attention. However, the past affects the present and therefore should not be ignored. Underlying emotions relating to past events will continue to have an effect at the unconscious level and in that way they will be even less under your control.

Facing the past in some instances may be unpleasant or even painful, but it can be psychologically and even physically beneficial. A number of studies suggests that confiding or confronting the perceptions and feelings associated with previously inhibited life experiences or traumatic events can help the person to come to terms with and integrate them. This, in turn, can improve the functioning of immune system and physical health in general[108].

Accepting the past (without being attached to it) allows you to move on. An initial stage may require going through a 'mourning' process. This can be beneficial if you don't remain stuck in it but eventually accept what has happened and free yourself from the grip of regret or remorse. Bear in mind that even bad experiences, mistakes and missed opportunities can be useful if you learn something from them or if they initiate a constructive change. The future cannot alter the past but it can often correct it.

REFLECTIVE LEVEL
Considering the following questions may help you clarify your relation to the past and the effects it has on your life: to what extent do you think that your present behaviour and attitude is affected by the past experiences? How do you feel and what do you do about past mistakes or missed opportunities? Is it helpful? What can we learn from the past? Does the past (your own, that your family, country, or the whole civilization) have a meaning and value and how it can be utilized?

PRACTICAL LEVEL

Re-visiting the past can help you decrease its influence, finish the old dramas and stop repeating them in the present. It can take the form of visualization or, alternatively, writing, drawing or speaking about a past event. It is observed that confiding, for example, 'allows individuals to 'forget' or to otherwise put the event behind them'[109]. This is because talking (and other methods) externalise the experience, which can help you work through, reframe and find meaning in it. It can also release the pressure of emotional reactions that may have been suppressed.

Whatever form you choose, the situation needs to be re-visited vividly, as it was. Do not get carried away by fantasy ('if only...'), just allow the spontaneous unravelling of your feelings and thoughts. Bear in mind though, that you are re-visiting the situation, not emotions you had (although they have to be acknowledged, repeating them my just leads to reinforcement). Don't forget that the reactions you had then may be different from the feelings you have now (e.g. you may have been afraid and run away, and you may feel ashamed for doing so now). They need to be tackled separately. It is especially important to remember that there is no need to be afraid any more of your reactions or people and events from the past (you survived, didn't you?).

Repeating this process should enable you to gradually accept the event and minimise its inhibiting effects on the present. It doesn't necessarily mean that unpleasant feelings will disappear or be replaced with pleasant ones, but, you will be able to control them, rather than letting them control you[110].

Writing autobiography can also help to come to terms with and make sense of the past. You can start at any point of your life and don't need to follow a chronological order.

RECOMMENDED MATERIALS
Schiffman, M. *Selftherapy* and Chapter 5 in Rainwater, J. *You're in charge* deal with this subject in more detail. *Remembrance of Things Past* by Proust can be inspiring.

31. THE FUTURE

> The future influences the present just as much as the past.
>
> Friedrich Nietzsche

Awareness of the future is uniquely human ability that significantly affects our lives. It might be obvious but nevertheless important to point out that the future does not exist. It is our mental construct that may (or may not) match to some extent with what will happen. The trick is to minimize discrepancies between these two. To achieve this, some common ways of perceiving the future is worth considering.

THEORETICAL LEVEL

Expectations mean believing that something is highly probable or likely to happen. They are necessary for normal functioning (we expect that day will come after night, or to find our home at the same place where it was before). However, unfulfilled expectations can lead to disappointment and frustration, because our sense of predictability and control are threatened. This can be avoided by minimizing attachment to expectations. Attachment usually takes place when we ignore other possibilities, fantasize about or invest emotionally into the outcome. So, accepting that something else may happen besides what we expect can reduce attachment and consequently disappointment. Especially attachment to unrealistic, improbable expectations that rely on wishful thinking rather than facts is counter-productive. Such expectations are usually the result of not accepting yourself, others or your situation. Idealizing the future can be a temporary escape, but it shifts the focus to an imagined world, which means missing the present, missing life. The old notion that happiness is inversely proportional to expectations and proportional to attainment is supported by both, analysis and empirical research. As one author summarises, 'the only overall way to increase happiness is to meet or reduce expectations.'[111]

Expectations that you are not attached to don't have an adverse effect on the present and allow more freedom. They are more satisfying because they are accompanied by the sense of ease if fulfilled, and create less disappointment if they are not. Not being attached to your expectations does not mean not having them, turning your back on the world or giving in to inertia. It is a state of mind characterised by being relaxed and attentive at the same time; being calm but open to recognize an opportunity and ready to take it. In this way, you can defeat impatience, but preserve liveliness. To minimize the pressure of expectations put them in perspective (e.g. by bearing in mind the transient nature of life). To maintain patience, deep convictions and faith can help.

Hopes are similar to expectations, but what we hope for is normally perceived as less certain, so it is easier to avoid attachment. Even so, hopes are more in the sphere of feelings than thinking, which is why they have a strong effect on motivation, performance and coping. It is well known that even extremely adverse situations can be endured if there is a hope. Losing hope, on the other hand, may be dilapidating.

Predictions refer to being aware of all the possibilities. Ignoring or rejecting the future can provide some respite, but it is counter-productive in the long run. Considering the alternatives is the way to avoid disappointment. Foreseeing possible setbacks also increases coping ability. Everybody can be weaken by an unpleasant surprise. If you put an effort into predicting in advance anything that can reasonably happen you will always know what to do and how to react. Being prepared is often enough to put you in a right frame of mind to overcome, avoid or minimize the effect of an undesirable situation. This does not mean worrying, expecting a problem or misfortune, but thinking through (and accepting) various possibilities, without giving in to either expectations or concerns. This is why it is better to base predictions on reason than affect. Besides thinking, intuition can also be a source of prediction but, like anything else, it can be mistaken. Moreover, intuitive predictions seem to be valid only if the situation continues to develop in the same direction. So, there is no need for fatalism, you can change the intuited outcome if you change the direction of the situation.

REFLECTIVE LEVEL
Examine to what extent you believe that the future is determined, what can affect it and how important it is for you. Beside your personal future, this can include your ideas about the future of your immediate environment, country or humankind.

PRACTICAL LEVEL
Looking in to see out. Visualise or draw a picture of a symbol that represents the future. A road is a common one: it can be straight or wavy, rough or smooth, busy or empty, going up or down. What does it tell you about the way you see and feel about you future?

Back to the future. Try to formulate a message that you would send to yourself in the past, especially concerning your expectations, hopes and predictions (it could be a recent or distant past). Then, imagine yourself in the future (again, a near or distant one) and consider what message you would send to yourself now.

Predictions check. It may be very useful to recall situations when you have *failed* to make a correct prediction and analyse the reasons why this has happened. For example, you'd thought a party was going to be great, and it was really a waste of time. Why had you got it wrong? How can you avoid such 'mistakes' in the future?

RECOMMENDED MATERIALS
Hope and Despair by A. Reading is one of few books on this subject. Becket's drama *Waiting for Godot* is a poignant illustration of the effects of false expectations.

32. RELATING TO THE SITUATION

God, give me the serenity
To accept what cannot be changed.
The courage to change what can be changed,
And the wisdom to know the difference.

St Teresa of Avila

This area examines three elements that define how we relate to our situation: perception of the situation (including the present, past and future), the basic attitudes (acceptance and rejection) and also evaluation of the situation (or life satisfaction).

THEORETICAL LEVEL

Perception of the situation is one of the basic human abilities and worth paying attention to. The research suggests that an ambiguous state of affairs is often more stressful than knowing even the most negative outcome[112]. The more we are aware of our situation the more we can direct and affect it, which increases the sense of control. Perception, of course, needs to be accurate, but this is not straightforward. How many time have you jumped to conclusion or have seen the situation in wrong light? This happens because we are affected by our previous experiences, expectations, intentions or feelings. So, first of all, an accurate perception requires separating it from our mental constructs; they can assist us in making sense of what we perceive, but they can also distort it (an exercise below may help in this case). Moreover, our perception is sometimes based on clues too complex or subtle to be rationally understood. An intuitive grasp of a situation is often an important contributing factor. It can be called *sense* (as in 'he had the sense of uneasiness in the room'). Sense is a quicker and more direct way of assessing the situation because it is not based on verbal interpretations, and is largely developed through experience. However, as perception needs to be separated from thoughts, sense needs to be separated from feelings that usually come *after* our interpretations and are more specific (and also, if possible, verified by other means).

Acceptance and rejection. How we feel about our situation does not depend only on the circumstances but also on a way we relate to the circumstances. Different people feel differently in the same situation. This depends on our aspirations, expectations, previous experience and often comparing with others. Realising that your views, feelings and thoughts about the situation are a part of yourself not the situation, increases flexibility. It is unlikely that your situation will ever be perfect. If you are dissatisfied, you can attempt to change or leave the situation you are in, but also you can try to change your feelings and thoughts about it (you can take that your glass is either half full, or half empty). Rejection may initiate change, but accepting your situation creates harmony within yourself and with the environment (which is a precondition for happiness). Shelving, at least temporarily, those desires that cannot be attended to at that moment can help in accepting the situation. This, of course, does not need to lead to resignation, giving up. It can be a firm starting point for an improvement. In fact, it is easier to affect the situation constructively if we face it, than if we reject it. Also, we are more likely to get support from our surrounding if we accept and find our place in it.

Evaluating the situation. Life satisfaction depends on how we evaluate our situation and this, in turn, depends on comparing it either with our past, future (expectations), or something in the present. The last one may involve comparing with others (keeping up with Jones's), or setting your own standards. Comparing with others may cause so called 'status anxiety'. It is, allegedly the main reason for dissatisfaction in the Western world despite the fact that (at least in this part of the world) we live better than ever, not only with respect to material wealth, but also security, relative freedom and health. So, it is far better to set your own standards, rather than using others as a measuring stick. Where you will draw the line is up to you, but bear in mind that too high standards may be frustrating and cause disappointment, while too low standards may be de-motivating.

REFLECTIVE LEVEL

On this level you can examine how you relate to your situation. Do you perceive your situation accurately? Are you satisfied with it? Which aspects of your situation do you accept and which ones do you reject? What can you do about it?

PRACTICAL LEVEL

Phenomenological reduction. What usually muddles the perception is our preconceptions. This exercise can help you perceive reality more directly. It consists of focusing on your surroundings while deliberately bracketing (or suspending) your interpretations, expectations and judgements. Start first from a simple and familiar situation (later you can expand it further) . For example, imagine that your room is new to you, examine and touch the objects, smell the air. If you notice that your pre-set feelings and thoughts (e.g. memories) interfere, let them pass without allowing yourself to be carried away by them, and try to keep the focus on immediate sensations. This exercise is not so easy as it may seem, but can be very refreshing.

Evening review. Going through the previous day in your mind before sleep can help you cleanse yourself from its residues and bring some clarity. It is important, however, not to give in to fantasies, worries or planning, but stick to what has happened, and leave all the unfinished business for another day.

Accepting the situation. Explore what aspects of your situation you find difficult to accept, try to find reasons and express your emotions about them. You can then try to change the perspective by, for example, focusing on positive rather than negative aspects of the situation or seeing what can be gained from what is perceived as negative.

RECOMMENDED MATERIALS

Part One in *Man's Search for Meaning* by Frankl can be inspiring. It is an autobiographical account that exemplifies how the way we relate to the situation can affect even extremely adverse circumstances.

THE WIND, ONE BRILLIANT DAY

The wind, one brilliant day, called
To my soul with an odor of jasmine.

'In return for the odor of my jasmine,
I'd like all the odor of your roses.'

'I have no roses; all the flowers
in my garden are dead.'

'Well then, I'll take the withered petals
and the yellow leaves and the waters of the fountain.'

The wind left. And I wept. And I said to myself:
'What have you done with the garden that was
                              entrusted to you?'

Antonio Machado
(translated by Robert Bly)

CHOICE GROUP

This group consists of the following areas:

Meaning is the root area of the group. The assertion is that choice is exercised only if an action is perceived as meaningful in some respect. To clarify the locus of this area it is necessary to distinguish two categories: *meaning of life* based on the belief that life has a purpose, that there is an overall plan, and *meaning in life*, reasons to live. Although these two can sometimes coincide (among, for example, revolutionaries or religious devotees), they do not depend on each other. This area is concerned only with the latter category, because the former does not comply with the criterion of universality (not everybody believes that life in general is meaningful).

Personal freedom and *Personal responsibility* are two polar areas that regulate the scope of choice. 'Personal' is added to distinguish these terms from, for example, political freedom or imposed social responsibilities respectively. Personal freedom is identified with autonomy, defined in this model as relative independence from physical, social and other determinants. Personal responsibility means accepting oneself as an agent. Freedom and responsibility understood in this way do not need to oppose, but can complement each other. Note that the area Personal responsibility relates to *Self-discipline* (p.76), but cannot be reduced to it. Responsibility is possible even without self-discipline (e.g. you can act responsibly by avoiding tempting situations, rather than trying to exercise self-control in them); conversely, in some cases people who have self-discipline can act without personal responsibility (e.g. soldiers who follow orders from their superiors).

The above three areas can be considered the necessary conditions *to be able* to choose. Just having a choice is not sufficient; one can be, for example, conditioned to react in a certain way without considering other options, even when they exist. The last area, *Deciding,* focuses on making a choice (presuming that the above conditions are met).

33. MEANING

> He who has a why to live
> can bear almost any how.
> Friedrich Nietzsche

Perceiving one's life and actions as meaningful is a universal need, but meaning cannot be generalised. So this area will mainly focus on the purpose and locus of meaning.

THEORETICAL LEVEL
Purpose. A number of psychologists point out that we require meaning to survive[113]. The most frequent reason given for suicide is that the person has no purpose for which to continue living. Research also shows that people who report 'a stronger sense of the purpose of their lives remain healthier in the face of stress'[114], and that 'feeling that one's life has some meaning and purpose is associated with happiness'.[115] Philosopher Bradley suggests that this is so because of the human need for coherence (or wholeness): 'if pleasures and achievements do not have any meaningful relation to one another, they will not give any satisfying overall character to one's life'[116] This suggests that the sense that life is meaningful can be lost if you are bound only to short-term day-to-day tasks. Overall aims, visions, deep affects, ideals (not as something above, but as a part of you) can provide inspiration and make a value of everyday life, rather than letting it be reduced to a succession of dreary experiences. It is true that being realistic with your ideals can save you from naivety and disappointment. However, a cynical attitude that mocks those sentiments on the basis that any ideals are either unattainable or not worth pursuing is usually a result of previous failures and, if directed towards others, can mask envy (because somebody else is persisting and may succeed). Cynical comments can weaken your commitment. To avoid this, you don't need to give up your ideals, but to be careful in front of whom, and how, you expose them.

Locus of meaning. Meaning in life is found (or created) by individuals, so a locus of meaning can be different for different people, which defines to some extent their life path. Being concerned only with yourself has a vulnerable and finite locus, so it provides temporary and partial fulfilment. Devotion to others (e.g. family, charity work, teaching, nursing, etc.) has a wider scope and can provide a more stable fulfilment (because even your death cannot diminish its meaningfulness). The universal as a locus is infinite and therefore gives lasting meaning. It does not exclude the first two, but includes them as a part of a wider perspective. The universal can be found in different forms (spirituality, nature, humankind, philosophical ideas, etc.). What is important is awareness that you are a part of a larger picture and willingness to harmonise your life and actions with it. In the words of Victor Frankl, meaning in life is found if you ask what life expects from you, not what you expect from life. This does not require following blindly an ideology or credo. Devotion is not submission. It has substance only if it is based on choice, rather than fear of punishment or expecting a reward. Freely accepting certain universal guidelines does not mean becoming enslaved by them. It may require, though, transcending individualistic 'freedom' that in fact often amounts to nothing more but being driven by some aspects of your personality (e.g. urges, emotions, intellect, a personal image, habits etc.). Doing so decreases inner conflicts, worries, uncertainty and hesitation, because your immediate desires lose their significance.

Commitment is an expression of meaning. When people describe their lives as meaningful, they usually mean that they are committed to, and are pursuing with some reasonable success, valued goals or incentives[117]. You can be committed only to something that has meaning for you. A committed person has in mind an aim or purpose, and is willing to invest an effort and make some sacrifices if necessary.

A commitment to finite activities or destinations provides temporary meaning. For example, if you are committed to a sport achievement, bringing up children, or a job, life may become meaningless when a physical peak is reached, children leave, or you retire. However, it is possible to be committed to a process rather than finite aims (e.g. pursuing knowledge), which provides lasting meaning. Although commitment implies durability, in some situations it may need to be altered. Commitment can cease to be meaningful because of a change of circumstances or new insights, for example. If not abandoned or modified when it happens, it may become an unproductive obstinacy.

REFLECTIVE LEVEL
You may consider on this level if there is a meaning *of* life[118] and how it relates to the meaning *in* your life (e.g. whether your happiness is the only ultimate aim). You can also clarify what you are, or wish to be, committed to (or you find commitment restricting).

PRACTICAL LEVEL
Imaginary dialogue. You can use guided imagination to clarify your thoughts in this area. Sometimes it is easier to consider certain matters in a dialogue form, which can be provided by externalising and personalising a part of yourself. Some authors suggest creating an image that represents wisdom for you and engaging in a dialogue with it[119]. It could be a sage, philosopher, or even an old friend, relative or teacher.

RECOMMENDED MATERIALS
Hanfling, O. *Life and Meaning* and Frankl's *The will to meaning* can be insightful. Sartre's *Nausea* is an illustration of grappling with the problem of meaning, while *The Remains of the Day* by Ichiguro offers a critical perspective on commitment.

34. PERSONAL FREEDOM

> Life is like a game of cards. The hand that is dealt you represents determinism; the way you play it is free will.
>
> Jawaharlal Nehru

Personal freedom or autonomy refers to freedom from innate or internalised determinants[120]. It is an ability to transform determinants into influences, causes into motives, which allows choice. This area focuses on the determinants that preclude the development of autonomy and on the factors that contribute to overcoming them.

THEORETICAL LEVEL

Autonomy is a specifically human characteristic based on an ability to exercise choice. Although some circumstances may be more favourable for the development of autonomy, choice is always possible regardless of circumstances. Lazarus, a well-know psychologist and an authority on human emotions, asserts (contrary to the prevailing views at that time) that 'person chooses rather than the environment, and sometimes this choice operates against even the usual environmental pressures.'[121] Without awareness that you can choose, any action is only a conditioned reaction. However, this is not enough. Autonomy also requires 'inner democracy', harmony in which everything has a voice, but nothing takes over. This means recognising your motives, but not allowing to be driven by any of them. It implies taking into account every aspect of yourself and also short and long-term consequences, rather than following a drive that is strongest at that moment.

The factors that lead to autonomy are self-discipline, independence and reflective thinking. Each of them is linked to the determinants described below. Beside these factors, autonomy can also be strengthened by increasing knowledge and determination. This is because knowledge allows us see more options, while determination enables us to carry them through.

Determinants are strong influences that create habitual responses, precluding autonomous choice and decisions. They can be grouped in three broad categories.

Physical: everybody is, to some extent, determined by inherited predispositions. However, it seems that these predispositions are potentials that can be affected and modified. Innate traits are not bad or good in themselves. If well directed, they can be utilised for constructive purposes, but if unattended or suppressed they may express themselves in an uncontrolled or destructive way.[122] Directing physical determinants is achieved through self-discipline, which is, as stated above, a prerequisite for autonomy. Self-discipline does not restrict, but in fact enables greater freedom.

Social determinants are often covert, but their effects can be long lasting. They consist of internalised directives imposed by others that create one's *script*[123]. Script is a 'life program' laid out by significant others, often in early childhood. It also includes cultural determinants, which are normally transmitted by significant others too. A certain level of independence leads to a greater autonomy in this respect. It does not need necessarily to lead to a change; you can maintain the same values or attitudes and still be autonomous if it is the result of your choice. At least some elements of social conditioning are useful. They provide security and social orientation, so a decrease of social determination needs to be accompanied with an increase of *personal responsibility* (p.146).

Personal determinants can be linked to the past, present or future:

We can be determined by our previous experiences. If you, for example, had a bad experience while trying to learn to ride a bicycle, you may become predisposed against cycling (or even sports in general) throughout your life.

Determination can be the result of a self-image that individuals want to create or maintain in the present ('I am such and such person, so I should (not)…'). For example, you may start smoking to look 'cool' (to others or to yourself) and then make a habit of it.

Also, we can be determined by our own expectations, what we want to become (e.g. a girl who promises to herself to be a better mother than her mother is). The philosopher Sartre proposes that 'the development of the project is determined by a "fundamental choice" made during youth, a private resolution to address the world in a characteristic style.'[124] Even forgotten promises may be still influential. For example, a boy may promise to himself never to be a wimp again, and find himself incapable of crying years later, although the original situation and the promise are long forgotten.

Reflective thinking, a critical look at yourself, is a good starting point in decreasing the influence of this factor.

REFLECTIVE LEVEL
Examine the purpose and value of autonomy (e.g. perhaps one could be more carefree without it?) If you believe in universal determinants (e.g. destiny, karma, the laws of evolution) you can also consider how these forces relate to your freedom.

PRACTICAL LEVEL
De-conditioning. Locate a situation in which your reaction is predetermined (you act in a certain way for no good reason or even if you don't want to). Try to find out why you are forced to act in that way. What does this situation remind you of, how far back can you recognise the pattern? When you have examined the causes, consider other possibilities. Imagine acting differently, observe emerging emotions and thoughts and establish to what extent they are justified. This may, but doesn't need to lead to a behavioural change. It is sufficient that you become aware and *feel* that you have a choice.

RECOMMENDED MATERIALS
Bern, E. *What do you say after you say hello?* (focused mostly on social determination) and Collinson, D. *Free Will* are recommended for further explorations.

35. PERSONAL RESPONSIBILITY

> The ability to accept responsibility
> is the measure of the man.
>
> Roy L. Smith

Responsibility means accountability, readiness to accept the consequences of your actions (for yourself, others, and the environment). However, the term responsibility is sometimes coercively used to actually indicate complying with externally imposed rules or order. Such a responsibility is reducible to conditioning and therefore not a part of this area. *Personal* responsibility implies accountability, primarily to yourself. This should not be confused with concern for personal consequences only, the attitude often nourished by an externally imposed responsibility. In fact, 'orientating oneself by one's conscience always requires the ability to situate one's perspective within the wider framework of universal guidelines.'[125] Personal responsibility may require some effort but it is more reliable and lasting, while an imposed responsibility disappears if it is not constantly reinforced. This area will highlight the importance and consequences of personal responsibility and indicate some ways in which it can be developed.

THEORETICAL LEVEL

Responsibility derives from awareness and acceptance that you are an active participant in life. This implies that you have choice and control over your actions to some extent. It can be a burden, people are sometimes prepared to sacrifice much (independence, autonomy, dignity) to avoid it. However, denying responsibility does not make you not responsible but irresponsible. Accepting responsibility for your life is a necessary part of the growing up process, becoming a person. It is a precondition for achieving and maintaining autonomy and independence. Personal responsibility first of all means taking your life seriously. After all, you have only one life. Wasting it is often the result of a deep-rooted sense of unfairness that has lead to giving up. However, it does not correct, but aggravates injustice. Taking life seriously is the first step in taking a grip on reality. It means focusing your will, realizing that avoidance is only a temporary solution and that it is possible to face the world and survive. This requires courage, so the process of developing personal responsibility needs to be gradual, starting from small decisions and actions. It is fully compatible with being child-like but not with being childish, with having a sense of humour but not with being frivolous. It can involve analysing reasons for your mistakes, but not looking for excuses. Let's consider some common excuses or strategies that serve to avoid personal responsibility:

Childishness implies not taking oneself and one's actions seriously. Unlike the child-like state, childishness lacks spontaneity, it is a mask, a role adopted to justify certain behaviour. It indicates that the person is not prepared to accept those aspects of oneself that may cause anxiety, shame and guilt, so that he can indulge in momentary pleasures, self-pity or irresponsibility. It could also be a compensation, an attempt to live out what one was not allowed as a child. Childishness has a negative effect on self-respect, because it involves denying one's agency.

Justifications are ways of *denying* one's responsibility. They can take two forms: passing responsibility onto somebody else or a group (so called collective responsibility). A few familiar examples are 'everybody does it', 'if we don't do it, somebody else will', 'I have only obeyed the orders'. The other form revolves around blaming others or circumstances (e.g. parents, teachers, economic or political situation, etc.)

Rationalisation means constructing a false but plausible explanation for one's behaviour. It must include actual self-deception to be effective. These are some common examples: 'the examiner's assignment is unreasonable, so it is O.K. to cheat', 'they deserve it', 'she really wanted...', 'if we didn't attack them, they would attack us'.

Trying to deny, hide or forcefully restrain the above ways of avoiding responsibility is not helpful. Only if they are allowed to emerge to the surface and become recognized for what they are, can you learn about their true motives or causes.

REFLECTIVE LEVEL
Questions such as 'can I make something of my life? On whom or what does it depend?', can have a profound effect on how you relate to personal responsibility. You may also consider the relationship between personal responsibility and personal freedom (for example, when they oppose and when they complement each other).

PRACTICAL LEVEL
Parent-child-adult. Developing personal responsibility is sometimes prevented by an internalised parental figure (usually operating by 'shoulds' and 'should nots') that allows the rest of the person to be seemingly released from responsibility. If you recognize that you are divided into the part that orders, punishes, reproaches and praises (*parent*) and the irresponsible, passive part that obeys or rebels (*child*) this exercise is for you. Try to find out first who is talking, who is giving orders or permissions, and whether you really can't manage without such 'help'. Then, establish a dialogue between these aspects of yourself and try to integrate them into a personally responsible adult.

RECOMMENDED MATERIALS
There are not many good materials on this subject. The chapter 'Responsibility' in Peck, S. *The Road Less Travelled*, can be stimulating, even if it needs to be read judiciously. In fiction, Dostoyevsky's *Crime and Punishment* can be thought provoking, while Camus' *Plague* is an example of how personal responsibility can have social consequences.

36. DECIDING

Without the possibility of choice
and the exercise of choice a man
is not a man but a member, an
instrument, a thing.

Archibald MacLeish

The focus of this area is on the process of deciding in general
and factors that facilitate it. Some specific types of decisions are
addressed within other relevant areas.

THEORETICAL LEVEL

There is the inherent paradox between choice and its
realization: we are free to choose, but making a choice
inevitably leads to renouncing choice – for every *yes* there must
be a *no*, each decision eliminating other options. Thus, a
possibility of a wrong choice can bring a burden of
responsibility and sometimes feelings of anxiety and guilt,
which may paralyse decision-making. A philosopher Ricoeur
points out that '…there is often a sense of sacrifice or loss
which accompanies choice, however great the exhilaration of
forward movement'[126]. This can affect the capacity to tolerate
and time a pre-decision state, which may lead to impulsiveness.
However, you are not in control of your decision-making if
your rush into decisions or procrastinate, so it is important to be
able to bear uncertainty for a while. To achieve this, it is useful
to put 'wrong' decisions in perspective. Regardless of
circumstances, each possibility gives us an opportunity to gain
and lose something. Learning from a 'wrong' decision can
sometimes be more valuable than the gains from a 'right'
decision. It is also important to assess the importance of a
particular decision, some may not deserve much time and
agonizing over them. In most cases, it is more efficient to aim
for an optimal decision (that takes into account the amount of
time spent on deciding) rather than persisting on finding the
best one. Emphasizing the quality of execution (the resolve to
do your best whatever you decide) rather than only a final goal
or direction, helps in alleviating anxiety.

REFLECTIVE LEVEL

Think about what factors are most influential in your decision making (rational thinking, intuition, feelings, the advice of others, or something else). Evaluate their reliability and on that basis consider if you would like to include some other factors.

PRACTICAL LEVEL

Decision-making focuses on various elements that may be involved in this process (not all of them are, of course, always necessary). Preparation can include gathering relevant information and defining a time limit. Then, the following faculties can be used:

Cognitive can involve predicting and comparing outcomes of each possibility (you can write down their advantages and disadvantages to make it clear); setting up priorities and assessing which decision fits with more important ones (see p.117); taking into account how each decision affects your personal values and considerations (e.g. other people); the assessment of the situation, probability: whether your decision making is based on a realistic scenario or on wishful thinking or inflated concerns.

Perceptive refers to reflective consideration of external influences, advice of others or applied techniques (e.g. *I Ching*). *Reflective* implies being open to, but not swayed by advice. A final decision must come from the person, not from the outside. *Signs* can also be included in this group. Taking signs as messages from an external source with universal meaning may lead to superstition that gives false and at the best temporary security but limits much. However, your mind is always looking for clues related to an immediate problem, so signs can be considered intermediaries that can be a source of inspiration and help you communicate with the unconscious. From this perspective anything can be a sign and they do not have universal meaning. Their choice and interpretation can differ from person to person, and from situation to situation. The same 'sign' can have a different meaning in different situation (or for somebody else in the same situation) because the clue is not in a sign, but in the way it is interpreted.

Affective: it is important to be aware of the difference between being influenced by emotions and making decisions in order to satisfy them, which can lead to impulsiveness. To avoid this, imagine that various options have already been realized, and examine how you feel in each case (you can feel very differently before and after an event).

Intuitive: intuition can help when there is no enough information or time for deliberation, but it should not be confused with impulsive decisions. Intuition seems to be affected by the state of mind we are in, so it should not be followed blindly. If you are in a negative state (e.g. dominated by guilt or fear) your intuitive decision can be in fact a self-fulfilling prophecy. The other limitation is that intuition seems to relate only to what we are focused on, rather than a broader picture and far-reaching consequences. It is also difficult to separate intuition from feelings, desires, or wishful thinking, so always consider if what seems to be an intuitive insight can have a different explanation. Practice seems to be the best way to develop intuition. Record your intuitive hints (without necessarily following them) and later compare them with the outcome. When you collect enough data, try to determine the difference between intuitive hints that have been correct and those that have not. Although even this method is not always certain (it is often hard to predict outcomes of all the possibilities), in time intuition should become more and more reliable.

RECOMMENDED MATERIALS
'How to Make a No-Lose Decision' in Jeffers, S. *Feel the Fear And Do It Anyway* provides some practical advice on decision-making. Nadel, Haims & Stempson *Sixth Sense* explores intuition in a comprehensive, but accessible way. Shakespeare's *Hamlet* is a classic example of how indecisiveness can have tragic consequences.

TO BE A SLAVE OF INTENSITY

Friend, hope for the Guest while you are alive.
Jump into experience while you are alive!
Think… and think… while you are alive.
What you call 'salvation' belongs to the time before death.

If you don't break your ropes while you're alive,
Do you think
Ghosts will do it after?

The idea that the soul will join with the ecstatic
Just because the body is rotten –
That is all fantasy.
What is found now is found then.
If you find nothing now,
You will simply end up with an apartment in the City of
Death.
If you make love with the divine now, in the next life you
will have the face of satisfied desire.

So plunge into the truth, find out who the Teacher is,
Believe in the Great Sound!

Kabir says this: When the Guest is being searched for, it is
the intensity of the longing for the Guest that does all the
work.
Look at me, and you will see a slave of that intensity.

Kabir
(15th Century)

DIRECTIVE GROUP

All the areas in this group play a role in directing our actions.

Desires is the area that focuses on the *what* (you want). Two kinds of desires can be distinguished: desires that fulfil your real needs (*end-desires*) and desires that serve to fulfil some other (perhaps unacknowledged) desires (*means-desires*). This difference is important because the means-desires can be misguided and even contradict our needs.

Aims are more specific than desires. They involve knowing not only where you want to be, but also the way to get there.

Intention refers to the resolution to fulfil your aim. An aim is something that you project outside you, something that you strive for. Intention is an inner force that sustains the process of achieving an aim. It is not possible to intend what you think is not possible to attain. Similarly, intentions are different from desires. As one expert on this subject puts it, 'wants are satisfied whereas intentions are carried out.'[127] Intentions are deliberate, desires are usually not: a person 'can knowingly have conflicting wants but he cannot knowingly have conflicting intentions.'[128] Desires and aims are linked to the end result, while intentions are linked to the process, so they are more closely related to action, although, of course, they cannot be identified with it. It is recognised that 'intending is a state or event separate from the intended action or the reasons that prompted the action.'[129]. Intention is also different from *deciding* (p.149). Deciding is the process of making choice; intention comes about when that process ends.

Gratification is the final area in this group. Gratification cannot be reduced to *pleasure* (p.107). It is an internal process involving tension or imbalance reduction, while pleasure is a sensation. Gratification does not need to provide pleasure (e.g. some smokers say that they don't even enjoy cigarettes; a food that can be fulfilling and nutritious even if you don't like it, is another more wholesome example). Pleasure also does not need to be gratifying (for instance, gambling may be pleasurable, but is usually not gratifying especially when you lose).

37. DESIRES

One must not lose desires. They are mighty stimulants to creativeness, to love, and to long life.

Alexander A. Bogomoletz

Desires are an important motivational force. However, because they are rarely examined, even fulfilled desires are often not satisfying and only too quickly replaced with new ones. This area suggests how to increase awareness of desires and how to affect them.

THEORETICAL LEVEL

Awareness of desires is the first step in controlling them. It requires not being ashamed, trying to block, hide or push desires aside, but bringing them to the surface, admitting them to yourself (if not to others). To paraphrase one author[130], in order to remain in control, it is necessary to be clear about your evaluations, and this in turn implies that there cannot be unacknowledged desires which seriously interfere with these evaluations. In other words, you have to be honest with yourself. This does not mean giving importance to every whim. However, desires that feel intense or reoccur should not be ignored or underestimated, but treated with respect even if you are not pleased with them.

Desires that reflect our needs can be called *end-desires*. Needs are important for our physical and psychological balance and development. They relate to our inner state and are typically less specific then other desires[131]. However, one desire can also substitute another (e.g. the desire to have a flashy car may mask the desire to impress others). These are *means-desires*. They can be so removed from the real end-desire that you may not even be aware of it. Recognizing your true need enables making a right decision, security in carrying it out, and adequate fulfilment. In the above example, a big car may not impress others or you may not be able to obtain it, but there are other ways to impress others; or you may realize that making an impression is only another means-desire for a deeper need.

Desire modification. Desires may control us, but we may control desires too. This is not achieved by suppressing them, which can be frustrating and can distort our thoughts and actions. Most desires, however, can be modified or transformed. This is possible because of the so called equitinality principle, stating that '... needs may be satisfied or goals accomplished through a variety of different means.'[132] It requires detaching a desire from a specific form. Less specific desires are easier to satisfy (e.g. a desire for chocolate may be a result of a need for carbohydrates that can be satisfied with many other types of food). The way of modifying desires depends on the category they belong to:

Unreal desires are desires that do not reflect your real needs (e.g. the desire to go to a football match, even if you don't care for football). They are always means-desires and they can be replaced with more adequate ones if you find out what your real need or end-desire is (in the above example it could be the desire to socialise, be with friends).

Inadequate desires are desires that conflict with your principles, beliefs, views, ideals, aims or, indeed, other desires. In this case, you can either adapt your principles (they may be inadequate, too) or, if they are more valued (more desirable) adapt your desires. What is important is to resolve the inner conflict before taking an action.

Unrealistic desires are desires that are unattainable or too costly. Awareness of the price and effort that satisfying a desire requires is what distinguishes realistic from unrealistic desires. It is important to avoid getting stuck with unrealistic desires and let them pass. This requires accepting that it is not possible to have everything and that not every desire can be fulfilled. It may provoke some emotional reactions (e.g. anger, grief etc.). They usually subside quicker if allowed to come out.

Realistic desires. Desires are passive, they are neither connected with their realization, nor with resources for their fulfilment. This is why, if they are to be fulfilled, you need to transform them into aims and intentions (see the following areas).

REFLECTIVE LEVEL

It may be beneficial to pay attention to how you relate to your desires (e.g. do you follow or disregard them without question, or you reflect on them first?) You can also consider how your immediate desires affect other aspects of yourself and your life. For example, are they the major driving force in your life? Can a prospect of fulfilling a desire make you forget others or your promises? If so, how do you feel about that?

PRACTICAL LEVEL

Uncovering end-desires. To find whether your desire is an end-desire or means-desire imagine that it is already fulfilled, and then change or exclude various components from the image, one by one (in the above examples, you could imagine attending a football match without friends, or that others are not interested in or impressed with your new car). If the so 'stripped' desire doesn't lose substantially on its intensity, it is likely to be an end-desire. If it does, examine which one of the excluded components is the strongest and start the process again, until you find a real underlying need.

Charting desires. Desires are hierarchically structured, which means that some are more important than others. This structure, though, does not seem either universal or stable, as some authors suggest. To increase the awareness of the order of importance and relationship among desires, you can name, draw, paint or even create a dialog with your desires, and then find each of them a place and connect them.

RECOMMENDED MATERIALS

There are many examples in literature about the effects of being driven by desires (e.g. Fitzgerald's *Great Gatsby,* Tolstoy's *Anna Karenina*). The chapter 'Wish and will' in Rollo May's book *Love and Will* addresses this subject is some depth.

38. AIMS

When a man does not know what harbour
he is making for, no wind is the right wind.

Seneca

Setting aims refers to an ability to conceptualise in specific terms not only what you want, but also how to attain it. This area clarifies what aims are and what is their purpose, and addresses factors that affect them.

THEORETICAL LEVEL

Purpose. The aim is different from the reward. Reaching an aim provides satisfaction because the action has been successful (which may, but does not need to bring some advantage). A reward, on the other hand, is not intrinsically connected to the action nor to the one who acts. The main purpose of aims is to give a sense of direction. Without aims, it is easy to become indifferent and allow circumstances to dictate our course. Specifying an aim is the first step towards the realization. Setting goals has a beneficial effect on performance, and influences attention, perception, information processing and remembering[133]. They enable you to have more selective choice, narrow perception and focus efforts and energy. Clear aims also increase motivation and persistence. Research indicates that 'having valued goals and experiencing progress in goal pursuit are vital to the experience of subjective well-being'[134]. On the other hand, following aims rigidly may have a negative effect on flexibility, adapting to new circumstances, and may lead to overlooking new opportunities or intuitive and affective hints. Attachment to aims can also cause anxiety, because there is always some uncertainty relating to any aim projected into the future (after all, our death can always put a stop to our endeavours). However, an aim can be a process rather than a fixed goal (e.g. the aim to learn), which means that it does not need to be confined to the future.

Setting aims. Translating desires into clear aims can bring peace of mind and increase confidence. A positively formulated aim (what you want) creates a higher motivation than a negatively formulated aim (what you don't want). The aim to stop smoking, for example, can be reformulated as an aim to be healthier, more fit, free from the habit, or relying on yourself rather than cigarettes to enjoy, be relaxed and feel confident in social occasions. To assess if a particular aim is worth pursuing several elements need to be considered: probability, circumstances, investment and consequences. Unrealistic aims can cause disappointment and the loss of motivation and confidence. The resistance between an aim and its realization can be minimized if every part of you is heading in the same direction. In other words, if you don't have inner conflicts relating to the goal. To avoid conflicts, consider your reasons and motives (whatever they are) and make a clear aim without doubt, shame, guilt, hesitation and reservations before an action. Once the aim is specified, it is not necessary to ponder on it anymore. *Cognitive dissonance*, or an overlap between deciding and acting (i.e. considering other options after already having taken a particular course of action) increases insecurity, susceptibility to influence and can be incapacitating. Doubt, as a part of the process of assessing and deciding, may be facilitative and may increase awareness, but it is unproductive when it interferes with the action. The sense of being on the right track, in the right place at the right time, increases confidence and decreases anxiety.

Flexibility. The above does not mean being rigid with your aims. New insights into the situation, for example, may require modifying the aim or the way to achieve it. Being flexible in this respect is often essential for success. It implies being able to accept the unexpected and change a direction if necessary. Also, rather than waiting for the right conditions, time and place that may never arise, a flexible person acts when and where an opportunity arises. This requires not being a slave of habits. Habits make life easier (we don't need to make new decisions from moment to moment) but can be very restrictive.

REFLECTIVE LEVEL

Consider what sort of aims you have (e.g. are they only short-term aims or also long-term ones?) and how important they are for you. If not much, what else is more important? You can also look at how you set your aims (e.g. what are your priorities), and how clear they are. Do you continue weighing them up even after you have taken action?

PRACTICAL LEVEL

The map of aims. Write down your aims, including major ones and small ones. Formulate them in simple terms (in a short sentence, without 'but', 'if', etc.). After that examine how these aims relate to each other. Aims can have different degrees of universality and importance (i.e. overarching aims and immediate aims), but they should be defined in such a way that they do not conflict; the smaller ones should flow into the bigger ones.

Aim breaking. If some aims look too big or far ahead, it may help to break them up into a few manageable ones and form a chain that will link them to the present (e.g. the aim to win a marathon may begin with an aim to run around the block every day).

Keeping on the track. In acute situations, when you feel that you are losing the sense of direction, guided imagination can help in focusing your mind on the aim again. You may imagine, for example, that you are heading with a boat towards the light-house, or aiming and shooting at the centre of the target.

RECOMMENDED MATERIALS

Goals! by Bran Tracy is a recommended self-help material. Melville's *Moby Dick* is an example from literature of how the obsession with a goal can distort one's life. On a more positive side, biographies of sportsmen, scientists or statesmen highlight the importance of goals.

39. INTENTIONS

If one advances confidently in the direction of his dreams, and endeavours to live the life which he has imagined, he will meet with a success unexpected in common hours.

Henry David Thoreau

Intention refers in this context to one's resolution to realize a goal. As a psychologist Donaldson puts it, it is 'a *built-in* guiding representation of a goal to be achieved... that sustains the act'[135]. This area addresses several factors that affect this process.

THEORETICAL LEVEL

Intention can be described as an inner tension that is the result of a difference between the present state and a goal. A tendency to resolve that tension links the person to his goal, which enables the goal to become a driving force. Carrying out intentions, however, is not straightforward, it depends on several factors.

Determination means resoluteness to do what you intend despite temptations, drawbacks, obstacles or contrary desires (your own or somebody else's). In other words, not giving in to yourself or others, following your intentions despite internal or external pressures that try to sabotage them. This implies that nothing should divert you from acting upon your decision except perhaps another decision based on new insights. The congruence between decisions and actions is a great personal support, because even if everything else fails, you know that you can always rely on yourself. Determination is supported by maintaining the focus on the aim, instead of on temptations or obstacles. Reminding yourself from time to time why you are doing something can help you not to get too attached to the process and so forget or miss the aim altogether (e.g. 'Do I want to make a book shelf, or a never finished DIY masterpiece?'). Incentives, rewards and feed-back (corrective, supportive and confirmatory) can also facilitate sustaining determination.

Resistance. Irresoluteness is either the result of weak motivation or strong internal resistance. Resistance is an opposite force from intentions, which decreases strength and efficiency. Indolence is probably the most common form, but it can have many causes. Internal resistance can be minimized if it is treated as a problem within a problem. If you find, for example, revising for an exam boring, you can deal first with boredom or try to find ways to make the task more interesting (e.g. by revising with somebody else). Providing that resistance cannot be decreased, you may consider modifying or even eliminating the aim (it may not be that important after all).

Persistence means not giving up even if the first round is lost. Losing is not yet defeat. If you feel that circumstances are against you, that your journey is an uphill straggle, it doesn't necessarily mean that you should change or abandon your aim. The method, the way you are trying to achieve the aim is worthwhile considering and changing first. On the other hand, persistence may become stubbornness if you don't know when to give up. Sometimes, for example, we continue pursuing unrealistic goals only because previous investments. A situation in which one spends more resources (time, energy, money) than appropriate, because there has been already 'too much invested to quit' is called *entrapment*. It can be avoided if you set a limit in advance on the future investments and resolve to stop when that point is reached.

Intensity refers to an amount of energy applied to carry out your intentions. A use of force can be sometimes justifiable (e.g. braking into a house in flames to save the occupants), but this is different from forcefulness. Forcefulness involves spending more energy than necessary or forcing yourself or others, which usually creates conflicts. Easiness, on the other hand, means accomplishing what you intend with an optimal effort. It implies achieving fulfilment without causing discomfort and with the minimal pressure on anything and anybody. While determination means not giving in to yourself or others, easiness means not mistreating yourself and others. It is characterised by being careful and gentle, treating with due respect (although not reverence) even objects (e.g. money). This minimizes conflicts and so increases inner content. It doesn't mean being irresolute, but being flexible with the ways of realising your intentions. In other words, choosing a direction of least resistance; going around walls, rather than destroying them. This is what makes the difference between determination and obstinacy.

REFLECTIVE LEVEL
Can you distinguish between a forceful and strong person, or between a weak and easy-going person (not only in theory, but in real life too)? More specifically, you may consider to what extent you are prepared to make sacrifices in the present for the sake of the future goals.

PRACTICAL LEVEL
Intention clarification. Intentions are difficult to carry through if they are dissonant with personality (e.g. intending to become a soldier, but finding hard to tolerate discipline). So, before attempting to realise your intentions see first whether you can recognise any inner resistance. If you can, consider what its cause is, and how it could be overcome. If you cannot come to terms with it, you may try to modify your intentions.

RECOMMENDED MATERIALS
'From Intention to Realization' in Assagioli, R. *The Act of Will*; 'Intention' in Farber, L. *The Ways of the Will* and chapters 9 and 10 in May, R. *Love and Will* focus on this subject. Hoff, B. *Tao of the Pooh* makes a case, in an accessible way, for an effort-less rather than forceful attitude when realising our intentions.

40. GRATIFICATION

> Lord, give me chastity – but not yet.
> St Augustine

Gratification (satisfying your desires) is important for our physical and psychological balance. However, not all desires are desirable. Gratifying some desires, or the way we do it, can have negative consequences. Also, an immediate gratification is not always appropriate. So, this area will deal with the ways to control and affect gratification.

THEORETICAL LEVEL

Denying gratification. It is not necessary to deprive yourself, but there is also no reason to become a slave of your wants. Always giving in to immediate desires limits our freedom and can be harmful. Moreover, not all of them reflect our genuine needs. Some forms of gratification are simply habits conditioned by previous experiences. Abstinence, however, can create an inner conflict and lead to excesses to compensate for what has been missed. To avoid a conflict, try to get rid of the desire itself, which requires reprogramming your thoughts and feelings (see the exercise below). Initially, some discomfort may be experienced, or the desire may intensify before starting to subside. If this happens, do not get obsessed about it, remember that it will pass, and let it go.

Delaying gratification. Some desires can be real and adequate, but it may still not be possible, appropriate, or convenient to satisfy them at that moment (common example being a desire to relieve oneself). Ability to delay gratification (patience) is central in controlling your desires. Research shows that an early development of this ability has far reaching effects on effectiveness, competence, confidence, self-assertiveness and coping[136]. It also increases the sense of self-control and freedom. Focusing on something else, possibly some other attainable desire or goal, may help to avert attention.

Gratification control. Inability to control your immediate desires may narrow your awareness, distort priorities, and lead to selfishness and disregard for others. Control is secured if gratification is not the result of blind submission to desires, but comes about willingly, with full awareness. It requires detaching yourself from them, at least for a moment. This would enable you to decide about gratification before it happens and approach an object of desire as a whole, without doubts and insecurity (there is no point in committing yourself to desires that you don't believe in – the result is seldom really satisfying). This, however, may be difficult if gratification depends on circumstances or others. Stable availability and proximity (not available, easily available and always available) do not add to a desire, while an increase or decrease of availability and proximity intensify already existing desires, which makes it harder to control them.

Moderation. Gratification itself rarely causes problems, but excesses often do. Moderation means avoiding extremes, being able to sense when it is enough and stop. This is not always easy: for example, the brain receives a message that we have eaten several minutes after food intake, so we can still feel hungry although in fact we have had enough. A pleasure is good only while it is really a pleasure, and quantity can destroy quality. This is why moderation is natural, while an excess indicates that gratification serves other purposes: it becomes a support (possessiveness); desire to recreate past experiences (habit); a substitute for another hidden need (compensation); or a response to denial and suppression (compulsiveness). An optimum is easier to achieve if you are clear about the need that gratification is supposed to fulfil. Going to an extreme is a sign of giving up freedom, allowing yourself to be driven by desires. Even traits that are considered positive, if taken to an extreme, can become negative: respectfulness can become submissiveness, modesty inferiority, assertiveness aggression, and so on. This means that one should be moderate with moderation too.

REFLECTIVE LEVEL
Examine first what has been really gratifying for you (e.g. visiting an elderly person may be more fulfilling than going to a night club, although the desire for the latter may be initially stronger). Then consider which desires that you have now would be actually gratifying if fulfilled.

PRACTICAL LEVEL
Reprogramming. Getting rid of unwanted desires may have to involve every aspect of life:
• *Motivation:* really wanting to do so, without any doubts, is essential. To strengthen determination, focus on benefits and positive counter-desires (e.g. to be fit and healthy).
• *Situation*: try to secure a relative stability in other areas of life.
• *Others*: ask those who are willing to support you, and learn to say no to those who would rather tempt you.
• *Thinking:* challenge those thoughts that support your desire (e.g. 'I need a drink to calm down'). Is it really true? What else can serve the same purpose?
• *Imagination*: use positive images about yourself (e.g. being strong) and negative images about the object of your desire (e.g. a slime covering the cake you just find irresistible).
• *Feelings*: associate a desire with unpleasant rather than pleasant feelings ('A cigarette feels or smells terrible').
• *Perception*: remove tempting items from your vicinity, or yourself from tempting situations, and redirect attention.

Time delay. If you feel that you cannot resist temptation, try at least to delay it for awhile (e.g. 15 minutes) and in meantime focus on something else. If you still have desire after the delay, go on, but extend the delay next time. Once you give in to a temptation, do it mindfully (with full awareness and responsibility). This will help you maintain the sense of control.

RECOMMENDED MATERIALS
Assagioli, R. 'The Direction of the Execution' in *The Act of Will* and Montaigne's essay 'On moderation' are suggested. Goethe's *Faust* is a poetic examination of this subject.

INVICTUS[1]

Out of the night that covers me,
    Black as the Pit from pole to pole,
I thank whatever gods may be
    For my unconquerable soul.

In the fell clutch of circumstance
    I have not winced nor cried aloud.
Under the bludgeonings of chance
    My head is bloody, but unbowed.

Beyond this place of wrath and tears
    Looms but the horror of the shade,
And yet the menace of the years
    Finds and shall find me, unafraid.

It matters not how strait the gate
    How charged with punishments the scroll,
I am the master of my fate:
    I am the captain of my soul.

W. E. Henley

[1] Latin for 'Unconquered'

PROBLEM GROUP

A problem is a situation for which one does not have a ready response. Problems are not intrinsically negative, in fact we often seek them (e.g. puzzles). They cause stress only if we don't believe that they can be solved, that is, if we don't know what to do. This group consists of four areas that are closely related to problems and dealing with them:

Strategy is the preparatory area of the group. It highlights the basic ways in which problems can be approached.

Achieving and *Coping* are the areas that relate to the active engagement with problems. Two different sets of problems are distinguished: one is related to possible gains (they can be called tasks) and another that is related to setbacks or occurred losses. *Achieving* refers to dealing with a task in order to maximize the gains. *Coping* refers to an active response to a stressful or distressing situation in order to minimize its effects. It is interesting that many people are good in dealing with problems belonging to one of these categories and poor in dealing with problems belonging to the other. This is probably the case because they are better motivated with certain type of problems.

Coping may seem similar to *tolerance* (p.121). However, these two areas of life cannot be identified. Unlike tolerance, coping is more pro-active (as indicated by its position in the map), it requires a change of the situation, perspective, or oneself. It can be said that coping starts when tolerance ends.

Control is the last area in this group. It is in a way a consequence of the previous three, though the sense of control has an important role in all of them (and many other areas). It is observed that 'the concepts of coping and mastery imply the exercise of *control* over events'[137]. However, there are also differences between these areas. If achieving refers to the ways the person affects the situation, and coping to the ways a person deals with the effects of the situation, control refers to harmonizing the person and the situation.

41. STRATEGY

*The game of life is not so much in holding
a good hand as playing a poor hand well.*

H. T. Leslie

Strategy is an ability to choose different responses to a problem. It is a global course of action, rather than an elaborate plan. People often choose a strategy automatically, out of habit, so it is common experience to be 'blind' to some solutions that become obvious only in retrospective. The purpose of this area is to minimize such situations.

THEORETICAL LEVEL
Putting problems off might bring temporary relief, but it often allows them to grow and increases insecurity in the long run. This is why it is important to face problems and adopt strategies how to deal with them. Two factors should affect their prioritisation: relative importance, and which ones will grow if unattended.

The first step in developing a strategy is to clarify what a problem really is. This is often neglected, and it is more difficult than it sounds. Saying, for example, 'I am not happy at work' is not sufficient. You need to specify the cause of discontent (e.g. boredom, the relationships, workload, etc.). Defining the problem accurately is essential because it influences what directions and solutions will be considered. This is easier if you distance yourself temporarily from the problem and look at it from different perspectives. One way to achieve this is to imagine, for example, that this is a problem of somebody else. Distancing does not imply neglecting your feelings, but attending to them separately, so that you can maintain objectivity. It can also help you to decide if tackling the problem is really worthwhile. If you are sure that it is, the next step is choosing a basic strategy. The factors taken into account should include the assessment of risk and possible consequences, what can be achieved and what can be lost.

General strategy. There are four basic ways of dealing with a problem:

	SELF	SITUATION
ACTIVE	Adaptation	Confrontation
PASSIVE	Isolation	Avoidance

Let's assume that, your problem is, for example, working with colleagues who have radically different moral or political views (e.g. they are sexists). You can: adopt their views (adaptation), try to change their views (confrontation), ignore them (isolation), or change the job (avoidance). The term *confrontation* refers to confronting a problem in order to change the situation, which does not necessarily involve arguments or fights with others. *Avoidance* also doesn't mean running away from a problem, but dealing with the problem by removing yourself from the situation. None of these methods is superior; it is always useful to consider all of them. They are possible in almost any situation, although not all of them can always bring a desirable outcome. Which one would work best in a particular situation depends on circumstances and the person(s) involved.

Specific strategies. Choosing a general strategy, of course, is not enough. You also need to find a way how to implement each step of the action. This requires taking a broader perspective, which may involve playing different scenarios in your mind. A good strategy means anticipating whatever may happen and finding solutions to possible obstacles. You can test whether you strategy is foolproof using the integration criteria (*congruence, consistency, completeness, cohesiveness*) described in the area 'Inner structure' (p. 65).

REFLECTIVE LEVEL
Think about the ways you have approached problems in the past. Have you always considered all the above strategies, or habitually used only one of them? What would you do now in the similar situations?

PRACTICAL LEVEL

When you feel stuck with a problem remember that there are always more possibilities than what immediately comes to mind. However, to find new solutions requires a new, fresh approach to the problem. Two main barriers to this are habit (choosing what you usually chose) and conformity (choosing what others usually chose). The following techniques may help you to overcome them:

Brainstorming. Jot down in quick succession as many ideas as possible that come to mind in connection with the problem. Don't evaluate them at this stage, sometimes the best solutions can be hidden in seemingly absurd thoughts. When this is done, pick one of these ideas and see what you can make of it, how it can become practicable. Go through the same process with the other ideas until you find a satisfactory solution.

Emulating a person: imagine that a person you admire and respect (e.g. a hero, spiritual guide, relative, friend) is in the same situation and consider what he or she would do.

Emulating a solution: try to find a similar problem the solution to which is already known (aircraft innovators, for example, studied how birds and insects fly).

Incubation is a period of unconscious mental activity assumed to take place while you are not focusing directly on the problem. So, if a satisfactory solution cannot be found, it may help to distract yourself with some other activity and allow intuition to take over. Of course, this should not lead to putting off or completely forgetting the problem.

RECOMMENDED MATERIALS

Most novels or films can be used to analyse various strategies. Some historical events, such as Kutuzov's skilful use of the retreat to defeat Napoleon (described in the novel *War and Peace* by Tolstoy) can also be insightful. A SF classic, *Foundation* by Asimov and *The Fire From Within* by Castaneda depict a variety of strategies in an accessible way.

42. ACHIEVING

Not in the clamour of the crowded street, Not in the solutes and plaudits of the throng, But in ourselves are triumph and defeat.

Henry Wadsworth Longfellow

Achieving refers to a satisfactory dealing with challenges or tasks. Motivation to master challenges (achievement motivation) is inborn, but life experiences may weaken or destroy it[138]. This area focuses on several stages in the process of accomplishing tasks.

THEORETICAL LEVEL

Dealing with tasks can include the following steps:

Analysis of the situation may include observing, collecting information, looking for the weak points; picking out essentials, discriminating between what is relevant and what is not; identifying assumptions and considering their acceptability; identifying restraining and facilitating forces that will affect an implementation of the strategy and the ways to reduce and strengthen them respectively (e.g. the available time to accomplish the task).

Preparation consists of finding the way and resources to implement a solution. It may involve assessing what you need (e.g. help from others) and how much time and effort is required. This step also includes removing from the environment and your mind everything that can be a distraction (e.g. switching off telephone).

Engagement is the central step. It requires confidence and determination. Entering this stage half-heartily or with conflicting motives, decreases the chances for success. A defeat and victory are begotten in the person, not the situation. Losing is external and depends on many factors, feeling defeated is internal and depends on yourself.

Emotions may be a powerful source of motivation at this stage, but if not properly channelled they can be counter-productive.

Re-balance allows you to express or meet needs suppressed during an action, such as the need for rest, emotional reactions, or body needs (food, drink, toilet etc.).

Evaluation consists of assessments such as what you have lost and what you have gained; what you can learn from the experience; what you can do next time to avoid mistakes. Although you may not always win, you can always learn something.

Not all of these steps are always necessary, but it is always useful to consider them.

REFLECTIVE LEVEL

A psychologist Csikszentmihalyi writes: 'when beating the opponent takes precedence in the mind over performing as well as possible, enjoyment tends to disappear.' [139] Do you agree with this? What is more important for you, the process or the end result? Can you lose without feeling defeated and have the sense of achievement even if you don't win?

PRACTICAL LEVEL

Achievement maximisation provides several steps that can increase your chances of success (of course, tasks vary greatly, so not all of them are always necessary).

• *Choose a task*: it is rarely productive to deal with several tasks at the same time, so make a list of priorities, and approach them one by one. It is also important to assess the size of a task. Too difficult a task may undermine self-esteem and self-confidence, too easy a one may not be challenging or interesting and solving it may not bring any satisfaction. A big task can be broken into several smaller ones – it will bring a sense of accomplishment sooner, and so maintain motivation. Consider each problem as a separate project. For routine tasks it is better to start from the hardest, while you still have a lot of energy. For challenging tasks start from the easiest because its successful accomplishment will give you self-confidence to tackle more difficult ones, or a more realistic view on other tasks if you can't complete even the easiest one.

- *Prepare*: collect first as much information as possible without interfering. For example, if you want to win a game, observe your opponent playing with others. In this way you can find out what her strong and weak points are, and establish what is needed to win. If you want to avoid an unpleasant surprise don't underestimate your opponents or obstacles. Something can be always learnt if you pay them full attention and respect.

- *Go for it:* if possible, choose a place and time for the action. If you are advancing, it may pay off to secure a chance for the retreat to avoid reaching the point of no return. It is always good to have something in reserve (e.g. contingency plans, back-up alternatives). This is especially important if you don't have sufficient information. A period of respite can be used to rest or prepare, bearing in mind that a pause will not last forever. If you are retreating, try to avoid defeatist attitude and remain alert and ready to take a chance. It is always better to concentrate on what can be gained or how to benefit from the situation than succumbing to negative emotions. For example, the force of your opponent can be used to your advantage if encouraged to go too far (like in judo). Opposing an attack in full strength is usually a waste of energy. It is better to wait for it to wear out and start receding. For instance, you can be more successful in an argument, if you hold on until the other person starts calming down. Sometimes it may be even beneficial to temporarily disengage or retreat into yourself. In any case, it is important not to become attached to a task at hand, but bear in mind what the goal is, and be able to give up when the cost is higher than a possible gain.

RECOMMENDED MATERIALS
There is rich literature on dealing with specific tasks. Of materials that deal with the subject more generally, Rubinstein & Pfeiffer *Concepts in Problem Solving* and poetically written *The Bhagavad-Gita* are suggested.

43. COPING

The decision to accept and carry on turns the worst failure into success.

Dr Claire Weekes

Coping is defined as an attempt to overcome or come to terms with difficulties or occurred losses. The area will first address the situations that involve coping and then point to various coping responses.

THEORETICAL LEVEL

Two broad groups of situations require coping: losing situations that cause *stress* (e.g. running late to work), and situations in which a loss has already occurred, that cause *distress* (being sacked for being late). Stress relates to setbacks, distress to loss. Distress usually has a more profound effect because a loss cannot be prevented any more, but stress is more common. It is usually instigated by the discrepancy between your perception of the demands on you and your ability to cope with them. In other words, stress is a result of a situation where there is a conflict between what you want or would like and what is actually happening. This means that, for example, you don't get stressed because you are in hurry, but because you have to force yourself to stop when in hurry. Such situations are common in modern society (lifts, queues, traffic jams, crowds etc.) but they are often made worse by poor time management. Accumulated stress can be an important factor in a number of physiological and psychological disorders (weakening of the immune system, heart attacks, nightmares, impaired sociability etc.). Factors that affect coping responses are: importance, intensity, duration and predictability of a (di)stressful situation; personal motivation, confidence, the sense of control; and social support.

A number of constructive coping strategies are listed below[140]. They are applicable in both stressful and distressing situations, but the latter may also require accepting the loss and reconstructing your reality.

Coping strategies

It is easier to cope with (di)stress if you separate the following components and deal with them one by one.

Perception

• Any problem can be turned either into an opportunity or learning experience. So, something might be gained even from loss. To do so, take (di)stressful situation as a challenge, a chance for a change or growth, try to find a gain in loss.

• You can transcend the experience by looking at the situation from a wider perspective (e.g. the world situation, spirituality).

• Distance, detach yourself (taking, for example, a professional attitude, as doctors often do to cope with their daily job).

Affect

• Blocking emotions may be necessary to deal with the situation effectively, but they should not remain permanently blocked.

• Emotional release (crying, shouting, screaming) can bring eventual relief, but only if it leads to acceptance (when grief dominates). Research shows, however, that when anger is dominant, letting off steam does not lead to improvement[141].

• Relaxation and meditation (see p.75) can calm you down.

Thinking

• You can decrease importance of an incident by observing it in context (count your blessings), or by comparing it with other possible misfortunes that may have befallen you.

• Humour can also be effective, not only because it reduces the importance of a problem, but tension too.

• Focus on a positive aim or outcome (e.g. you may cope with exhaustion or pain in sport by thinking about the victory).

Action

• If something can be done, you can focus on the problem (get more information, try to find solution, confront or negotiate)

• If nothing can be done, you can distract yourself by activities (sport, hobbies, work), entertainment (TV, music, etc.), having company, observing (a scenery or other people), rest (sleeping, reading, fantasying), various pleasures, or mood altering consumption (food, moderate drink, or medications)

• Sharing, asking for advice or help, and receiving comfort may also significantly reduce the effects of (di)stressful situation.

REFLECTIVE LEVEL
Reflecting on what causes you stress and distress and how you cope (e.g. which of the above strategies you are using and whether they are effective), can prepare you to face and deal with such situations with more confidence in the future.

PRACTICAL LEVEL
Being positive. Unfavourable events can be taken either as misfortunes or as a challenge. The former prepares you to lose, the latter to win. So, it is important to recognise and confront defeatist thoughts (e.g. thinking how unlucky you are), before they start influencing your decisions and coping ability. You can oppose them by accepting the situation (count your blessings) and trying to find something positive in it.

Time-out. If you feel that you do not have the strength to face the problems that surround you, withdrawing and letting them lie for while can provide a break to recuperate (it may need only a couple of minutes). Redirecting attention can help you to let go of worries and other circular thoughts in these moments. You can design something that is always at hand specially for this purpose. Anything pleasant that you can focus on and 'lose' yourself in it can be used: an object (e.g. a ring, stone, photo), a pet, view etc.

Dealing with impatience. If having to wait makes you nervous, use the situation as a chance for a mini break, cue to relax (e.g. focusing on breathing and muscle relaxation is useful in itself and also can distract you from expectations that cause impatience).

RECOMMENDED MATERIALS
Stress and Coping by Monat & Lazarus is very comprehensive, but not an easy read. A number of books that provide practical advice on how to deal with stress are regularly published. Boethius' *The Consolation of Philosophy* can be very inspiring.

44. CONTROL

To rule is easy, to govern difficult.
Goethe

Having a sense of control is a universal need. An infant's crying, for example, is a way to control her environment. Yet, what it means to have the sense of control and its importance is often poorly understood. This area will address consequences, types and factors that affect control.

THEORETICAL LEVEL

Consequences. A sense of control is an important factor in many areas of life. Both, animal and human experiments, clearly show that 'the organism responds differently to conditions characterized by controllability on the one hand, and lack of control on the other.'[142] Control, for example, affects coping response and also decreases after-effects of distressing situations. The evidence from several sources indicates 'that the sense of control is an important factor not only in coping with stress, but for health more generally.'[143] This is because it reduces physiological stress responses (such as adrenaline and cortisol secretion). A diminished sense of control, on the other hand, increases feelings of insecurity and discontent, and affects efficiency.

Types of control. When the person believes that the situation depends on her it is called in the literature internal control. If the person on the other hand believes that she has little impact on outcomes (that they depend on other people, fate, luck etc.) it is called external control. Research[144] shows that subjective well being is greater in those scoring high on internal control, as also in those who believe that they have much choice in what they do. However, exaggerated internal control can induce an unjustified sense of personal failure, responsibility and guilt.

In relation to the situation and others, the internal control can be directive and imposed. The former means that that you consider yourself a part of the situation, an 'insider', while the latter means that the situation is approached from 'outside'. Directive control takes into account the circumstances, it neither opposes, nor gives in to the forces around, but uses them (like a sailing-boat the wind). This means adapting, directing and coordinating. Imposed control enforces a particular course of action regardless of circumstances. It needs more energy, but it can sometimes be more efficient (like a motor boat). Focusing on a situation (what needs to be done) increases directive control, while trying, for example, to control others (e.g. by trying to please or intimidate them) may enable temporary imposed control, but usually doesn't have a lasting effect.

What control is. Control means being aware of personal power and knowing how to use it. Therefore, it is a state of mind, based on the belief that we are able to affect the situation. A sense of control is not directly related to the amount of control we exhibit in a given situation, but to the possibility, to the confidence that we can if we want. Controlling behaviour is often the result of the need to prove (to ourselves or others) that we are in control and in fact betrays a lack of the inner sense of control. One who is in control, does not need to show it. Therefore, control is derived from the sense of confidence rather than the other way around. People who are in control take the initiative only if necessary. Letting others take over the helm or sharing power does not mean losing control as long as it is voluntary. Control however always requires your presence. Thinking about what could have happened or been done may help you prepare better for the future but it is an impediment in the immediate situation. Excitement and intensified emotional reactions are inversely proportional to controllability. They usually reduce directive control, although they are sometimes used to increase control over others.

REFLECTIVE LEVEL
Consider what attitudes affect your sense of control (e.g. how significant is the terms lucky or unlucky for you). You can also compare directive and imposed control (e.g. in relation to the environment) and think about when control becomes over-control.

PRACTICAL LEVEL
The following exercises can help you maintain your sense of control:
Control feeling. When you feel that you are in control, try to remember physical and psychological manifestations of that state (e.g. feeling 'on top'), so that you can recall it when necessary. Any image, word, or sensation can serve as a reminder to bring it back.

Control image. Guided imagination can also assist the sense of control. For example, visualize yourself at the helm of a ship, gradually increasing the control over its direction.

Dream control. Establishing the sense of control in your fantasies and dreams can have positive effects in real situations, too. Nightmares, for example, are often related to the subjective sense of the lack of control. If you wake up in the middle of a nightmare, go back in imagination in your dream (however frightening or unpleasant it is), and then continue the action to its satisfactory ending, not the interrupted one. Do not run away, or allow yourself to be defeated. This does not necessarily require fighting. You can ask for help or even transform the enemy into an ally. Remember, you are in control!

RECOMMENDED MATERIALS
There is a rich literature not only on how to maintain control, but also on how to behave in a position of power and control. 'Managing with Heart' in Goleman's *Emotional Intelligence*, and in fiction, Frank Herbert's SF classic *Dune* and *Memoirs of Hadrian* by Margaret Yourcenar are some good examples.

NEW EVERY MORNING

Every day is a fresh beginning,
Listen my soul to the glad refrain.
And, spite of old sorrows
And older sinning,
Troubles forecasted
And possible pain,
Take heart with the day and begin again.

Susan Coolidge

ACTIVITY GROUP

Human activity, in its broad sense, includes several elements that are covered here by the following areas:

Motivation is the root area of this group. It consists of two interrelated aspects. The aspect related to the external domain consists of our motives. They are reasons (external or internal) for a certain course of action. The aspect related to the internal domain can be called internal motivation. It is an incentive to act based on the belief that the action is worthwhile. This distinction is important because those two aspects don't always go together. It is possible to have a strong motive and yet lack internal motivation (e.g. one may need to support family, and yet lack motivation to look for a job). Similarly, one can be highly motivated without a strong reason (e.g. to climb to the top of the mountain).

Energy. Using the term *energy* in relation to human beings is admittedly problematic. Energy is difficult to define even in physics, and that the term is often overused, misused and abused in alternative literature makes it even more confusing. In this context, the term is used to encompass common experiences referred to as strength, vigour, élan, energy, effort, tiredness. This area belongs to the internal domain.

Organization addresses structuring, organizing and planning activities within the time-space framework. It belongs to the external domain and is a counterpart to the previous area because it is concerned with the distribution and direction (the use) of energy.

Performance. The above areas can be considered the necessary conditions for an activity. *Performance* is the final area in this group that focuses on activity itself. It is also the last area in this category. It is concerned only with deliberate, conscious actions (actions such as walking or writing that are usually automatic or unconscious are not considered). Performance normally involves an interaction between the internal and external, so it encompasses both domains, as indicated by its position in the model.

45. MOTIVATION

Every man without passions has within him
no principle of action, nor motive to act.

Claude Adrien Helvetius

Motivation is an inner incentive to act. Psychologists suggests that it 'is an innate human need and begins in infants as an undifferentiated need for competence and self-determination'[145]. There is no doubt that the ability to control one's motivation can be beneficial. Little can be accomplished without it. We are all too familiar with the debilitating effect that a lack of motivation can have. Learning about motivation is important not only to be able to motivate yourself, but also to be able to motivate others. This area will consider various types of motivation and how it can be increased.

THEORETICAL LEVEL

Intrinsic and extrinsic motivation. Intrinsic motivation is motivation to engage in an activity for its own sake, because you find it interesting or enjoyable (e.g. a hobby); it can also be the result of perceiving an activity as worthwhile (e.g. helping those in need or self-improvement). Extrinsic motivation is motivation to engage in an activity as a means to an end (a typical one is to earn money). In some cases, extrinsic motivation can be internalised (e.g. the sense of duty or guilt).

There is evidence that intrinsic motivation fosters creativity[146] and can promote learning and achievement better than extrinsic one[147]. An offer of a reward (as an extrinsic motivator) to perform a task that is already seen as enjoyable or interesting can, in fact, lead to a *reduction* in intrinsic motivation[148]. This, of course, also depends on the kind of reward. Research shows that 'informational aspects of rewards (e.g. praise) are likely to enhance intrinsic motivation, while tangible rewards (e.g. money, prizes etc.) are more likely to be perceived as controlling events and to decrease intrinsic motivation.'[149] It is an important point, because we tend to rely (in work place, education and personal lives) excessively on external rewards to motivate others and ourselves. This is not to say that these types of motivation cannot be combined when it makes sense, nor that extrinsic motivation cannot help if the intrinsic one is not present or cannot be incited.

Negative and positive motivation. Negative motivation (the aspiration to preserve the existing state and avoid whatever threatens to make it worse) is associated with negative feelings (e.g. fear). Positive motivation (creating, achieving, expanding, improving,) is associated with positive feelings. Negative motivation can be sometimes stronger, but the positive is more effective in the long run. Negative motivation often results in experiencing a lack of energy and desire for rest – not from the trigger, but from the unpleasant feelings that one is motivated by. Whether motivation is positive or negative often depends on the perspective (you can run *from* an attacker, or run *for* safety). To transform negative motivation into positive, you need to accept the immediate situation and from that position focus on what can be gained, rather than on what has been or can be lost. Ruminating on losses and missed opportunities doesn't achieve anything, but prevents you from being present and recognising future possibilities.

Affecting motivation. Motivation is important because it strengthens determination and energizes, but it needs to be nurtured and reinforced. Besides already mentioned enjoyment and interest, several other sources of intrinsic motivation are suggested: challenge, curiosity, the sense of control and imagination[150]. Motivation is also affected by expectancies about the outcome. Highly motivated people believe that their actions can make a difference. So, positive expectations can increase motivation (unless they become self-satisfying fantasies). Another way of controlling motivation is by creating and balancing motives (or reasons) for an action. Unlike aims, motives don't need to converge (reaching the destination may entail turning left and right). By manipulating different motives, motivation can be maintained throughout a prolonged period. Such incentives can be a sense of achievement, rewards and other benefits, enjoying a game, or enhancing one's self-esteem. Emotions and ideals can also be a motivational force (e.g. love for one's country, belief in progress). Social factors such as cooperation, competition, praise, even criticism can also strengthen motivation. In a group setting motivation can be mutually reinforced, but exaggerated enthusiasm may not be always appropriate and can even deflate motivation of others.

REFLECTIVE LEVEL

It may be beneficial to explore how you motivate yourself (and others) and what type of motivation is dominant in your life. You may also consider the effects on yourself and others of being overly enthusiastic about certain activity.

PRACTICAL LEVEL

Invoking motivation. The purpose of this exercise is to become familiar with the sensations associated with the desire to act, so that they can be invoked when needed. Recall a situation in which you have been highly motivated. The focus should remain on the feeling of motivation, not on the ensuing activity. Allow yourself to experience all the related sensations. If some of them are negative (e.g. the anxiety that motivation may be too strong) examine their validity, or shape the impulse until it feels right.

Enhancing motivation. Rather than forcing yourself to act, try to find something positive (interesting, challenging) in the task at hand and imagine vividly all the advantages and benefits, until you come to the point of beginning to act without having to apply pressure. Do not forget that getting started is the hardest part.

RECOMMENDED MATERIALS

There is abundant literature on motivation, but many materials focus on the basic motives (e.g. hunger) and other subjects that may not be of much practical use. Chapter 12 in *The Act of Will* by Assagioli and *Why We do What We Do* by Edward Deci may be of wider interest.

46. ENERGY

Energy is eternal delight.
William Blake

Energy is the capacity for activity and it can have various sources: physical, emotional, mental, sexual etc. A level of energy not only affects our ability to perform tasks, but also our emotional state and intellectual capacities. This area will focus on the ways energy can be affected, increased and directed.

THEORETICAL LEVEL

Control of energy. Personal power does not correlate to the amount of energy you possess but to the ability to focus and utilize it. Being a potential, it depends on you how your energy will be distributed. The awareness of and adjustment to your level of energy (which fluctuates even within a day) can increase productivity. This means, for example, doing hard tasks when you feel strong, and easy ones when you don't, rather than following a prearranged plan. Negative effects of giving in to bursts of energy, or blocking or forcing its natural flow are often greater than possible gains (e.g. forcing yourself to work when tired may result in mistakes correcting which may take longer than a brief rest). The processes of building up and spending energy need to alternate. Doing something without enough energy reserves is futile. On the other hand, if accumulated energy is not invested or released it may become destructive, cause restlessness, stress and even aggression (examples of this may be found among confined people and even animals). This should not be confused with boredom or the need for stimulation (although these factors may also be present). Even activities that are not particularly exciting or interesting but allow spending energy, can be effective in this respect. Excessive energy can also accumulate in an unusable form (as in the case of 'couch-potatoes'), which is destructive in the long term.

Preservation and enhancement of energy. Tiredness is a sign of a lack of energy, which is the result of overcoming internal and external resistance. Several factors can have a positive effect on your energy level:

Rest. Full and effective rest requires first of all changing continuity or routine. So, a rest can be active or passive, depending on what you are resting from. Sleeping and dreaming enable both types of rest, but they may become an escape from reality.

Being active (exercise, sport, etc.) can make you temporarily tired, but in the long run it increases the flow of energy, strength and stamina. Research suggests that regular physical exercise is not only beneficial for physical health but also contributes to a reduction of stress, acute anxiety and depression[151].

Body-care is crucial for maintaining an optimal level of energy. It requires listening to your body, providing good conditions (hygiene, warmth, nutrition) and minimizing its exposure to harmful effects. Poised posture and the balanced use of body (e.g. distributing a weight evenly rather than carrying it on one side) save energy and prevent wear and tear of the spine, joints, ligaments and muscles, as well as protect against injury.

State of mind. The effect that a state of mind can have on the level of energy is well documented[152]. Emotions can increase energy extraordinarily but they can also have a debilitating effect, as in the case of depression. Psychological blocks and inner conflicts consume energy and make you weaker. On the other hand, good moods, enthusiasm and laughter release energy trapped by tension or worries and can strengthen you.

Transformation of energy. Energy can be transformed from one form to another. So, any form of energy that can be evoked (e.g. excitement, emotional or sexual energy) may be re-directed and used for a different purpose (providing, of course, that the process of evoking energy doesn't become a distraction).

REFLECTIVE LEVEL

It is worthwhile paying attention to which factors, situations and activities energize you and which ones deplete your energy. It is important to include after-effects too (e.g. alcohol consumption may make you feel temporarily energetic, at the expense of lacking energy the next day). Consider what you can do to achieve a more balanced flow.

PRACTICAL LEVEL

Tactical use of energy. If you lack energy examine first why it is so. If nothing can be done about it, the energy can be saved by reducing waste. You can temporarily withdraw, contract yourself (to minimize exposure), and be, think and feel on a smaller scale. This may involve decreasing expectations from yourself, avoiding challenging tasks, focusing on only necessary activities and performing them in the simplest way. Take into account that emotional reactions (positive and negative) can also consume a lot of energy.

Energy flow. Imagine inhaling energy, which then fills your body (the head, chests, stomach, genital area, limbs). Depending on your personal views, you can identify energy with oxygen flow, or it can be seen as an immanent entity. It is important to monitor if its flow is anywhere interrupted, and examine why, if it is. This exercise can moderately enhance your energy level and provide some insights into how the energy is distributed.

Stretching the body accompanied with a vocal release (e.g. a hum) can reduce tension and emotional pressure, which should result in the increase of energy flow.[153]

RECOMMENDED MATERIALS

Blanche, C. *The Book of Energy* provides some practical advice on how to increase one's energy level from various perspectives. Chapter 9 in Rainwater, J. *You are in charge*, and Lawen, A. *Bioenergetics* are also relevant for this area.

47. ORGANISATION

It turns out that an eerie type of chaos can lurk just behind a facade of order – and yet, deep inside the chaos lurks an even eerier type of order.

Douglas Hofstadfer

Organizing and structuring reality is a universal human characteristic, even on the level of perception (e.g. we tend to automatically perceive a triangle when we see three isolated points). This area, however, focuses on organization on a larger scale – namely the ways we structure our lives and activities. Organisation is usually identified with an externally imposed structure, which can be boring and weaken motivation. However, there is another way of organising activities, so these two types will be compared first. The issues of time, change and planning will also be addressed.

THEORETICAL LEVEL

Innate and imposed order. The world does not seem to be fully pre-determined and predictable. The chaos theory finds its place not only in weather or social sciences, but even in engineering and electronics.[154] However, this does not mean that we live in completely disorderly reality. Although it may sometimes look chaotic and unpredictable, the world seems to have its own innate order (the succession of the seasons can be one example). In organising our activities we can either follow this natural flow, or impose an order from the 'outside'. For example, you can eat (or feed somebody) when hungry, or at pre-fixed times. Both ways have their advantages and disadvantages. Following an innate order enables coordinating your activities with the rhythm of your needs or the surrounding and adapting quickly to a change. It leads to better harmony and a minimal waste of energy. Imposed order is, however, more predictable and more efficient in group settings, when activities of many people need to be synchronised.

Change. Both frequent changes and attempts to keep things unchanged can create a conflict with the natural flow of events, which leads to waste of energy. Preventing the change can temporarily provide a state of constancy, control and predictability and in that way alleviate anxiety, but lasting stability can be achieved only if we accept that everything changes, that only change itself is permanent. In practice, it requires flexibility to shift between the steady periods and the periods of rapid change. This means avoiding to be either idle or hurried, knowing when the time is for action and when for rest and acting upon it. Just accelerating your activities can, in fact, decrease effectiveness. This is why it is important to do it gradually, so that you can check if you are still in control and have not lost yourself in the process. Everything is possible to accomplish if excesses are avoided, and trying to do too much is also an excess.

Time is the basic framework within which we organize our activities. The ability to operate within this framework is a necessary condition for normal functioning. However, an attachment to time can be limiting and de-motivating as much as disregarding time. This happens when the focus is on the time itself rather than on what we do (e.g. when how long we will be engaged in an activity is determined by time units, rather than by an accomplishment, enjoyment or tiredness). It is worthwhile to bear in mind that the quality of time is more important than the amount of time at your disposal. Perception of time can be stretched and condensed. However, there is no activity that doesn't need time, so to prevent an impasse, it is better to do the most important projects first.

Planning. A good plan is not just a time-space construct, but an organization of a string of activities with regard to circumstances. It should include answers to what, how, when and where, and solutions for conceivable obstacles. Planning can greatly contribute to accomplishing a task and enhance motivation, but focusing on a plan can result in forgetting that which it stands for. If it is rigid, it can be limiting and counterproductive. A flexible plan minimizes the possibility of conflict when changes in the situation or unpredictable events occur. For that reason a plan should always be below rather than above you. This means considering a plan only as a means to an end, rather than an end in itself. Holding to your intentions is persistence, to plans – stubbornness.

REFLECTIVE LEVEL
Consider the two types of organisation proposed above. To what extent is it possible and practical to follow a natural order, and to what extent is it necessary to impose an external organization? You can also examine your relation to time (whether you usually try to kill, save or fight time) and to what extent planning daily activities can be helpful.

PRACTICAL LEVEL
Backwards schedule. To get a more realistic picture of how you use your time, write down without interfering (for a week or so) how much time you have spent on various activities (making a schedule of what has happened, not what you want to do). You may be surprised.

Background planning can help you benefit from plans without being bogged down by them. Make a plan of your daily, weekly, monthly and yearly activities, look at what can be achieved regarding available time, play with it, and then leave it aside. Come back to this plan only when you feel confused, want to check your progress or change something.

RECOMMENDED MATERIALS
Assagioli, R. 'Planning and Programming' in *The Act of Will,* and Koch, R. *The 80/20 Principle: The secret of Achieving More with Less,* are suggested.

48. PERFORMANCE

> Do what you can, with what you
> have, where you are.
>
> Theodore Roosevelt

This area describes the factors that constitute *competent* performance. Psychologists claim that 'human beings have an innate need to be competent, effective and self-determining'[155]. So, the assumption here is that most people, in most cases, desire to do well when they deliberately undertake an action. Therefore, (unlike in the other areas) the other side of the spectrum will not be considered.

THEORETICAL LEVEL

On the whole, competence depends more on how effectively we utilise our abilities (whatever they are), than what abilities we have. So, shortcomings and imperfections cannot be used to justify inactivity. Trying always to do well regardless of the importance, value or a possible reward increases your chances to perform competently even under pressure because it becomes a habit. It doesn't guarantee success, sometimes we may fail for reasons beyond our control, but even a failure is easier to accept when we know that we have done our best. If your priority is to satisfy yourself rather than others, praise or criticism will not have a negative effect on quality of your performance (in such a case comments of others are not primary motivators). Doing well does not mean striving for a maximum but an optimum. That means taking into account all the factors: quality, time, purpose, circumstances, your mood, and an accurate assessment of your (and others') abilities. Beside extrinsic gains that it can bring, such as a financial reward, recognition and so on, competent performance also enhances self-esteem and interest, and has a positive effect on the sense of achievement and purpose.

Some features that characterize competent performance are highlighted on the next page.

Preparation consists of considering, before you start, all the steps of the process and how they are related, and also what you may need (tools, assistance etc.).

Practicality requires keeping in mind the aim before and during an action. It can be a safeguard from spreading too much or getting bogged down with details. This, however, does not apply when the process is more important than the final result.

Efficiency means doing things at the right time, at the right place, with as little waste of energy as possible. Procrastination often increases inner resistance, so an action should follow a decision as soon as possible. Rushing, however, can also reduce efficiency.

Carefulness is achieved by, once you have started, keeping the focus on the activity, rather than thinking about something else or whether what you are doing is useful or not.

Elegance makes a performance look spontaneous, natural and easy. It is achieved through a persistent and attentive practice.

Improvisation implies flexibility in thinking, seeking actively new ways of accomplishing a task. This may be important if something unpredictable happens. However, complicating matters needlessly is not improvisation but a waste of time. The easiest, the simplest way is often the most effective. There is usually (although not always) a good reason why a particular manner of doing something is customary.

Creativity is an ability to produce something new, and it can make any work more pleasurable. Creative ideas arise more easily in the process, rather than prior thinking.

Effectiveness means completing what you have started. Incomplete tasks can leave you open and continue to affect you. Projects too big to be accomplished without interruptions can be divided into manageable segments. This will increase the sense of achievement and improves motivation. Not everything can be accomplished though. Sometimes a project has to be abandoned. That also means finishing, as long as it is a conscious decision, rather than just leaving an unfinished work behind to linger.

REFLECTIVE LEVEL
It is worthwhile considering how the importance of an activity or its results affect your performance and what other factors influence it (e.g. feed-back from others).

PRACTICAL LEVEL
Inventory of activities. To avoid wasting time, it is important to invest energy into activities that are likely to return or increase it in one form or another. This, of course, is not to say that an activity must be 'useful'. An intrinsically valuable, satisfying activity is usually beneficial. So, you can make an inventory of your activities, check if the enjoyment or returns (for yourself or others) are higher than the investment, and get rid of those in which this is not the case.

Preventing sabotage. This exercise can help you minimize possible drawbacks before undertaking an action. Consider what and who can endanger your project (including possibly a part of yourself, an inner 'saboteur'); who could gain if the project falls through. If it is another person, you can get in his shoes and imagine what he would do to sabotage the project. Then, you can prepare for it in advance, or negotiate, confront or deal with him. You can approach your own internal saboteur in a similar way.

The final performance. To avoid careless doing, some authors recommend imagining as if it is the last thing you will do in your life. This can indeed improve the quality of a performance because it focuses the mind on the present. However, a caution is called for, because such an attitude may lead to forgetting a larger context.

RECOMMENDED MATERIALS
Csikszentmihalyi, M. *Flow* and Pirsig's novel *Zen and the Art of Motorcycle Maintenance* may be inspiring and lead to better and more enjoyable performance.

DIFFERENT

Not to say what everyone else was saying
not to believe what everyone else believed
not to do what everybody did,
then to refute what everyone else was saying
then to disprove what everyone else believed
then to deprecate what everybody did,

was his way to come by understanding

how everyone else was saying the same as he was saying
believing what he believed
and did what doing

Clere Parsons

IDENTITY GROUP

This group is concerned with the identity formation within the social framework. In other words, it focuses on the relation (and a possible, but not necessary tension) between individuality and sociality. It includes the following areas:

Dependence is the first area in the group because it affects all the other areas. All human beings are inter-dependent to some extent (although the level of dependence varies). Two forms of dependence are considered: *acquisitional* and *social*. In the former, others have an instrumental function, in the latter, an intrinsic one. Which is why the area takes a position in the model that incorporates both the *agency mode* and the *existence mode*.

Individuality refers to the distinctiveness of each person. We would all agree that 'every individual embodies and contains a uniqueness, a reality, that makes her unlike any other person or thing.'[156] Of course, qualities that make an individual don't have to be unique, but the way in which they are combined and expressed always is. In a way, individuality makes us what we are, which is why this area belongs to the *existence* mode.

Influence is in some way the counterpart to *Individuality* and belongs to the *agency mode*. To influence means to have an effect on what someone thinks, feels, says or does. All human interactions involve some extent of mutual influence, so it is considered unavoidable. However, some influences have only instrumental aims (influencing people to achieve something else), while others are concerned with the persons involved (with their personal change). This area attempts to clarify the difference between them.

Belonging is the final area that focuses on the relationship between an individual and a group. Every human being (however isolated) belongs to some groups or categories (at least to humankind). However, the sense of belonging, the awareness that one is a part of a larger community, may be lost. This can cause alienation, which is frequently linked to a number of personal and also social problems.

49. DEPENDENCE

Our language has wisely sensed the two sides of being alone. It has created the word 'loneliness' to express the pain of being alone. And it has created the word 'solitude' to express the glory of being alone.

Paul Tillich

This area is not only about dependence, of course, but independence too. Full independence is hardly possible though, so this term in the text refers to its optimal, not absolute level. The optimal level of independence varies from person to person, so you will need to judge for yourself where you stand in this respect. Two different types of (in)dependence are addressed below: *acquisitional and social*.

THEORETICAL LEVEL

Acquisitional dependence refers to a human need for social support and help. We all depend on others to some degree: children depend on their carers for food and shelter or on teachers to learn; adults are also dependent to some extent (e.g. on public services or other family members). A high level of dependence can provide security with minimal responsibility, but it is not always reliable and limits freedom. It can put the person in an inferior position, which may create feelings of worthlessness and powerlessness. An increase of acquisitional *independence* is a normal part of personal development, fostered in every society, but its optimal level depends on circumstances and varies from society to society. The consequences of independence are increased responsibility, but also greater freedom and self-confidence. However, the move towards independence may cause insecurity and anxiety until self-reliance takes over. They can be minimised by making a gradual shift. The process may also be held back by the feeling of guilt (sometimes perpetuated by a provider). This is why it is important to understand that becoming independent is not betrayal. In fact, it releases others from the burden of responsibility for you. It shouldn't hurt anybody if it goes with respect and doesn't mean abandoning them. Of course, confidence that you are capable of taking care of yourself and being able to do so, doesn't exclude occasional help from others. Asking for assistance when it is necessary is not a weakness. Even if help is not needed, the value of its availability should not be undermined (do you feel the same about policemen when you need them and when you don't?).

Social dependence refers to dependence on the company of other people. In other words, to an ability or inability to be alone. It may be related but not necessarily, to *acquisitional dependence*. Unlike the latter, there is a clear indicator when your social dependence is too high: a feeling of loneliness. Loneliness should not be confused with the desire to be with others. This is only one of the possible reasons for it. Loneliness is not a motivator of sociability, but possessiveness. The feeling of loneliness is not innate, it is usually a product of some other factors: anxiety (clinging onto others), boredom (consuming others), habit (being wrapped up with others), or emptiness (seeking approval or confirmation that you exist). Loneliness may intensify if you feel bad about yourself for some other reason. It can be eased by seeking company, but this increases dependency even further. If others recognise that they are used for instrumental reasons (to alleviate loneliness), it can create discontent and diminish their respect. So, they may pull away and not make themselves available when you really need them, or they may try to abuse your dependency on their company. Learning to be comfortable when alone leads to greater social independence (e.g. you don't have to compromise just to keep company). The time spent alone is different from the time spent with others, but it is also valuable. It may not always be pleasant (as company isn't either) but it certainly could be. This does not mean avoiding other people. In the words of a famous psychologist Karen Horney, an independent person is not compelled either to move away from people or to move towards or against them.

198

REFLECTIVE LEVEL
Are you content with the level of your acquisitional dependence? If you are not, think about at least one thing that you could do to change it. How about your social dependence? Do you ever feel lonely and if you do, how do you deal with it? More generally, it may be interesting to consider how far co-dependency and inter-dependency between people, even from different parts of the globe, and between people and other life forms, go.

PRACTICAL LEVEL
Alone but not lonely. This exercise aims to help you increase control over your social dependence. Loneliness doesn't appear because one is not with other people, but because one is afraid that he cannot be if he wants to (a reduced choice). So, choosing to spend some time on your own can, in fact, decrease the sense of loneliness. Design a period when you can be alone (excluding also substitutes such as telephone, internet chats, TV or imagined conversations). It is important to accept fully the decision to be alone and try to create a quality time without others. Time on your own may be more predictable, but allows greater freedom and depth, so if bored, you can be creative or replace the excitement of unpredictability with the quality. Pay attention from time to time to what you feel. If loneliness creeps in, try to find its cause and deal with it. This exercise may need repeating and experimenting, until you come to the point where being in the company of others doesn't have an overall priority and the fear of loneliness doesn't affect your decisions.

RECOMMENDED MATERIALS
Fromm's *Escape from Freedom* is an excellent and accessible analysis of the possible consequences of the fear of independence. Dowrick, S. *Intimacy and solitude* part 3, points out the importance of social independence, even in intimate relationships. Montaigne's essay 'On solitude' and the writings of Thoreau can also be inspiring.

50. INDIVIDUALITY

Rabbi Zusua said that on the Day of Judgement, God would ask him not why he had not been Moses, but why he had not been Zusua.

Walter Kaufman

Although we have much in common, everybody is a different, separate individual, with our own distinctive set of characteristics and life experiences. Individuality is therefore something given, so this area will focus on factors that restrict its expression.

THEORETICAL LEVEL

Conformity means compliance with the attitudes, behaviour, dress code etc., of a group. Where conformity dominates, individual judgments tend to converge and group norms become a relatively permanent frame of reference. This can be a result of indolence or the need for security and approval. Another powerful force towards conformity is the feelings of separateness and anxiety that showing individuality may bring. These feelings may be experienced not only by those who do not conform, but also by the rest, who may fear for the group cohesion. Individuality, however, does not need to be a threat to, or create a conflict with, the society or group. It doesn't mean being egocentric, but accepting that you are, like everybody else, different, and allowing yourself (and others) to be so. Valuing what we share does not preclude respecting what we don't. In fact, individuality may add something worthwhile to the group and increase its flexibility[157].

Copying may be useful when learning new skills. However, copying the manners or appearance of somebody else with the hope that some essence will also rub off, is misleading at the least. Copying others may temporarily increase your self-esteem but it requires suppressing your individuality, which creates an inner conflict and diminishes self-respect. To copy means, in a way, giving up your own life, losing yourself. So, even if you achieve a desired goal but alienate yourself in the process, you will not be able to enjoy it, because you will not be there. Everybody has their own way, and what has worked for one person may not work for another. Besides, an imperfect original is usually more valued than even a successful copy of a masterpiece.

Self-consciousness. The opinions, judgments and other reactions of others towards us are important because they provide social orientation and security. Pretending that they are not may increase their influence on the unconscious level. However, being aware of and respecting the opinions of others is different from judging yourself only through their eyes, using them as a mirror and the only measure of your own worth. If others become a more important criterion than yourself, it may lead to losing individuality and incorrect self-assessment (they may, for example, be in a bad mood or react in a particular way for reasons completely unrelated to you). Exaggerated concern about the impression you leave also increases insecurity. A more accurate way of determining the adequacy of your behaviour than trying to guess what others think (or will think) about you, is a sense or feeling that you have about the whole situation. This requires focusing really on the atmosphere and others, rather than on yourself through them.

Pleasing others. If adapting to the desires or demands of other people is the strongest factor that influences your behaviour, it can be interpreted as a weakness and abused. Always giving in or trying to fulfil the expectations of others doesn't earn love but the loss of respect. People usually value more a person who can't be manipulated, because it shows that she is not an object, but an individual. This doesn't imply being irresponsible, but not allowing others to take you for granted. It simply means being aware of your needs and desires too, and contributing to decisions and plans rather than just following them. You may still need to adapt, but *to the situation* rather than to others.

REFLECTIVE LEVEL
Have you ever considered what the consequences are of
uniformity and diversity (for both, individuals and the society)?
When is it better to follow an established route and when to find
one's own way (regarding a dress code, behaviour, opinions,
beliefs etc.)? You may take into consideration in this respect
your immediate surrounding (e.g. neighbours), as well as public
authorities (e.g. politicians, religious leaders, scientists).

PRACTICAL LEVEL
What do I really want? Make a habit, in social situations, of
checking from time to time your own feelings and desires.
Whether you really want to be there or do what you are doing –
or you are just complying with the wishes of others or doing
something to leave an impression. Even if the latter is the case,
it does not mean that you have to immediately change
something, though. The awareness of what your priority is at
that moment is enough (you may, for example, decide to put up
with the situation out of consideration for others, which is
different from being submissive).

Being watched. Imagine, while for example walking or waiting
for a bus, that somebody is observing you (for no specific
reason). Monitor how you feel and in what way it affects your
behaviour. If you react strongly, try first to find out why it
matters to you. Then, relax and make a conscious attempt not to
be much bothered (perhaps saying to yourself something like
'So what?'). You can also imagine (but don't get into details)
that people are talking about you, and do the same.

RECOMMENDED MATERIALS
Individuality seems a popular theme for non-fiction and fiction
writers alike. Here are only some examples of the rich literature
on the subject: May, R. *Man's Search for Himself*; Wilson, C.
The Outsider; Emerson's essay 'Self-Reliance', Huxley, A.
Brave New World and Salinger's *Catcher in the Rye*.

51. INFLUENCE

> People are usually more convinced by reasons they discovered themselves than by those found by others.
>
> Blaise Pascal

Influence is unavoidable, but some influences and their effects are desirable and some are not. It is often difficult to distinguish between them, so in this area the special attention will be paid to differences between various types of influence.

THEORETICAL LEVEL

The reasons for accepting an influence. Psychologists have recognised three major reasons for accepting an influence[158]: *compliance* – influence is accepted to avoid unfavourable or achieve favourable reactions (as in case of coercion or a threat of punishment); *identification* – influence is accepted because the power to make decisions is handed over to others (e.g. an authority or a group); *internalisation* – influence is accepted because it makes sense (e.g. a sound argument). Only the last one is compatible with autonomy.

Types of influence. Influences can be intentional and unintentional. Unintentional influences can have a strong impact, but the focus here will be on intentional ones, because they can be shaped. There are two types of such influences:

Instrumental influences are concerned with immediate goals, rather than with the persons involved or long term outcomes. Such influences often emphasise the way they are delivered (e.g. shouting) in order to divert attention from weak points in the content. They can be *direct* (coercions by force, threat, punishment, reward) or *indirect* (manipulations such as flattery, veneer friendliness, flirtation, emotional blackmail, hints). This type of influence can have a short term and superficial effect, but if unsuccessful, they create an even stronger resistance.

Intrinsic influences are concerned with a personal change, rather than only immediate outcomes. They can also be direct and indirect. An indirect intrinsic influence is influence by an example. It creates the least resistance and can be profound, but it is not always practical (it usually takes time). Direct intrinsic influences are verbal interventions. There are several types: *prescriptive* (giving advice, judging, evaluating); *informative* (providing information); *confronting* (challenging the person's attitude, behaviour or belief); *catalytic* (facilitates self-directed problem-solving or coming to conclusions); *supportive* (influence through being approving, confirming, validating). Each of these interventions can be effective if used in appropriate circumstances, but they can also be misused. It is important to remember that intrinsic influence is not about controlling others (trying to make others do what you want creates a conflict, either with them or within them, and therefore it is likely to make somebody unhappy).

The process. Unlike a behavioural change, an inner change cannot be forced, it happens only when the person is ready and willing to change. Unsolicited advice also undermines the competence of the person advised. Influence is more profound if limited to helping people arrive to desired conclusions themselves. This requires willingness to look at the situation from their perspective. Generally, suggestions will be accepted more readily if a pleasant (loving, secure, pacifying, supportive) atmosphere is created. Persuasion can work if there is common ground and if there is trust, openness and a sense of security. Otherwise, even a sound argument will only create resistance, and increasing intensity or forcefulness of persuasion will not bring desired results. The more somebody is excited, the easier he can be influenced in the same direction, but it is more difficult to initiate a change. Appealing to person's weaknesses (e.g. vanity) rather than virtues may sometimes be effective, but it is easy to cross the line between using and abusing the weaknesses of others. If talking doesn't work, you can also influence others by altering your behaviour (e.g. a change from being warm to being cold) causes uncertainty and may result in both weakening or strengthening resistance.

Feedback is the most common form of direct influence. Some people feel awkward even when praised, so feedback always requires sensitivity. Choosing a right time and place is also important. Feedback can be useful only if it doesn't undermine confidence and if it is accepted. Confidence is not undermined by constructive criticism, but when negative feedback aims at the person rather than an act, or when positive feedback is perceived as insincere. Feedback is more likely to be accepted when it is specific, includes examples, and when the person can do something about it.

REFLECTIVE LEVEL
You may consider what methods are effective in influencing you and how you influence others. Also, you can look at when (if ever) instrumental influences are justified.

PRACTICAL LEVEL
Influence work out. Arrange with (or imagine) somebody to alternately criticise and praise you. To start off, issues can be invented; they don't really need to relate to you. Resist the temptation to answer back and observe how criticism and praise affect you. Repeat the exercise until you can accept them in a non-attached way. This doesn't mean creating barriers or ignoring the comments, but not being defensive or carried away by them. In time, issues with which you feel less secure can be brought up. If you are doing this with a real person, you can reverse the roles. This would enable you to see how you praise and criticise others (e.g. whether you tend to criticise an act or the person).

RECOMMENDED MATERIALS
Back K. & Back, K. 'How others influence you' in *Assertiveness at Work* and the updated version of one of the first ever self-help book, *How to win friends and influence people* are suggested.

52. BELONGING

> No man is an island, entire of
> itself; every man is a piece of the
> continent, a part of the main.
> John Donne

This area focuses on the individual as a part of social networks or groups. Groups can consist of only a few people (as in the case of a team) or be very large (e.g. a nation). They often promote the sense of belonging, but in some cases groups can have an opposite effect and create a sense of exclusion (for non-members and some members too). So, it is worthwhile looking at how groups are formed, what they require, and also at the attitudes that contribute to becoming a part of a group.

THEORETICAL LEVEL

Taxonomy. There are three major ways of forming groups:
Physically determined groups (e.g. race, nation, gender, age) were dominant in the past, but are losing their importance today (at least in some parts of the world).
Socially determined groups (religion, family, country, culture) also decrease slowly in importance, but are still very powerful.
Self-determined groups (e.g. partners, friends, political or professional groups, clubs) are chosen on the basis of personal desires, shared interests and mutual acceptance.
Of course, in practice there is not such a clear cut between these categories. For example, belonging to a club or even one's partner may be socially determined, or belonging to a religion may be the result of personal choice.

Purpose. Belonging increases one's sense of security and productivity (a group can do more than individuals), reduces the risk of errors and minimises personal responsibility[159]. On the other hand, the group often limits individual freedom, it is more inert and slow, and usually operates at the level of lowest common denominator. Being a part of a group may decrease dependence on individuals (because there are always others), and also on a larger community. However, if you are concerned only with the interests of the group that you belong to, the rest of the world may be alienated (and even perceived as hostile) which makes you more susceptible to group control. A wider social framework can protect the person from the pressure of the group, so it is always beneficial to maintain some outside contacts.

Joining a group. It is noted that those individuals who are accepted 'observe the group to understand what is going on before entering in, and then do something that shows they accept it; they wait to have their status in the group confirmed before taking initiative in suggesting what the group should do.'[160] Following these hints may maximise your chances, but is not, of course, a guarantee that you will be accepted. Even so, the sense of belonging still depends on you rather than others. If not accepted in one group you can turn to others, as long as you are flexible enough in your choice.

Group requirements. To function properly a group needs:
A common purpose: to be accepted by a group you need first to accept the group, which means primarily recognising and accepting its purpose (even if it is not explicitly stated).
Recognition of boundaries: a group wouldn't be a group if it didn't have boundaries (however flexible they are), so, it is important to be aware of them.
Organisation deals with where, when, what and who. The last point requires having your place or role within the group.
Participation: groups rely on the contribution of its members (in one way or another), so how much you will get from a group depends to a large extent on how much you invest in it.
Non-dependence on individuals: a group that depends on an individual does not last long, so nobody should make herself (or be made by others) irreplaceable.
Cohesion doesn't need to become conformity. Groups usually accept individual differences as long as they are not an imposition or interfere with the functioning of the group.

Belonging does not require giving up individuality, but may require giving up pride that you have individuality.

Commonly accepted norms: every group has implicit or explicit norms (e.g. rules, customs, laws) that enable its functioning. Although they can be sometimes transgressed, groups have a tendency towards self-preservation; so if a margin of abuse is surpassed, it will sooner or later turn against the perpetrators. Some norms may be perceived as imperfect, unfair, or infringe on individual freedom, but if the whole system of norms is bad, the group would not be able to survive.

Ability to adapt: although individuals are expected to accept the norms, any group needs to adapt and evolve, so there is always room for those who want to make a change or improvement.

REFLECTIVE LEVEL

It may be useful to consider whether you have the sense of belonging, or it doesn't matter to you, or you feel isolated or excluded. Whatever the answer is, the following questions may help you clarify your relation and attitudes towards groups you are part of: which groups have you chosen and which ones have been chosen for you? Which ones are important and why? What do you (dis)like in each? What purposes those groups fulfil? Do they function well and how can you contribute to further improvements?

PRACTICAL LEVEL

You and the group. Visualise your connection to different groups you belong to, and observe your emerging feelings and thoughts. If you are not content, you can examine what is a problem and what can be done about it, or search for alternative groups.

RECOMMENDED MATERIALS

Johnson, D & Johnson, F. *Joining Together* and *Group dynamics* by D. Forsyth are worthwhile looking at. A novel *The Shipping News* by Proulx also explores this subject.

FIRST THEY CAME FOR THE JEWS

First they came for the Jews
and I did not speak out –
because I was not a Jew.
Then they came for the communists
and I did not speak out –
because I was not a communist.
Then they came for the trade unionists
and I did not speak out –
because I was not a trade unionist.
Then they came for me –
and there was no one left
to speak out for me.

Pastor Niemöller

SOCIAL ATTITUDES GROUP

The term social attitudes refers to the way we perceive, value, assess and threat each other. There is no need to emphasise how important these attitudes are on the group level (e.g. cultures) as well as on the individual level (in personal relationships). This group consists of the areas that affect their formation:

Moral sense is the root area of this group. Recognising and cultivating our own *personal* moral sense is important nowadays not only because the existing sets of moral rules and principles appear hardly adequate to respond to the increasing complexity of human interactions, but also because morality itself is becoming more and more personal. Although most of us appreciate the value of moral considerations, we are not prepared any more to accept without questioning rules imposed from above. Developing our own moral sense can provide something to rely on that is compatible with personal autonomy. In other words, it enables us to avoid moral relativism ('everything goes') on the one hand, and social indoctrination on the other[161].

Protection refers to an ability to prevent or minimise undesirable effects of the social environment and is one of the basic abilities of any living organism. Its purpose is the preservation of the being from external forces. This means that protection is essentially re-active, which is why it belongs (as the other areas in this group) to the *existence* mode.

Relating to others is the counterpart to *Protection*. Its focus is not on interactions with others, but on some affirmative attitudes that enable contacts and connections between individuals and groups (i.e. respect, acceptance, tolerance).

Symmetricity is a new term for the area that examines comparing with others and a 'vertical' relation between individuals (e.g. equality, superiority, inferiority). This feature is a universal occurrence not only among humans but the other primates as well (expressed, for example, in a hierarchical organisation of a group). Symmetricity is the final area in this group because it is based to some extent on the other areas.

53. MORAL SENSE

In every act of moral self-affirmation man contributes to the fulfilment of his destiny, to the actualisation of what he potentially is.

Paul Tillich

Moral sense refers to a universal human ability to evaluate actions in terms of good and bad (even when they do not affect the evaluator) and is necessary for social functioning. Moustakis writes that 'moral sense... is not a law or a definition but... the internal directive that establishes meaning and value'[162]. Recognising that we have moral sense is important because it is not always possible to clearly formulate and rationally justify what is morally good and bad. Support for its existence can be found in psychology, philosophy and even bio-neurology[163]. An indirect indicator of moral sense is that sympathy, compassion, fairness, regret, guilt and concern for others can occur spontaneously among children (unlike shame that needs to be socially induced). In fact, the inability to recognise and evaluate consequences of one's actions (and actions of others) is considered to be a sign of mental disorder. This is not to say that moral sense implies moral uniformity. Moral sense is only a potential, shaped by society and personal experiences, and expressed within a particular social framework. It can be embodied in different moral interpretations and conducts, or even stunted. However, although moral sense often coincides with socially accepted morality, they may conflict and should not be identified. This area will focus on the consequences and development of moral sense.

THEORETICAL LEVEL

Consequences. Acting in accord with your own moral sense feels good, behaving contrary to it does not, although these feelings can be distorted by other gains or losses. A result of the latter may provide temporary and partial satisfaction, but the former creates lasting positive feelings and a sense of completeness. Disregarding moral sense is sometimes attractive because it may offer immediate relief or gratification, but it alienates and isolates the person from other people and a part of himself. This causes an inner conflict indicated by disturbed conscience and the accompanying feelings of regret or guilt (this is why justifications are so common – nobody wants to see himself as bad). Conscience is absent only if the social aspect of a person is partly or completely cut off. But, as psychologist Horney points out 'we cannot suppress or eliminate essential parts of ourselves without becoming estranged from ourselves.'[164] However, guilt or remorse may be also socially conditioned, rather than being the result of conscience. They can be triggered by the fear of punishment, which does not need to involve one's conscience. The absence or presence of fear is what indicates the difference.

Development of moral sense can be vertical (qualitative) or horizontal (quantitative). The former increases its sensitivity (an ability to deal with complex and intricate situations)[165]. The latter increases the scope or locus of concern, so moral sense becomes more inclusive (selfish or parochial people, for example, are not developed in this way)[166]. Both, vertical and horizontal development are supported by the development of the *will* (character, virtues) *reason* (principles) and *affect* (empathy, care) [167]. Moral sense and conduct requires all these faculties. Personal moral conflicts are usually the result of an imbalance between them (e.g. moral principles conflict with weak will), so balancing their development minimises the chance of such conflicts. An action can have, however, a moral connotation only if it is the result of choice, so a certain level of autonomy and personal power are also needed. General moral rules and principles can have an important supportive role, but they can be limiting. They are a simplification and therefore do not always account for the complexity of a situation (they can be too rigid or too broad).

It needs to be borne in mind that harm can be caused or perpetuated through inactivity and ignorance, not only malevolent actions. Therefore, moral sense is not only concerned with avoiding harmful actions, but also with an active promotion of good causes.

REFLECTIVE LEVEL
It may be useful to clarify the following issues: why be moral? Do we need a reason? To what extent would you change your conduct, if the law and punishment did not exist? Does being good make one weaker? What is the difference between morality and good behaviour? Is it immoral to do something self-destructive or destructive with consent (e.g. masochism, euthanasia, etc.)?

PRACTICAL LEVEL
Overcoming partiality. A frequent problem regarding fairness is a tendency towards partiality (it is related to the horizontal development of moral sense mentioned above). A political philosopher Rawls' suggestion to imagine that one does not know on which side he (or any other party) will end up can promote impartiality (a trivial example of this method is that one cuts the cake but another chooses a slice). The other way to achieve impartiality is to analyse some situations in which you don't have any interests, and then apply the conclusions to your own situation (e.g. you can come to the conclusion what is fair by imagining first a similar situation that doesn't involve you or people close to you).

RECOMMENDED MATERIALS
There are many materials on this subject. Buber's *Images of Good and Evil,* Nietzsche's *Beyond Good and Evil,* and Dostoyevsky's *Crime and Punishment* are suggested because they can stimulate further thoughts in this respect.

54. PROTECTION

The offender never pardons
George Herbert

When protection is really needed is not always clear, so it is sometimes misused (e.g. to justify aggression) or abandoned (to avoid appearing aggressive). This is why it is worthwhile to look closely at adverse behaviour and responses to it.

THEORETICAL LEVEL

Adverse behaviour can be active (e.g. aggression) and passive (e.g. ignoring the other). The latter may be less conspicuous but equally destructive. Beside instrumental reasons (i.e. a prospect of some gains), adverse behaviour can be a result of several factors. Their better understanding may contribute to diffusion of such behaviour (in yourself and others).

Social factors: aggressive behaviour can be a learnt response (e.g. imitating others). It can also be the result of alienation and deprivation. A harsh or rejecting environment may push some individuals or groups to adopt an adverse attitude. This is supported by a belief that regard for others can make one weak, less capable to cope. However, such a belief is false. Being a good person does not mean being soft – it is compatible with strength and firmness. In fact, it contributes to the personal strength, because it enables an individual to act as a whole.

Psychological factors include, for example, the sense of unfairness or injustice, and powerlessness to correct them. They often lead to displacement (e.g. a child that is treated unjustly may hit another child to vent her frustration). Thwarted expectations and other perceived threats to our sense of control cause anxiety and may also trigger an outburst of anger.

Neuro-biological factors (e.g. low blood sugar) and *environmental factors* (e.g. ambient temperature, crowding) that cause frustration, pain and other discomfort can significantly contribute to aggressive behaviour, so a special care is needed if they are present.

Purpose of protection. Indiscriminate liking or loving can become a self-satisfying pattern not really related to experience or others. Such an ideology has little to do with reality. Not all people have always good motives, sometimes they act out of malice, spite, envy, desire to manipulate, etc. It is easier to become a victim if this possibility is not accepted. Always blaming oneself and finding excuses for others is equally maladaptive as always blaming others, and finding excuses for oneself. If love and benevolence are not accompanied by strength and caution, they can be abused. Aspiring to be a good person cannot be an excuse for passivity and submissiveness. A good person is good towards herself too, which includes being able to protect oneself. Giving in to abuse is not a sign of love. Some people go as far as one allows them, so it is important to be able to set a limit. Tolerating malevolence has not only adverse effects in the immediate situation, but also allows it to grow. However, it is important to be aware what is protected, and if protection is really needed (why certain behaviour is interpreted as hostile). Overprotection makes you closed and so limits experience. Furthermore, protecting your weaknesses or character flaws (e.g. vanity) can prevent further development.

Response. Hostility can either be *avoided* (if it does not have long term consequences), *diffused* through, for example, humour or acknowledging the feelings of the other person (listening, clarifying), or *confronted* (making clear how you are affected). In any case, it is important to preserve confidence and calm. Difficult people are encouraged when they notice that one is taken in by their behaviour and starts overreacting. Fear doesn't help (unless you are running away). An angry response or frustration may achieve short-term goals, but it hides insecurity and increases a risk and uncertainty. Genuine calm leaves a more authoritative impression and is usually more effective than agitation. To maintain calm, focus on the situation (resolving the problem) rather than fighting others or yourself. And remember, asking for help to protect yourself or others is not cowardly.

REFLECTIVE LEVEL

It may be worthwhile examining your attitude towards adverse behaviour: what situations (or people) tend to arouse aggressive feelings in you? How do you react in such situations? Do you think that there is a better way to deal with them?

PRACTICAL LEVEL

Dealing with protective reactions. It often happens that an emotional response to an adverse behaviour is suppressed in the actual situation by another emotion (e.g. fear may suppress anger). This may create an inner conflict and keep you attached to the situation that has caused your grievances. To avoid this, one of the following ways can be used to express the original emotions without directly involving the elicitor:

(i) *Imagination*: visualise the person who has upset you when you are on your own, and speak or shout at her (in imagination or aloud). It is important to do it from a subjective perspective, imagining the other person, rather than observing yourself in imagination.

(ii) *Talking* about the situation and the related emotions (e.g. to a counsellor or friend).

(iii) *Writing, drawing:* you can express your emotions through writing a letter to the elicitor (but wait awhile before sending it). Drawing can serve the same purpose.

(iv) *Action:* you can vent your emotions on a sack, cushion or other object.

Although beneficial, self-expression is not always sufficient. A resolution also requires developing a strategy to deal with the situation and deciding on an attitude towards the elicitor (e.g. to forgive her, confront her, or minimise the contact and forget her).

RECOMMENDED MATERIALS

Ferrucci, P. 'Tigers of Wrath' in *What We May Be* and Elgin, S. *The Gentle Art of Verbal Self-Defence* are suggested. An episode in a short novel by Richard Bach, *Illusions,* exemplifies the importance of being able to protect oneself.

55. RELATING TO OTHERS

Tolerance is the positive and cordial effort to understand another's beliefs, practices, and habits without necessarily sharing or accepting them.

Joshua Liebman

This area refers to the attitudes that enable people to get along and relate to each other constructively (respect, acceptance, tolerance). Such attitudes are often taken for granted ("Of course I respect others!"). Yet, it may be worthwhile examining why (and when) they make sense, what can influence them, and why it is sometimes difficult to stick with them.

THEORETICAL LEVEL

Respect simply means treating people as subjects not objects. This implies recognising that every person has an intrinsic value because one is (*existence*), and because one does (can make choices and act upon them, which is called *agency*). Treating people as objects might increase the sense of control, but because it means not being really aware of *persons*, it induces feelings of loneliness and boredom even when among others. This may increase the intensity of compensatory desires, which can lead to further alienation. Also, you are more likely to be treated with respect if you treat others with respect. Respecting others, though, doesn't need to become a burden. Giving equal attention to everybody doesn't require giving them equal time.

Acceptance increases your chances of being accepted and rejection of being rejected. Acceptance is also more fulfilling than rejection because it involves openness and sharing that expands and enriches the person. It is supported by attempting to understand the other, rather than emphasising his 'faults'. If you are aware of somebody's shortcomings you don't need to be troubled by them. Assessing others on the basis of *their* qualities rather than *your* expectations minimises a chance of disappointment.

Acceptance is different from tolerance. Tolerance is a capacity to bear, put up with others, suggesting that they are a problem, pain, burden to be endured. Unlike acceptance, it implies being closed and a sometimes covert superiority (of those who tolerate). Acceptance may include tolerating something, but it doesn't mean putting up with everything. In fact, it is easier to openly disagree with what one does if the person himself is honestly accepted (sometimes people allow to be taken advantage of in order to hide their true feelings and appear tolerant). Accepting the others as they are and trying to understand their motives can be the first step to elicit a positive change. However, there are several reasons why accepting others may be difficult:

Insecurity (as a result of uncertainty or a real or imagined threat) makes some people to form their attitudes on the basis of superficial similarities or differences (e.g. nationality), which often leads to an incorrect judgment[168]. For the same reason even mundane unfamiliar customs (such as food preparation or dress code) can be perceived as a threat.

Projection. You may find some characteristics of others difficult to accept because you recognise the same characteristics in yourself. So, an inner conflict is projected outside.

Comparison. A sense of superiority (e.g. cliquishness) or inferiority (e.g. envy) are barriers to accepting others. Conceit or envy are usually the result of distorted perception, when one aspect of your own or somebody else's life is extracted from the whole. However, nobody has everything. It is likely that the one who envies has something the envied one would desire (privacy, free time, no responsibility). Similarly, those looked down on are likely to have something to offer if one is open enough to recognise it.

Generalisation. To assess people on the basis of their individual merits requires an effort, time and intelligence, so some people try to simplify this process by generalising some superficial information. It can happen on several levels: crude generalisations are based on physical (race, age, physical ability, gender, nationality) and social determinants (culture, religion). They both undermine individual differences and are misleading. There is reliable evidence that physical characteristics, for example, do not correspond to personality traits or psychological or behavioural characteristics[169]. Generalising some other superficial features (e.g. the way one dresses, talks or looks) can also be misleading.

The other type of generalisation is when a whole community or group is judged (or rejected) on the basis of limited experience with one or a few individuals. Variety in intelligence, moral capacity, communication skills etc. is usually, in fact, greater among members of the same sufficiently large group, than between groups.

REFLECTIVE LEVEL
Do you think that everybody should be respected, or that respect depends on what one does (i.e. when do you lose respect for somebody? Is it related to self-respect of that person?) You can also examine your attitudes towards new people (is your usual initial reaction curiosity, trust, suspicion, anxiety or animosity?) What indicators do you use to form your opinion about them and how quickly does it take? Perhaps too quickly?

PRACTICAL LEVEL
On the way to acceptance. Choose an individual or a group that you find difficult to accept. Locate exactly what is not acceptable and detach it from that individual or group. It should be easier to accept people when that which bothers you is excluded. Now, turn to that aspect itself. Why does it really concern you? Are you making any generalisations? Can these people do anything about it? Can you? (E.g. talk to them, change your view…)

RECOMMENDED MATERIALS
Downie, R. S. *Respect for Persons* provides some theoretical background to this subject. Lee, H. *To Kill a Mockingbird* might look somewhat outdated nowadays, but it is still a good analysis of how people form their attitudes and what affects them.

56. SYMMETRICITY

Remember, no one can make you feel inferior without your consent.
Eleanor Roosevelt

It is hardly necessary to point out the importance of an area that relates to equality and inequality. Society, however, seems ambiguous about this subject. Equality is nominally advocated, but asymmetrical relationships pervade many areas of life. The first issue addressed here is what can be compared and what cannot. Based on this, the attitudes of superiority, inferiority and equality, and their adequacy are examined, with an emphasis on the difference between personal and functional (a)symmetry.

THEORETICAL LEVEL

Comparing. A commonly overlooked misconception is that objects and people can be compared. In fact, it is possible only to compare their characteristics (if 1, 2 and 3 are persons or objects, only their attributes a^1, a^2 and a^3 are comparable). To say 'He is better', or 'She is superior' is logically incorrect. Such statements are used either for the sake of simplicity or as a generalisation. Comparing one or a few characteristics and then generalising from them may be sometimes practical, but it does not do justice to the complexity of human beings and human life. One can drive, play or look better, but it does not mean that she is a better or superior person (one who plays better may not cook better, and so on). This is easily overlooked if an attribute or role becomes more important than the whole person, which can be abused to justify some instrumental aims (e.g. an inequality in a position or affluence). Not even all characteristics can be compared, but only those that can be measured using the same criterion. So, comparing should be used judiciously, bearing in mind that nobody is a better or worse person and that everybody is, in fact, an unrepeatable and essentially incomparable individual.

Personal symmetry. From the above perspective, equality does not imply that we are all the same, but that we are not comparable. Equality allows differences, it only means that standards of assessment, rights and opportunities should not depend on them. In other words, 'an inequality in treatment must be justifiable in some way.'[170] This implies that attitudes of inferiority or superiority are inadequate. They may be perpetuated by others or circumstances (sometimes people act from a superior position only to probe the strength of the other), but ultimately where you stand depends on you and your way of thinking. Reminding yourself that we are all mortal can significantly decrease the importance of other differences. Nobody is really superior, but some people may be more confident because they do not bother with comparing, or appear so because they suppress 'weak' aspects of themselves. Inferiority and superiority are connected. Believing that there is somebody below implies believing that there is somebody above, too (and the other way around). Looking down on others is usually a compensation for a lack of genuine self-respect. An impression of inferiority or superiority may also arise because dependence, needs or the importance attached are not reciprocal. Not admitting it to yourself and attempting to maintain a pretence of equality only exacerbates the situation. Sometimes we may even willingly put ourselves in an inferior position (e.g. as a response to a favour). However, this is more likely to be perceived as a punishment than a reward. Personal asymmetry always has a negative effect on spontaneity, friendship and intimacy. On the other hand, abandoning thinking in terms of superiority and inferiority decreases tension and nervousness, and makes those involved more open and relaxed.

Functional asymmetry. The above does not make comparing obsolete, but its generalisation. Sometimes functional asymmetry is important, even necessary, but it does not give anyone a license for abuse, degradation or humiliation. Parents and teachers, for example, usually have superior knowledge, experience and skills than children, but this does not make them superior people. The way to avoid inferiority in a subordinate position is to accept it – hiding or denying that you are in this position only proves inferiority. Respecting the qualities of others and freely accepting limited subordination in order to learn or perform a task, do not create inferiority. For example, one will learn to drive better if the superiority of the instructor's *skills* is accepted, but this does not require accepting an unequal relationship.

REFLECTIVE LEVEL
Many everyday situations may be used to examine your attitude towards personal and functional (a)symmetry. For example, do you habitually think that others are more important than you, or that you are more important than others? Does it vary from situation to situation? Or, if you are into competitive sports, can you make a difference between a desire to win and a desire to beat your opponent (to prove that you are better)?

PRACTICAL LEVEL
Challenging asymmetries. Visualise yourself with somebody else you know. Observe how you relate to each other (e.g. what your positions are, whether the other person seems bigger or smaller than in reality). If you detect a sense of superiority, try to find what it is a compensation for. If you look (or feel) inferior, consider if your mutual needs are asymmetrical and how they can be balanced, whether that person is irreplaceable and whether you really depend on her. Imagine a situation in which the attributes that make the person superior are irrelevant (e.g. one's social status on a deserted island or one's looks in a combat). See if you feel differently.

RECOMMENDED MATERIALS
The psychologist Alfred Adler wrote extensively on this subject. His book *What Life Could Mean To You* can be worthwhile reading.

DON'T BE LITERARY, DARLING

Don't be literary, darling, don't be literary
If you're James in the morning you're Hemingway in bed
Don't talk of yourself in the style of your own obituary –
For who cares what they say of you after you're dead.

Don't be always a thought ahead and a move behind
Like a general reconnoitring dangerous ground,
This is a game it's much better to enter blind
And the one who wins is the one who is caught and bound.

If you can't be straight then just say nothing instead.
I'll know what you mean much better than if it was said.

Sasha Moorsom

INTERACTION GROUP

This group consists of the areas that constitute human interactions:

Appearance is usually the first signal to others. The ability to create an impression is a universal and irreducible phenomenon that is achieved through various means (clothes, make-up, posture, way of talking or behaving etc.)

Awareness of others deals with skills that allow us to become aware of what other people think or feel: listening, observing and empathy. This type of awareness is different from awareness of objects around you, for example. While the latter mostly depends on our senses, awareness of others is more indirect. We need to extrapolate about the thoughts and feelings of others on the basis of sensory information. This means that awareness of others involves an active process that requires willingness and effort, which is why this area (as the other areas in this group) belongs to the *Agency mode*.

Communication focuses on information transmission. It can be considered a counterpart to the above area that, as already mentioned, includes listening and other receptive aspects of an interaction. It may look strange to separate listening and communicating in discrete areas when they are often interlinked. However, it is not uncommon to use one without the other (e.g. giving a speech, listening to the radio) which indicates that they consist of distinctive skills that can be approached independently.

Behaviour has been defined in the academic world as 'a class of events which occurs during co-presence and by virtue of co-presence.'[171] Putting it in more familiar terms, behaviour refers to a manner of conducting ourselves during an interaction with others (which is close to the common meaning, rather than to the much more inclusive use of the word in psychology). It overarches and, at the same time, relies on the other areas in the group (but it cannot be reduced to them).

57. APPEARANCE

> May the outward and the
> inward man be at one.
>
> Socrates

Appearance has a multiple purpose: to attract or protect; to help us situate within a certain role; to signal mood, character, profession, position or status. This area focuses on some basic factors that affect appearance: congruence, flexibility and appeal.

THEORETICAL LEVEL

Congruence. An appearance is incongruent if it does not correspond to the person. Sometimes people deliberately try to appear different than they are. This can have various motives: to trick others, to hide or protect, to preserve privacy, to compensate for the subjective sense of personal inadequacy or inferiority, or to prove something to oneself or others. Emphasised impressions usually indicate the opposite. For example, an over-jovial appearance may hide melancholy (sometimes with the hint of what is hidden to provoke curiosity); or somebody who feels submissive may appear aggressive (and the other way around). Incongruent appearance can have a temporary effect, but it creates barriers between the person and others, causes tension and never fully satisfies. Closeness is avoided for fear that the real person will be revealed and consequently rejected. Trying to impress others with a pretence also diminishes individuality and may have the opposite effect from desired if recognised. An attempt in deception is usually a compensation, admitting that one lacks certain qualities (e.g. a genuinely tough guy does not need to make an impression of a tough guy). It is often a sign of an inferior position and if the person himself is not aware of it, others may be. Even if they are temporarily deceived, an idealised image is not effective in the long run because it is hard to live up to created expectations, and gains are usually smaller than losses when the discrepancy is recognised.

Congruent appearance, on the other hand, is based on one's character and preserves spontaneity. It still allows presenting yourself in various ways, which can be achieved through emphasising different aspects of your personality. Without an ability to undertake different roles in various situations social interactions would be limited. So, creating an image is not a problem, as long as it is genuine.

Flexibility. Even if you do not pay attention to your appearance, you still leave an impression, which affects the assessment and attitude of others towards you. This can, in turn, affect your own self-esteem. An image, therefore, can be important, which does not mean that you should take it more seriously than yourself. Appearance is only the means to convey certain information about yourself. Identifying with it makes you inflexible. If a so fixed image is negative, it may create a sense of worthlessness. Being attached to even an agreeable image can be restricting and can prevent full interaction. Besides, an image that is useful in some situations may be counterproductive in others (e.g. a person with the image of a tough guy may find it difficult to be intimate). If you are not attached to your images, you can use and change them depending on the situation, which increases your freedom and flexibility, and enables you to adapt better.

A fixed image can also be imposed by other people. Allowing this, limits your choice and makes you controllable by those who have created and have their own reasons to perpetuate it.

Appeal cannot be reduced to a sum of characteristics that one possesses, or physical looks (this may be sufficient only for instrumental purposes, i.e. mating). Research confirms that 'people who are seen as attractive are usually those with interesting or lively personalities.'[172] An appearance has appeal if it is a result of an organic whole, which means that every part corresponds to the whole and expresses the whole and that the whole expresses all its parts. This does not imply symmetry or regularity, but connectedness, some level of coherence between inner and outer, between what is expressed and how it is expressed. This is why the attractiveness of the same person may vary, depending on his state of mind at that moment. For example, insecurities about your look can diminish your appeal more than actual imperfections. The above also indicates that beauty can take different forms, it does not require complying with certain standards (i.e. fashion). Creating a particular within the universal, using various means to create beauty in accord with your personality is what makes your style.

REFLECTIVE LEVEL
Consider whether your image and appearance are freely chosen, accepted or adopted. Related to this issue, you can examine to what extent the pressure of others and society in general plays a role in this area (e.g. why do people follow fashion?)

PRACTICAL LEVEL
Playing with appearance. You can experiment with different appearances first on your own (using a mirror if necessary) and then in front of others. Fixed images can be countered by creating opposite ones, but make sure that they resonate with your character. To preserve spontaneity, analyse the effects on others afterwards, rather than while being with them.

RECOMMENDED MATERIALS
'Self-image and Self-presentation' in Argyle, M. *The Psychology of Interpersonal Behaviour;* Chapter One in Asbell, B. and Wynn, K. *Look Yourself Up* and Goffman, E. *The Presentation of Self in Everyday life,* are suggested. Photos and footages of public figures can also be serve to analyse how appearances are used to produce certain effects (why do politicians, for example, tend to appear more often in casual clothes nowadays, but film stars almost never?)

58. AWARENESS OF OTHERS

> When the pickpocket meets a
> saint, he sees only pockets.
>
> Anonymous

Awareness and understanding of others are based on listening, observing and empathy. These skills are often neglected, despite their great value in any sphere of social life.

THEORETICAL LEVEL

The focus of attention can be on the other person, the content, or both. It is important to decide what is your priority, because they require different approaches. Focusing on content may require memorising facts, taking mental notes and so on, while focusing on the person may include empathy, emotional and other non-verbal cues. The focus can also be widened or deepened. The former is based on registering as much information as possible in order to be able to form a complete picture. The latter involves focusing on selected pieces of information in order to penetrate to deeper levels of meaning.

Listening. The conversation skills consist of listening as much as talking. This is to say listening to others, not to yourself (i.e. using the time while the other is talking to think what to say next). It is important to acknowledge that something has been heard (through body language or verbally). Understanding the reason why somebody is telling something will help you adopt the right attitude (e.g. the person may seek advice, sympathy, or a chance for an emotional release). Open-mindedness doesn't require accepting the view of the other, but being willing to see things from a different perspective. Attention is, however, easier to maintain if you can relate what is said to your own experience and interests. Sometimes a conversation has overt and covert meaning. Ambiguity can be resolved either by asking for clarification or by ignoring a hidden meaning (taking a statement at face value) but not by going along with it (assuming, without a confirmation). A good listener does not assume, but checks that he has understood things properly by occasionally rephrasing what has been said. You can also use questions to clarify something or point at contradictions, but trying to reveal what somebody is unconsciously or deliberately avoiding, demanding honesty and openness, usually has the opposite effect.

Observations. The body reflects the state of mind, so paying attention to appearance and body language (especially if verbal statements seem inconsistent or incongruent) can provide the listener with additional information and clues. Research shows that the benefits of being able to read non-verbal cues include being better adjusted emotionally, more popular, more outgoing, and more sensitive[173].

Empathy is not only important for moral development, it also enriches one's life. The experience of those who cannot 'put themselves in others' shoes' is impoverished. Empathy also enables better understanding of others and their motives (which plays an important role in acceptance and forgiveness). However, empathy is not always productive (e.g. in physical defence) or constructive (e.g. it may trigger envy). False empathy, when you attribute to the other person what you would experience under the circumstances of that person, can also be counter-productive and misleading.

An assessment of others and their actions should take into account the circumstances, intentions (that are based on perception, motives and judgment), the act itself (based on motivation and abilities) and consequences. This is because good intentions can lead to an incompetent act, a bad consequence can be the result of a good action, and so on. For example, helping others for their own benefit has a different value from helping them out of pity, desire to feel superior, or impress others.

REFLECTIVE LEVEL

Think about who is a good listener of people you know and who is not, what makes the difference and where you would put yourself in that respect. Also, you can consider what factors are most important for you in forming an opinion about other people (e.g. looks, background, profession, behaviour, what is said, or how it is said) and whether they are really reliable and accurate, or just perpetuate already existing views.

PRACTICAL LEVEL

Bracketing. Distortion of one's perception is usually the result of personal pre-assumptions (e.g. stereotyping). This method can minimise their effect. It consists of a deliberate attempt to put in brackets your assumptions, expectations, judgments, opinions. Try, when listening, to focus only on clarifying what you hear and refrain from interpretations and jumping to conclusions. Later, you can compare information so obtained with your expectations and assumptions and analyse the differences.

Developing empathy. Pick up a character from a film or a book, and try alternately to empathise with her, put yourself in her shoes, be aware how she feels and what she experiences, and then take a detached, more "objective" position. You can change characters, pick ones of different gender or background or ones that you do not like, and see what difference this change of perspectives makes.

RECOMMENDED MATERIALS

Bolton, R. 'Listening Skills' in *People Skills*; 'The Roots of Empathy' in *Emotional Intelligence* by Goleman and still informative Desmond Morris' *Manwatching* are suggested. Sophisticated observations of others, found in good fiction (such as *War and Peace* by Tolstoy, for example), can be even more illuminating.

59. COMMUNICATING

A word is not a crystal, transparent and unchanged; it is the skin of a living thought and may vary greatly in colour and content according to the circumstances and time in which it is used.

Oliver Wendell Holmes, Jr.

We are all aware how important effective communication is. Several factors that contribute to the quality of communication are addressed below.

THEORETICAL LEVEL

Preparation can be useful in predictable situations, for example when communication goes only in one direction (a speech, acting, etc.) or is limited to a factual level (e.g. at an exam). However, preparation may not always facilitate conversation. The responses of others are rarely fully predictable, so it can hamper spontaneity. Words need to match an immediate mood and situation to have a desired effect. Of course, thinking through an issue is different from preparing what to say and is usually useful.

Flow. To maintain the flow of conversation a pause is as important as talking. It gives participants time to digest what has been said, to rest, or a chance to reply. Interruptions can also be sometimes functional. They can speed up and build up a conversation if they are closely related to what has been said. However, making a leap forward, changing the topic, or speaking to somebody else breaks the flow and is perceived as undermining the other person. It may also result in missing something important or prevent the one who is talking from expressing himself fully on other levels beside informative (e.g. affective). So, in balance, it is usually better to allow others to finish before speaking. How long one should speak depends on how much others are willing to listen. Feedback can be derived from replies, and also from body language, facial expressions, mood or a level of tension.

Maintaining attention is a central issue. What's the point of talking if nobody is listening? Although it is hard to generalise, maintaining attention almost always requires talking that is:

Interesting: an interesting talk is also relevant, imaginative and (if appropriate) includes humour. It is worth remembering that what is interesting for you may not be interesting for others. If you want to be listened to, take into account who is on the other side and try to find a common ground. This does not refer only to mutual interests, but also pace, intensity, depth and knowledge. Take going into depth, for example. If what you are talking about does not have the same significance for the other, it can be devalued. This can be avoided if those involved are synchronised, so that they can reach depth together.

Clear: it is worth checking first whether what you want to say is clear to you; if it is not, it will certainly not be clear to others. Some other common 'mistakes', such as assuming that others know what you know, being ambiguous or confusing, and making things too complicated, can also affect clarity.

Concise: not everything needs to be spelled out. Interest often arises out of what can be extrapolated rather than what is said. Most people prefer to make their own conclusions, because it puts them in a more active position and appeals to their intelligence. Generalising your own opinion infringes on the right of others to have theirs. Repeating, especially, rarely improves an impression. It is more likely that what has been said is ignored than not heard or understood.

Convincing: how something is said may be as important as what is said, in this respect. Talking calmly leaves an impression of authority and control, and it *can* be compatible with intense emotions. Changes in intensity, pitch, intonation and pace, on the other hand, break monotony. Loud speaking may convey some power or openness and grab attention temporarily, but it could also be unpleasant and suggest a lack of depth, thoughtfulness and respect. People are more attentive if one speaks softly, but too quiet talking can make listening an effort. Body language and eye contact are also a part of the message. Not looking at all or staring at the listeners usually create an atmosphere of inequality.

The content. These two features are especially relevant regarding the content:

Sincerity. To what extent one can be sincere should depend on the listener's ability to accept it, not his function or importance. Intelligent people respect sincerity even when what is said does not please them. Lying may help avoid some immediate undesirable consequences of your actions, but it always implies giving power to another person. It also involves a risk, creates a barrier towards the other and requires an effort (lies need to be remembered). Even if you find lying to others sometimes beneficial, it is always better to be honest with yourself, which means being aware that you are lying and why.

The locus. A restricted use of *I* may leave an impression of insecurity, but its frequent use may have a self-centred effect. In any case, a locus of conversation should not be restricted to yourself: 'self-preoccupation excludes the listener and, by so doing, explicitly discredits and derogates the importance of the other person.'[174] Self-praise too, rarely produces desired effect. Trying to force admiration from others only alienates.

REFLECTIVE LEVEL
Reflecting on your speaking manners may be beneficial (e.g. do you always talk for the sake of others, or sometimes for your own sake, just to be heard?). Consider also who you (dis)like to listen to and why. It may improve your own style of conversation. When lying might not be morally wrong (e.g. if used to protect somebody) is worthwhile examining, too.

PRACTICAL LEVEL
Listen to yourself. You can tape some of your speeches, conversations or replies and then analyse them from the perspective of a listener (if it is done in an inconspicuous way it should not affect spontaneity). A well-intended feedback can serve the same purpose.

RECOMMENDED MATERIALS
How to Communicate by McKay, Davis & Fanning, and *People Skills* by Bolton, R. are among many materials on this topic.

60. BEHAVIOUR

Suppose you scrub your ethical skin until it shines, but inside there is no music, what then?

Kabir

Social behaviour often leads to duplicity and the loss of spontaneity, so this area will pay special attention to the integration of behaviour with the rest of the person.

THEORETICAL LEVEL

Regulators of behaviour can be external and internal:

Conventions are external norms that regulate public behaviour. Their purpose is to ensure that all participants have some control over the situation (predictability) and can maintain desired distance and regard. However, conventions do not guarantee genuine respect for others, and may be a barrier to closeness. They can also be restrictive (although there is always some freedom within a common framework). Familiarity with conventions makes spontaneity easier, because it provides confidence in assessing to what extent and when they can be safely transgressed.

Consideration is the internal regulator based on taking into account the effect of your behaviour on others. It primarily means not infringing on or depriving them (e.g. by making them feel excluded or ignored). Consideration does not imply permissiveness or timidity, but being aware of others and their needs: knocking on their door, but not insisting or forcing your way in if it does not open; also sensing when it is time to stop before exhausting those around or yourself (e.g. staying no longer than is necessary or a pleasure for everybody). Consideration requires genuine respect and more attention and flexibility than conventions, because behaviour needs to be adjusted from a situation to situation and from person to person (and to the way they feel at that moment). However, it allows more freedom and can be more rewarding than following conventions.

Congruent behaviour (based on one's personality) has the following characteristics:

Authenticity means behaving in accord with one's character and experience. Behaviour emerges from the person and is an integral part of the person, while inauthentic behaviour 'does not really involve the selves of those who take part in it'[175]. Authenticity relies on confidence that you *can* be accepted as you are (not necessarily that you will be). It does not involve comparing with others, so forming equal relationships is easier. Authentic behaviour enables directness and openness, leading to a quicker contact and greater exchange between participants, which enriches the quality of experience.

Spontaneity is not impulsiveness, acting upon the thoughts and feelings of the moment. Behaviour governed only by emotions creates affectation, not spontaneity. Spontaneity means being aware of your inner state (being honest with yourself) but also taking into account others, the flow of the situation and the purpose of the interaction, and allowing your behaviour to emerge from these without much interference. It enables a natural adaptation to circumstances and quicker reactions, but it may be more risky because it is less predictable. There are several factors that may affect spontaneity:

Rational control. Spontaneity can be hindered by a desire for perfection and moral purity or (self)imposed principles, if they are forced upon or lead to disregarding other aspects of yourself. They often create a barrier between the person and others, and affect the quality of experience. Rational control may increase the overall sense of control and security, but may limit freedom and beget boredom. This can be avoided if you allow your ideals to sink in and behaviour to emerge spontaneously from them.

Planned behaviour may minimise uncertainty, but it can be inadequate if the situation is not predicted accurately, or if it loses the power of spontaneity.

Trying to leave a good impression can be counterproductive if it impedes spontaneity. The more you stretch yourself to appear better, the more vulnerable you are.

Forms of behaving addressed below are especially relevant in new situations.

Politeness is a congenial way of interaction, but it loses its value if it becomes servility or cliché. To produce a positive effect, balancing closedness, the sense of equality and spontaneity is required. For example, if you feel intimidated by somebody, being closed helps to conceal it, equality helps to assure mutual respect, and spontaneity helps to find a common ground despite the differences.

Stridency sometimes may be necessary, for example to attract attention, or when the initiative has to be taken but there is no time for explanations. Strident behaviour requires confidence in your judgment and intentions. It relies on emotional impact (that is usually temporary), so promptness and speed of your reaction are important.

REFLECTIVE LEVEL

It may be worthwhile examining the purpose and value of conventions that you follow. You can also consider in which situations you are authentic and spontaneous and in which you are not, and what makes the difference.

PRACTICAL LEVEL

Freeing behaviour. A behaviour can easily become a habit, which can be very limiting. To increase flexibility, experiment with different forms of behaviour (e.g. a boisterous one can be replaced with a placid one, and the other way around) and observe the reactions. Comparing the behaviour of others and its effects can also be insightful.

RECOMMENDED MATERIALS

Buber, M. *I – thou*; Berne, E. *Games People Play*; Zimbardo, P. *Shyness* and Chapter 3 in Rainwater, J. *You are in charge* can contribute to the further exploration of this area.

THE PROMISED GARDEN

There is a garden where our hearts converse,
At ease beside clear water, dreaming
A whole and perfect future for yourself,
Myself, our children and our friends.

And if we must rise and leave,
Put on identity and fight,
Each day more desperate than the last
And further from our future, that
Is no more than honour and respect shown
To all blocked from the garden that we own.

There is a garden at the heart of things,
Our oldest memory guards it with her strong will.
Those who by love and work attain there
Bathe in her living waters, lift up their hearts and
Turn again to share the steep privations of the hill;
They walk in the market but their feet are still.

There is a garden where our hearts converse,
At ease beside clear water, dreaming
A whole and perfect future for yourself,
Myself, our children and our friends.

Theo Dorgan

RELATIONSHIP GROUP

This group focuses on the relationship process and the basic types of relationships. It consists of the following areas:

Relationship dynamic is the root area of this group because it is relevant for any type of relationship. Relationship process requires both, being receptive and also being proactive, so it encompasses *existence* mode and *agency* mode.

Intrinsic relationship is a relationship that is an end in itself – its main purpose is to *be* with others (which is why this area belongs to the *existence* mode), and usually includes an affective component. Although it is not restricted to friends, a more common term friendship will be sometimes used as a synonym for this type of relationships.[176]

Instrumental relationship is a relationship that is the means to an end – the primary reason for its existence is not the relationship itself but another goal (e.g. professional relationships). It mainly operates on the cogitative level. This area belongs to the *agency* mode because its main purpose is to *do* something with others.

Although the two above types or relationships are counterparts, they are not mutually exclusive. One can develop friendships with co-workers or benefit from friends. What makes the difference is where the emphasis in a relationship is.

Intimate relationship consists of intrinsic and instrumental aspects, but beside cognitive and emotional, it also includes a physical component: it 'involves cooperative and shared activity, including the giving and receiving of attention, objects, comfort, and concern. It frequently involves body contact, such as caressing, cuddling, and kissing'[177]. This of course, does not imply that this type of relationship consists only of positive experiences. Those that may not be constructive or pleasant can also be present. Although other relationships may also include some elements of intimate behaviour the focus in this area is on relationships based on personal choice (love between adults).

61. RELATIONSHIP DYNAMIC

I was angry with my friend: I told my
wrath, my wrath did end.
I was angry with my foe: I told it not, my
wrath did grow.

William Blake

This area focuses on various stages of the relationship process: initiating a relationship, a change (with an emphasis on dealing with conflicts) and ending a relationship.

THEORETICAL LEVEL

Initiating a relationship can occur on several levels:

Cognitive revolves around possible mutual benefits, common interests or novelty. It is easier to start a relationship on this level if you focus on what can be shared rather than on what you can gain. There are telltale signs indicating whether people are interested in each other: the conversation tends to gravitate around themselves more than unrelated subjects, and also eye contact is more frequent and maintained for longer'[178]

Affective stems from simply liking to be with others or feeling love for others. These affects can be stimulating and refreshing because they save us from being preoccupied with ourselves. A person who is not capable of giving love will not be able to receive it either. However, others cannot be expected to return it – loving may be enriching even if not reciprocated. The less you feel the need to be loved the more you will be able to love (a person in need is hardly in a position to give – unless for instrumental reasons, which is usually intuitively sensed).

Physical (sexual) is another frequent motive to initiate a relationship. Showing that you are attracted to another person is not an offence, but imposing your desire is. People generally do not like to be treated as objects (of one's sexual desire). Mature people do not have sex because they are tricked, sacrifice themselves or surrender to somebody's advances, but simply because they want to. Sexual desire is natural, however, those who are dependent on sex lose the freedom of choice and devalue themselves, which makes *them* less desirable.

The process. Until they stabilise, relationships usually fluctuate between closedness and openness, self-affirmation and relationship-affirmation, strength and softness. This may lead to conflicts. It is observed that conflict 'is growing at the very time when the relationship is growing too'[179]. It is not necessarily a negative event though, it 'can help maintain or even develop a relationship if it is managed right'[180]. There are several ways to deal with conflict: denial, avoidance, domination, capitulation, compromise, collaboration. Only the last one, however, can lead to long term improvements, so the other ways can be used if the short term results are more important than the relationship. A tendency to avoid conflict, for example, 'can be destructive if it prevents a couple from dealing with the issue that causes the concern.'[181] Always giving in to keep the other works only temporarily. Unsettled issues with others are more difficult to resolve without them. This does not mean that arguments and fights are inevitable. Research unambiguously confirms that the ability to communicate effectively is essential for a successful relationship[182]. *Distributive tactics* make unproductive conflicts, while *integrative tactics* make a conflict productive. The former are characterised by competitiveness, the aim to win, preferring personal goals to common goals, and usually use threats, sarcasm and shouting. The latter consist of looking for common ground, maintaining an essentially positive image of the other person and his intentions even at the point of disagreement, prioritising mutual interest to personal ones.

Changing your attitude is another way of affecting a relationship. This is not achieved by fantasising about what you could do and say or by acting differently, but by changing your inner stand towards that person. A way we relate to somebody is a result of our frame of mind, so if it is changed, behavioural change will come spontaneously. If only behaviour is changed, countless details difficult to control consciously will betray the real state (e.g. behaving as an equal if you feel inferior is unlikely to work).

Separation. Attachment to the other person often creates a network of connections that break up when the relationship ends. So, not only can separation cause the feeling of loss, but it also requires reconstructing one's internal and external life. This is why predicted separations are easier to handle[183]. Moreover, a separation initiated only by one side may have a negative effect on the self-esteem of the other, so it is important, if possible, to prepare the other person for separation and accompany it with genuine respect.

REFLECTIVE LEVEL

Consider typical strategies you use to initiate or end relationships, and how you deal with conflicts. You can also reflect on some of your existing relationships: how they have developed and in what direction you would like them to move in the future.

PRACTICAL LEVEL

Conflict resolution. There are several steps that can lead to a constructive conflict resolution. You can do them first on your own and then perhaps with other(s) involved.

- Establish first the common ground, what you share with the other party (e.g. a mutual aim, interest, basic values).
- Define the problem, where you differ. If this involves a criticism, it should consist of describing the effects of the situation rather than judging the other. Referring to an act rather than the person is more likely to be accepted and lead to a change and reconciliation.
- After discussing the problem, look for possible solutions, select the one that can be acceptable for both, and plan who will do what, where, and when (and stick to mutually agreed plans!)

RECOMMENDED MATERIALS

Resolving Conflicts by Grant and *I Only Say This Because I Love You* by Deborah Tannen are suggested. N. Hornby's novel *About a Boy* is also interesting because it describes several different ways of dealing with conflicts.

62. INTRINSIC RELATIONSHIP

Of all the means which are procured by wisdom to ensure happiness throughout the whole of life, by far the most important is the acquisition of friends.

Epicurus

This area is based on a universal human need (sometimes called 'affiliative need') to be with others. For all practical purposes it can be identified with friendship. Such relationships have been always important, but even more nowadays when the family ties have loosened.

THEORETICAL LEVEL

Intrinsic relationships have the aim in itself, so it can be developed only if instrumental expectations do not interfere. A real friendship cannot be used as a trading chip, to obligate others, or to feel obliged because of it. Constraints in a true friendship come from inside the relationship, rather then being imposed from the outside.

Several factors contribute to this type of relationship.

Equality. Mutual acceptance and equality (see the area *Symmetricity* p.219) are the foundations of any friendship. An intrinsic relationship is difficult to maintain if the persons involved do not consider themselves equal. This is why it is important to show respect and at the same time that you are a match for the other.

Reciprocity. Friendship is not only a matter of receiving, but also giving. A relationship that is not reciprocal is quickly rejected. Moreover, concentrating only on getting creates dependency, obsessiveness, possessiveness, and selfishness, while giving contributes to openness, equality, friendship and love. Giving can be pleasant in itself, not only because of gratefulness or praise. Some people believe that being unselfish would make them more vulnerable. In fact, the opposite is the case, because the direction is *from* the person who is giving rather than the other way around. To be able to give, it is first necessary to be aware that you have something to give (goods, attention, support, affection, a helping hand, time etc.). Giving is meaningful only if it is voluntary, so there is no point in giving what you don't really want to give. Indiscriminate giving is not productive. You may be taken for granted if you leave the impression that you would yield to any demand. What is easily obtained is usually less valued. By the same token, imposing yourself, forcing on others what they do not want, is not a sign of friendship but rather a need for self-gratification.

Openness and trust. It is recognised that 'the main feature that stabilises, establishes and develops relationships of all types is proper and dexterous control of *self-disclosure*, that is, the revelation of personal layers of one's self, one's personal thoughts or even one's body.'[184] Friendship involves a greater level of openness and revealing oneself than formal behaviour. This implies that people *share* themselves (their inner selves, which requires openness) with each other. Being closed may give protection, but it prevents fuller exchange between people. This is not to say that total candour is necessary. That people remain to some extent a secret for each other can make a relationship more appealing. If you reveal everything about yourself too quickly, you may cease to be interesting. This does not mean acting secretively. Mystery can increase interest only if interest already exists, otherwise it just puts people off.

Opening up, though, involves certain risk and if not mutual, it may affect the balance of control. To what extent you can 'place yourself in a friend's hands', depends, of course, on the extent to which you can trust that person. The level of openness should also correspond to the level of closeness that all involved seek to achieve. It is usually safe to open to a degree that could not endanger your self-respect and the sense of equality. This simply implies not going further than you feel comfortable. Getting involved or giving yourself to others should not lead to losing yourself. It is important to be aware what effect openness has on others too. Opening up suddenly rather then gradually may provoke anxiety and destabilise the relationship.

Care. Openness cannot be an excuse for being inconsiderate, rude or hurtful. It needs to be balanced with care and support for the other, which are highly beneficial. Research suggests that close, confiding and supportive relationships even enhance health by preserving the immune system and encouraging good health habits[185]. Care primarily means acceptance, being there for the other and showing that she matters. Affirmative and optimistic views (that include rather than exclude the other) also increase the sense of security and hope. This doesn't mean being indiscriminate or biased. Security is based on the trust of your friend that even if she has failed or done something wrong, she will not be rejected, but supported in her resolve to change or improve.

REFLECTIVE LEVEL
Consider how important relationships that don't have any instrumental purpose are for you and what is really important in such relationships and what is not (e.g. does a good friendship require perfect people?)

PRACTICAL LEVEL
Improving friendships. Imagine vividly an ideal friend (could be a real one or fictional) especially regarding equality, reciprocity, openness and care. Now, imagine that you are an ideal friend (using the same criteria). Compare a relationship between such friends with the ones you have. If you find that there are differences, think about how they can be bridged.

RECOMMENDED MATERIALS
Duck, S. *Friend for life* is a good introduction to this subject. Miller, S. *Men and Friendship* is an insightful personal search for friendship. From fiction, Jane Austen's *Emma* and Barnes, J. *Metroland* can also be inspiring and thought provoking.

63. INSTRUMENTAL RELATIONSHIP

Tact is the art of making a point without making an enemy.

Howard W. Newton

This area focuses on relationships that are the means to some other ends. There are three basic types of such relationships.

THEORETICAL LEVEL

Self-benefit relationship. When somebody is concerned only with his own benefit, others are treated as objects, the means to an end. This results in ignoring their needs and valuing them only if they are useful. People are replaced with their roles or functions, which often leads to desire to dominate and control. This can happen in a wide range of interactions, from cheating to the attitudes of some employers. If you are on the rough end of the stick, you have to choose how to respond. A response can be submission, avoidance or confrontation. The risk and short and long term consequences should be taken into account (e.g. giving in to a persistent salesman may look an easy way out, which can be regretted later). If you choose confrontation, enter it without any doubts to avoid insecurity. Prepare for every possibility rather than expecting fair play. In case you don't have enough power and resources to deal with the situation, work on building them up, before acting. It may be useful, for example, to try to win support from others.

Sometimes self-benefit motives may be hidden behind inauthentic behaviour (e.g. over-friendliness). If you recognise this, the best strategy is to discontinue the interaction or disrupt the game by bringing up possible underlying motives. If this is not possible, you can close down, and remain alert to the actions and behaviour of the other (e.g. inconsistencies or sudden changes of behaviour, even for the better, warrants caution). Distancing yourself minimises the effect of unpleasant feelings usually experienced in such situations, and enables you to take a wider perspective, which precludes naivety.

Mutual-benefit relationship can have several forms:

Cooperation. All the participants have the same goal (e.g. a sports team). It increases productivity (a group can do more than individuals) and reduces the risk of errors. Cooperation requires that individual aims do not override the common aim.

Reciprocation. Those involved benefit in different ways (e.g. trading – one person gets money and the other goods).

Co-dependency. The interests of all the participants depend on the other participants (e.g. sharing a flat).

All of them may involve discussing, arguing, negotiating: in the first case about the ways and the means to achieve a goal, in the second about the aims, and in the third about rights and duties. Reminding yourself (and others if necessary) about the purpose of interaction can save time and energy. Your negotiating position can be improved in any situation by making yourself more valuable (e.g. by doing something better than others). As with conflicting desires, it is easer to find an acceptable solution for all if the participants move away from specific objectives to the underlying reasons (i.e. why they want something). This is because it opens a way to a greater number of possible solutions.

Assertiveness plays a significant role in these interactions. It is not about winning, but negotiating. It doesn't mean being intolerant or closed-minded. Changing your mind is compatible with assertiveness, and is not a weakness. It is an ability to clarify your own views to others and their views to yourself, in order to find an acceptable solution for all. This is why preparation and knowledge are important (e.g. knowing and clarifying to others, if necessary, the rights of everybody involved). Confidence and self-acceptance also play an important role. Taking responsibility for your decisions and actions will help you to be clear and direct. The intimidating effect of somebody in a position of authority can be reduced if you see the human being behind the role or function. You have acted assertively if you don't have residual negative feelings afterwards.[186]

Others-benefit is an interaction that has an aim to help others. It reduces self-centredness and selfishness, and is one of the most powerful mood-changers[187]. However, if asked for help, it is worthwhile bearing in mind that a refusal is less disappointing than an unfulfilled promise, so it is better not to promise more than you can and are willing to do. Also, excessive help can deprive others of the benefits of being in charge of their lives[188].

REFLECTIVE LEVEL
Examine your attitudes towards various types of instrumental relationships. For example, you may help others (without expecting anything in return) and see how it makes you feel (e.g. whether it has been a waste of time or worthwhile).

PRACTICAL LEVEL
Defusing intimidation. An intimidating effect can be defused if you visualise the person that you are apprehensive of in a mundane or even humorous situation (e.g. playing with kids, sitting on the toilet, belly-dancing or diminishing is size). This can really help, but it is important not to get carried away. Doing this with a vengeance may produce the feeling of guilt, which can increase anxiety in the real situation.

Assertiveness rehearsal. Practise expressing your feelings. It can take the form of positive statements (e.g. 'I feel ignored') or questions (e.g. 'Why did you interrupt me?'). It is important to match the content with the way it is expressed. A question should not sound like a statement, and a statement should not sound like a question.

RECOMMENDED MATERIALS
Alberti & Emmons *Your Perfect Right;* Cornelius & Faire *Everyone can Win* and Fisher & Ury *Getting to Yes* are some examples of rich literature on this subject.

64. INTIMATE RELATIONSHIP

> Love does not consist in gazing at
> each other but in looking outward
> together in the same direction.
> Antoine de Saint Exupery

Intimacy is a close relationship that includes cognitive, emotional and physical components (e.g. touch, tenderness). The two main types of intimate relationship are considered: *passionate love* and *compassionate love*.

THEORETICAL LEVEL

Passionate love is an intense desire for union with the other person. The common view is that its occurrence cannot be controlled (hence, *falling in* love). In fact, passionate love is usually triggered by identifying fulfilment of one's needs and desires with somebody else. In other words, projecting one's ideal onto the other. Passionate love is usually temporary because sooner or later inevitable differences between these two cannot be ignored anymore. Infatuation is an inability to accept the difference, which leads to either disappointment or an attempt to force the other to adjust to one's ideal. It is closely linked to low self-esteem, dependency and insecurity, anxiety and deprivation[189].

Passionate love can affect other aspects of your life, but other intense experiences (positive and negative) can also enhance passion[190]. Its intensity is also based on the sense of novelty, opening to new possibilities, which can be perpetuated by imagination. This is why unrequited love or delayed fulfilment can (up to a certain point) enhance passion. Passionate love is characterised by excitement, moments of exultation, feeling accepted, safe and even a sense of union and transcendence. However, foiled passionate love intensifies low self-esteem, a sense of loneliness, and may trigger the feelings of emptiness, anxiety, despair and jealousy[191]. To avoid this, it is important to be aware if passion is all that holds the relationship, and recognise and accept when it wears off.

Compassionate love may be less intense but is lasting. At the beginning, passion can serve to counteract anxiety and melt barriers between the partners, but later it may even become an obstacle to a deeper connection. Attraction is rarely sufficient to sustain the relationship. Something else is also needed. Compassionate love is based not only on a desire to *be* and *do* with somebody, but also on a desire to *stay* and *grow* together.

Being with the other refers to acceptance, care, respect (including self-respect), and mutual equality. Research also suggests that '...reciprocal positive evaluative behaviour plays a crucial role in maintaining a satisfying and loving relationship'[192]. *Doing with the other* means having shared goals or activities and mutual interests that transcend individual ones. It also includes helping, comforting and protecting the other if necessary. *Staying with the other* is based on commitment: a good relationship is not found, but constantly created in a dynamic process, which requires an effort and perseverance. Intimate depth and closeness are also important. They are not only psychologically and physiologically beneficial, but also enhance the quality of experience, which decreases the need for intensity and variety. *Growing with the other* involves transcending oneself, a willingness to change. Focusing on the relationship itself rather than the person leads to a genuine change instead of accommodation or compromise. Ingredients that enable growth are understanding, sensitivity, trust, honesty (including emotional honesty), and, most of all, never taking your partner for granted, or the relationship can become stale.

On the other hand, certain factors frequently associated with intimate relationships are actually not necessary. *Similarity* can make life easier but is not essential for a good relationship. Accepting somebody different requires courage, however, such a person can fulfil and supplement the other more than one who is just a self-reflection. *Proofs*: proving love rather than showing it, or seeking a proof indicates underlying insecurity either in oneself, the partner, or the relationship. *Enclosure*: although some predictability is desirable, a relationship also needs novelty[193], so it is enriched by nurturing individuality and outside interests. Focusing only on each another prevents development. *Possessiveness* is a result of a desire to have, which leads to treating the other as an object, not subject (because possessing or having implies control, it deprives the other of her own will). This cannot contribute to a constructive relationship. *Jealousy* is not a result of love but insecurity, which has a negative effect on intimacy. However, this type of a relationship may require the exclusion of others to an extent that is mutually agreed.

REFLECTIVE LEVEL

What do you expect of an intimate relationship (existing or imagined)? What are your priorities, where would you set boundaries? It may also be interesting to consider the statement 'unless one loves oneself one cannot love another'[194].

PRACTICAL LEVEL

Falling in and climbing out. This exercise can help you regain control if you are experiencing unrequited passionate love or excessive attachment. Write down in one column your thoughts and fantasies about the person. Then deliberately take a critical view and record it in another column. In the third column try to distance yourself a bit and be objective, separating your projections from a real person. This should enable you to assume a more realistic and adequate attitude towards that person. And remember, she cannot be the right one if she does not recognise that you are the right one.

RECOMMENDED MATERIALS

Part Two in Peck, S. *The Road Less Travelled*; Fromm, E. *Art of loving* and Beck, A. *Love is Never Enough* are recommended. In fiction, Tolstoy's classic *Anna Karenina* unravels side by side the story of compassionate and passionate love, while *The Romantic Movement* by Alain de Botton is an insightful contemporary analysis of intimacy.

EXERCISE TOOLBOX

There are over hundred practical exercises in the materials. To make it easer to used them, they are all grouped here in four big categories: *understanding* (as the basis); *dealing with* (to get from minus to zero); *regulating* (to maintain a zero point) and *improving* (moving from zero to plus). Each of them have subgroups relating to yourself, experience, actions and others.

UNDERSTANDING (27)
Yourself: Self-representation; Self-characterisation; Focusing on feeling; Revealing hidden feelings; Laddering; Dream analysis; Self-disclosure; Keeping a diary; Writing autobiography; (9)

Your experience: Evening review; Systematic elimination; Uncovering fear; Looking in to see out; Back to the future; Predictions check; (6)

Your actions: Imaginary dialogue; Where do I want to be?; Uncovering end-desires; Intention clarification; Charting desires; The map of aims; Backwards schedule; (7)

Your relationships: Bracketing; Overcoming partiality; Developing empathy; Falling in and climbing out; (4)

DEALING WITH (28)
Yourself: Unblocking emotions; Re-living the past; Dream control; Altering moods; Developing self-acceptance; Resolving inner conflicts; Mind Mapping; Dealing with your 'saboteur'; Parent-child-adult; (9)

Your experience: Exposure; Worry reduction; Anxiety control; Desensitisation; Combating boredom; Being positive; Accepting the situation; (7)

Your actions: Brainstorming; Incubation; Emulating a person; Emulating a solution; Preventing sabotage; Visualising confidence; Time-out; (7)

Your relationships: Defusing intimidation; Dealing with protective reactions; On the way to acceptance; Assertiveness rehearsal; Conflict resolution; (5)

REGULATING, MAINTAINING (27)

Yourself: Peaceful images; Meditation; Dis-identification; Centring; Breathing exercises; Progressive relaxation; Autogenic Training; Energy flow; Stretching; (9)

Your experience: After fear; Matters of death; Coming to terms with death; Letting go; The pyramid of priorities; Importance regulation; (6)

Your actions: Keeping on track; Control feeling; Control Image; Dealing with impatience; Inventory of activities; Life house; Tactical use of energy; (7)

Your relationships: Alone but not lonely; Challenging asymmetries; Being watched; Influence work out; What do I really want?; (5)

IMPROVING (28)

Yourself: De-conditioning; Making change; Reprogramming; Time delay; Good discipline; Invocation by image; Evoking moods; Uplifting learning; Thinking straight; Developing creativity; (10)

Your experience: Phenomenological reduction; Awareness control; Openness control; Enhancing experience; Mindful eating; Mindfulness; On the top of a mountain; (7)

Your actions: Decision-making; Aim breaking; Background planning; Enhancing Motivation; Invoking motivation; Achievement maximisation; The final performance; (7)

Your relationships: Playing with appearance; Listen to yourself; Freeing behaviour; You and the group; Improving friendships; (5)

To find where these exercises are, please, look at the index.

FILMS

Movies can also be inspiring. Here are some suggestions related to each area:

01. SELF-AWARENESS: Spellbound (1945); Magnolia (1999)
02. RELATING TO ONESELF: Fight Club (1999)
03. PERSONAL CHANGE: Fried Green Tomatoes (1992)
04. SELF-VALUATION: It's a Wonderful Life (1946); Pride and Prejudice (2003)
05. FEELINGS: Ordinary People (1980)
06. EMOTIONS: The Sound of Music (1965)
07. EXCITEMENT: Grease (1978)
08. MOODS: Girl, Interrupted (1999)
09. LEARNING: Educating Rita (1983); Little Man Tate (1991)
10. REASONING: Twelve Angry Men (1957)
11. CREATIVE THINKING: F/X murder by illusion (1986)
12. INNER STRUCTURE: The Truman Show (1998); The Matrix (1999); Dark City (1998)
13. HARMONISATION: Barbarian invasion (2004)
14. STABILITY: The Driver (1978)
15. SELF-DISCIPLINE: All that jazz (1979)
16. DEVELOPMENT: The Wizard of Oz (1939)
17. COURAGE: Born on the fourth of July (1990)
18. CONFIDENCE: Billy Elliot (2000)
19. ANTICIPATORY ATTITUDE: As Good AS It Gets (1997)
20. SECURITY: Fearless (1994)
21. EXPERIENCE: Zorba the Greek (1964)
22. OPENNESS: Don Juan de Marco (1995)
23. INTEREST: Dead Poet Society (1990)
24. PLEASURE: Chocolat (2001)
25. RELATING TO DEATH: The Seventh Seal (1956)
26. IMPORTANCE: Citizen Kane (1941)
27. ATTACHMENT: Paris-Texas (1984)
28. TOLERANCE: Falling down (1993)
29. THE PRESENT: Groundhog Day (1997)
30. THE PAST: Three Colours: Blue (1993)
31. THE FUTURE: What dreams may come (1998)
32. RELATING TO THE SITUATION: Life is beautiful (1998)

33. MEANING: Mr. Holland's Opus (1996)
34. FREEDOM: Lawrence of Arabia (1962)
35. RESPONSIBILITY: The Conformist (1970)
36. DECISIONS: Casablanca (1942)
37. DESIRES: Piano (1983)
38. AIMS: Field of Dreams (1989)
39. INTENTIONS: Forrest Gump (1994)
40. GRATIFICATION: Bright Lights, Big City (1988); 28 Days (2000)
41. STRATEGY: Thomas Crown Affair (1999)
42. ACHIEVING: An Angel at My Table (1990)
43. COPING: The Colour Purple (1985)
44. CONTROL: The Godfather (1972)
45. MOTIVATION: Fly Away Home (1996)
46. ENERGY: Chariots of fire (1981)
47. ORGANISATION: Up, Close and Personal (1996)
48. PERFORMANCE: Gattaca (1997)
49. DEPENDENCE: Easy Rider (1969)
50. INDIVIDUALITY: Rebel without a Cause (1955)
51. INFLUENCE: Pay it Forward (2001)
52. BELONGING: About a boy (2002)
53. MORAL SENSE: Third man (1949)
54. PROTECTION: Edward Scissorhands (1990)
55. RELATING OT OTHERS: To Kill a Mockingbird (1962); Kiss of the Spider Woman (1985)
56. SYMMETRICITY: Blade Runner (1982)
57. APPEARANCE: Clueless (1995); Tootsie (1982); Some Like it Hot (1959)
58. AWARENESS OF OTHERS: The Green Mile (1999)
59. COMMUNICATING: Rashomon (1950)
60. BEHAVIOUR: American Beauty (1999)
61. RELATIONSHIP DYNAMICS: Annie Hall (1977); Four Weddings and a Funeral (1994)
62. INTRINSIC RELATIONSHIP: Jules and Jim (1961); Midnight Cowboy (1969)
63. INSTRUMENTAL RELATIONSHIP: Broadcast News (1987)
64. INTIMATE RELATIONSHIP: The Four Seasons (1982)

INDEX

260

BIBLIOGRAPHY

THE STRUCTURE

Aristotle, *The Nicomachean Ethics* (chapters: II, III, IV, VI) Oxford: OUP, 1983.

Gilling, D. and Brightwell, R. (1982) *The Human Brain* London: Orbis Publishing

Cattel, R. B., Saundrs, D. R. and Stice, G. K. (1950) *The Sixteen Personality Factor Questionnaire* Shampaign, Ill: Institute of Personality and Ability Testing.

Donaldson, M. *(*1992*) Human Minds* London: Penguin.

Elliott-Kemp, J. (1986) 'The Whole Picture: towards a map of whole human potential' in *The Management of Stress and Human Potential* Sheffield: PAVIC Publications.

Epstein, S. (1998) 'Personal Control from the Perspective of Cognitive-Experiential Self-Theory' in Kofta, M., Weary, G. and Sedek, G. (eds) *Personal Control in Action* New York; London: Plenum Press.

Ford, M. E. and Nickols, C. W. (1987) 'A taxonomy of human goals and some possible applications' in Ford, M. E. and Ford, D. H. (ed.) *Humans as self-constructing living systems*: *putting the framework to work* Mahwah, NJ: Lawrence Erlbaum.

Gardener, H. (1993) *Multiple Intelligences* New York: Basic Books.

Hall, G. and Lindzy, G. (1978) *Theories of Personality* 3rd ed. New York: John Wiley.

Hampden-Turner, C. (1981) *Maps of the Mind* London: Mitchell Beazley.

Harre, R. (1983) 'Psychological dimensions' in *Personal Being* Basil Oxford: Blackwell.

Hopson, B. and Scally, M. (1986) *Lifeskills Teaching Programmes,* No. 3 Leeds: Lifeskills Associates.

Jung, C. G. (1921) *Psychological Types* London: Routledge and Kegan Paul, 1947.

Kolb, D.A. (1979) 'On management and the learning process', in Kolb, D.A., Rubin, I. M., and McIntyre, J. M. (eds) *Organisational Psychology, A Book of Readings* 3rd ed. Englewood Cliffs: Prentice Hall.

Kosko, B. (1992) *Nuronetworks and fuzzy systems* Eaglewood Cliffs NJ: Prentice Hall.

MacNulty, C. (1990) 'Setting the Scene: The Future for Education' in *Learning without Limits*: *The Dilemma of Knowledge* The Saros Seminar transcript.

Metzner, R. (1971) *Maps of Consciousness* New York: Collier Books.

National Forum for Values in Education and the Community (1996) *Consultation on values in education and the community* London: SCAA.

Rogers, C. (1951) *Client-cantered therapy* Boston, Mass: Houghton Mifflin.

Rogers, C. (1959) 'A Theory of Therapy in Personality and Personal Relationships' in Koch, S. (ed.), *Psychology: A Study of a Science,* Vol 3. New York: McGraw Hill.

Shotter, J. (1982) 'Contemporary Psychological Theory – Human Being: Becoming Human' in Dufour, B. *New Movements in the Social Sciences and Humanities* London: Maurice Temple Smith.

Thurstone, L. L. (1938) *Primary Mental Abilities* Chicago: Chicago University Press.

Trevarthen, C. (1987) 'Split-brain and the mind' in Gregory, R. (ed.) *The Oxford Companion to the Mind* Oxford, New York: Oxford University Press.

SELF CATEGORY

FORMATIVE GROUP

Dowrick, S. (1991) 'Self: Is that who I am?' in *Intimacy & Solitude* New York; London: W. W. Norton.

Mulligan, J. (1988) 'Mapping your life' in *The Personal Management Handbook* London: Sphere.

Self-Awareness

Asbell, B. & Wynn, K. (1991) 'The Secret Life of Your Mind' in *Look Yourself Up* London: Fourth Estate.

Ferrari, M. and Sternberg, R.J. (ed.) (1998) *Self-awareness* New York: Guilford Press.

Freud, S. (1916) 'Part II. Dreams' in *Introductory lectures on psychoanalysis* London: Penguin, 1973.

Goleman, D. (1995) ' Know Thyself' in *Emotional Intelligence* London: Bloomsbury.

Hall, J. A. (1983) *Jungian Dream Interpretation: A Handbook of Theory and Practice* Toronto: Inner City Books.

Hobson, J. A., and McCarley, R. W. (1977) 'The brain as a dream state generator: An activation-synthesis hypothesis of the dream process' *American Journal of Psychiatry*, Issue 134.

Langs, R. (1988) *Decoding Your Dreams* London: Henry Holt.

Parlett, M. and Page, F. (1990) 'Gestalt therapy' in Dryden, W. (ed.) *Individual Therapy* Milton Keynes; Philadelphia: Open University Press, 1992.

Perls, F., Hefferline, R., Goodman, P. (1951) 'Orienting the Self: experiment 8' in *Gestalt Therapy* New York: Julian Press.

Rainwater, J. (1979) *You are in charge* (chapters 1, 4, 5 and 6) California: DeVorss, 1989

Underwood, G. (1982) *Aspects of Consciousness,* Vol. 3: 'Awareness and Self-Awareness' New York; London: Academic Press.

Relating To Oneself

Dryden, W. (1998) *Developing Self-Acceptance* New York: John Wiley & Sons.

Freud, S. (1915) 'Repression' in *General psychological theory* New York: Collier, 1963.

Isenberg, A. (1980) 'Natural Pride and Natural Shame' in Rorty, A. (ed.) *Explaining Emotions* Berkeley; London: University of California Press.

Rogers, C. (1961) *On Becoming a Person* Boston, Mass: Houghton Mifflin.

Taubman, S. (1994) *Ending the Struggle Against Yourself* New York: Putnam Publishing Group

Personal Change

Asbell, B. & Wynn, K. (1991) 'Can We Change Our Personalities?' in *Look Yourself Up.* London: Fourth Estate.

Martin, G., and Pear J. (1983) *Behaviour modification: What it is and how to do it,* 2nd ed. Englewood Cliffs, NJ: Prentice-Hall.

Prochaska, J. O., Norcross, J. C. and DiClemente, C. C. (1995) *Changing for Good.* New York: Avon.

Rusk, T. and Read, R. (1978) *I want to change but I don't know how* London: Thorsons.

Sharpe, R. and Lewis, D. (1976) *The Success Factor* Zagreb: Prosvjeta.

Watzlawick, P., Weakland, J. H., Fisch, R. (1974) *Change* New York: W. W. Norton.

Self-Valuation

Adler, A. (1927) *Understanding Human Nature* New York: Fawcett, 1954.

Aristotle, 'Pride' in *The Nicomachean Ethics* Oxford: Oxford University Press, 1983

Branden, N. (1994) *How to Raise your Self-esteem* New York: Bantam

Coopersmith, S. (1967) *The Antecedents of Self-esteem* San Francisco: W. H. Freeman

Darwall, S. (1977) 'Two kinds of respect' in Dillon, R. (ed.) *Dignity, Character and Self-Respect* London: Routledge, 1995.

Hill, T. E. (1985) 'Self-Respect Reconsidered' in Dillon, R. (ed.) *Dignity, Character and Self-Respect* London: Routledge, 1995.

Hinton, S. (1991) 'Self-esteem' in *Developing Self-Discipline* London: UCL.

James, W. (1890) 'The Consciousness of Self' in *Principles of Psychology,* Vol 1. New York: Dover Publications, 1950.

Mulligan, J. (1988) 'Self-esteem' *The Personal Management Handbook* London: Sphere.

Sachs, D. (1982) 'How to distinguish self-respect form self-esteem' *Philosophy and Public Affairs,* Vol 10, Fall.

Suissa, J. (1995) *Modesty as an Educational Ideal* MA thesis, University of Jerusalem.

Tayor, G. (1980) 'Pride' in Rorty, A. (ed.) *Explaining Emotions* Berkeley; London: University of California Press.

Taylor, G. (1985a) 'Shame, Integrity and Self-Respect' in Dillon, R. (ed.) *Dignity, Character and Self-Respect* London: Routledge, 1995.

Taylor, G. (1985b) *Pride, Shame, and Guilt* Oxford: Claredon Press.

Thomas, L. (1983) 'Self-Respect: Theory and Practice' in Dillon, R. (ed.) *Dignity, Character and Self-Respect* London: Routledge, 1995.

White, P. (1996) 'Self-Respect and Self-Esteem' in *Civic Virtues and Public Schooling* New York: Teachers College Press

AFFECTIVE GROUP

Arnold, M. B. (1960) *Emotion and Personality* New York: Columbia University Press.

Arnold, M. B. and Gasson. J. A. (1954) 'Feelings and emotions as dynamic factors in personality integration' in Arnold,

M. B. and Gasson, J. (eds) *The human person* New York: Ronald Press.

Averill, J. (1980) 'Emotions and anxiety: sociocultural, biological, and psychological determinants' in Rorty, A. (ed.) *Explaining Emotions* Berkeley; London: University of California Press.

Ewert, O. (1970) 'The Attitudinal Character of Emotion' in Arnold, M. B. (ed.) *Feelings and Emotions* New York, London: Academic Press.

Ford, D. (1987) 'Energizing Selective Action and Emotional Arousal' in *Humans as Self-Constructing Living Systems* Mahwah, NJ: Lawrence Erlbaum.

Frijda, S. (1993) 'Moods, Emotion Episodes and Emotions' in Lewis, M and Havilland J. *Handbook of Emotions* New York; London: Guilford Press.

Kelly, A. (1989) *The Metaphysics of Mind* Oxford: Oxford University Press.

Lazarus, R. S. (1991) *Emotions and adaptation* Oxford: Oxford University Press.

Lyons, W. (1980) 'Physiological changes and the emotions' and 'Emotions and feelings' in *Emotion* Cambridge: Cambridge University Press.

Pribram, K. H. (1987) 'Feelings as Monitors' in Arnold, M. B. (ed.) *Feelings and Emotions* New York; London: Academic Press.

Ryle, G. (1949) 'Emotion' in *The Concept of Mind* London: Penguin Books.

Feelings

Deurzen-Smith, E. van (1988) 'Understanding emotions' in *Existential Counselling in Practice* London: SAGE

Dunlop, F. (1984) *The Education of Feelings and Emotion* London: Allen & Unwin.

Gendlin, E. (1980) *Focusing* New York [etc.]: Bantam Books.

Goleman, D. (1995) *Emotional Intelligence* (chapters 1, 2, 3 and app. A and B) London: Bloomsbury

Greenberg, L. S. (1996) 'Allowing and Accepting of Emotional Experience' in Kavanaugh, R.D., Zimmerberg, B. and Fein, S. (eds) *Emotion, Interdisciplinary Perspectives* Mahwah, NJ: Lawrence Erlbaum Associates.

Hanfling, O. (1976) *The Grammar of feelings* Milton Keynes: Open University.

Herzog, H. A. (1988) 'The moral status of mice' *American Psychologist* Issue 43.

Izard, C. E. (1977) *Human emotions* New York: Plenum Press.

Kenny, A. (1963) 'Feelings' in *Action, Emotion and Will* London: Routledge & Kegan.

Macquarrie, J. (1972) 'Feeling' in *Existentialism* London: Penguin Books.

Schiffman, M. (1967) *Selftherapy* Berkeley: Bookpeople, 1990.

Strongman, K. T. (1987) *The Psychology of Emotion* New York: John Wiley.

Emotion

Arnold, M. B. (1970) 'Perennial Problems in the Field of Emotion' in Arnold, M. B. (ed.) *Feelings and Emotions* New York; London: Academic Press.

Assagioli, R. (1965) 'Catharsis' in *Psychosynthesis* London: Crucible, 1990.

Bantock, G. H. (1967) 'The Education of the Emotions' in *Education, Culture and the Emotions* London: Faber and Faber.

Blundell, J. (1975) 'Emotions and aggression' in *Physiological Psychology* London: Methuen.

Ekman, P. and Davidson, R. J. (1994) *The Nature of Emotion* New York: Oxford University Press

Goleman, D. (1995) *Emotional Intelligence* (chapters 5, 12-14) London: Bloomsbury

Heron, J. (1982) 'Education of the affect the unexplored domain' in Habeshaw, T. *Three Ways to Learn* (no info.): SCEDSIP.

Lawen, A. (1976) *Bioenergetics* London: Penguin.

Lazarus, R. (1975) 'The Self-Regulation of Emotion' in Levi, L. (ed.) *Emotions: Their Parameters and Measurement.* New York: Raven Press.

Lewis, M. and Havilland, J. (1993) *Handbook of Emotions* New York: Guilford Press.

Oatley, K. and Jenkins J. (1996) *Understanding Emotions* Oxford: Blackwell.

Perls, F., Hefferline, R., Goodman, P. (1951) 'Orienting the Self: Experiment 7' in *Gestalt Therapy* New York: Julian Press.

Peters, R. S. (1970) 'The Education of the Emotions' in Arnold, M. B. (ed.) *Feelings and Emotions* New York; London: Academic Press.

Sousa, R. de (1994) 'Emotion' in Guttenplan, S. (ed.) *A Companion to the Philosophy of mind* Oxford: Blackwell.

Warnock, M. (1986) 'The education of the emotions' in Cooper, D. (ed.) *Education, values and mind* London: Routledge & Kegan Paul.

Wellek, A. (1970) 'Emotional Polarity in Personality Structure' in Arnold, M .B. (ed.) *Feelings and Emotions* New York; London: Academic Press.

White, J. (1984) 'The education of the emotions' *Journal of Philosophy of Education,* Vol. 18, No 2.

Zillmann, D. (1993) 'Mental Control of Angry Aggression' in Wegner, D. and Pennebaker, J. (eds) *Handbook of Mental Control* Englewood Cliffs: Prentice Hall.

Excitement

Fromm, E. (1973) 'Excitation and Stimulation' in *The Anatomy of Human Destructiveness* London: Jonathan Cape.

Strelau, J. and Eysenck, H. (1987) *Personality Dimensions and Arousal* New York; London: Plenum Press.

Moods

Asbell, B. & Wynn, K. (1991) 'Your Moods and Mental States' in *Look Yourself Up.* London: Fourth Estate.

Boss, M. (1977) *Existential foundations of Medicine and Psychology* New York; London: Aronson.

Morris, W. (1989) *Moods, the Frame of Mind* New York: Springer-Verlag.

Nowlis, V. (1970) 'Mood: Behavior and Experience' in Arnold, M. B. (ed.) *Feelings and Emotions* New York; London: Academic Press.

Podvoll, E. M. (1990) *Seduction of Madness* London: Century.

Salovey, P., Hsee, C. K. and Mayer, J.D. (1993) 'Emotional Intelligence and the Self-regulation of Affect' in Wegner, D. and Pennebaker, J. (eds) *Handbook of Mental Control* Englewood Cliffs: Prentice Hall.

Thayer, R. E. (1996) *The Origin of Everyday Moods* New York: Oxford University Press

COGNITIVE GROUP

Flew, A. (1975) *Thinking about thinking* London: Fontana/Collins.

Gilhooly, K. J. (1982) *Thinking* New York; London: Academic Press.

Hudson, L. (1967) *Contrary Imaginations* London: Penguin.

Matlin, M (1983) *Cognition* London: Holt, Rinehart and Winston.

Sanford, A. (1987) *The Mind of Man* Brighton: The Harvester Press.

Thomson, R. (1959) *The Psychology of Thinking* London: Penguin Books.

Learning

Blundell, J. (1975) 'Learning and memory' in *Physiological Psychology* London: Methuen.

Dearden, R. F. (1967) 'Instruction and learning by discovery' in Peters, R. S. *The Concept of Education* London: Routledge & Kegan Paul.

Gellatly, A. (1986) Section II: Memory Skills in *The Skilful Mind* Milton Keynes: Open University Press.

Hamlyn, D. (1978) *Experience and the Growth of Understanding* London: Routledge.

Honey, P. and Munford, A. (1992) *The Manual of Learning Styles* Maidenhend: Honey.

Macquarrie, J (1972) 'Knowledge and understanding' in *Existentialism* London: Penguin

Mowrer, O. H. (1950) *Learning theory and personality dynamics* New York: Ronald

Smith, F. (1992) 'Remembering, Understanding, and Learning' in *To think* London: Routledge.

Reasoning

Baron, J. (1988) *Thinking and Deciding* (Parts I, II and IV) Cambridge: CUP.

Baron, J. B. and Sternberg, R.J. (eds) (1987) *Teaching thinking skills* San Francisco: W. H. Freeman.

Beck, A. T. (1976) *Cognitive therapy and the Emotional Disorders* London: Penguin.

Fisher, R. (1990) 'Critical thinking' in *Teaching Children to Think* Oxford: Blackwell.

Geach, P. (1957) *Mental Acts.* London: Routledge & Kegan Paul, 1971.

Garnham, A. and Oakhill, J. (1994) *Thinking and Reasoning* Oxford: Blackwell.

Gellatly, A. (1986) 'Skill at reasoning' in *The Skilful Mind* Milton Keynes: Open University Press.

Price, H. H. (1953) *Thinking and Experience* London: Hutchinson.

Smith, F. (1992) 'Thinking critically' in *To think* London: Routledge.

Thouless, R. H. (1956) *Straight and Crooked Thinking* London; Sidney: Pan Books.

Wason, P. C. & Johnson-Laird, P. N. (1972) *Psychology of Reasoning* London: Batsford.

Creativity

Bandura, A. (1986) *Social Foundations of Thought and Action* Englewood Cliffs; London: Prentice Hall.

Baron, F. (1958) 'The Psychology of Imagination' in Parnes, S. J. and Harding, H. F. (eds) *A Source Book for Creative Thinking* London: Charles Scribner's Sons, 1962.

Barrow, R. (1990) 'Imagination and Creativity' in *Understanding Skills* Ontario: Althouse.

Branthwaite, A. (1986) 'Creativity and cognitive skills' in *The Skilful Mind* Milton Keynes: Open University Press.

Davis, G. (1973) *Psychology of Problem Solving* New York: Basic Books.

De Bono, E. (1970) *Lateral thinking: A Textbook of Creativity* London: Ward Lock.

Fisher, R. (1990) 'Creative thinking' in *Teaching Children to Think* Oxford: Blackwell.

Garnham, A. and Oakhill, J. (1994) 'Creativity' in *Thinking and Reasoning* Oxford: Blackwell.

Gilhooly, K. J. (1982) 'Daydreaming' and 'Creative processes' in *Thinking* New York; London: Academic Press.

Noel, J. (1999) '*Phronesis* and *Phantasia*: Teaching with Wisdom and Imagination' *Journal of Philosophy of Education,* Vol. 33, Issue 2.

Rainwater, J. (1979) 'Games People Play in Their Heads: Constructive and Destructive Uses of Fantasy' in *You are in charge* California: DeVorss & Company, 1989.

Ricoeur, P. (1950) *Freedom and Nature* Evanston, Ill: Northwestern University Press.

Smith, F. (1992) 'Imagination' and 'Thinking creatively' in *To think* London: Routledge.

Thomson, R. (1959) 'Creative Thinking' in *The Psychology of Thinking* London: Penguin Books.

Tyler, L. E. (1978) 'Creativity: The Recognition of Possibilities' in *Individuality* San Francisco, London: Jossey-Bass Publishers.

Inner Structure

Bandura, A. (1977) *Social Learning Theory* Englewood Cliffs; London: Prentice-Hall.

Buzan, T. (1974) *Use Both Sides of Your Brain* E. P. Dutton.

Ellis, A. & Harper, R. (1975) *A New Guide to Rational Living* Englewood Cliffs, NJ: Prentice-Hall.

Fransella, F. (1990) 'Personal construct therapy' in Dryden, W. (ed.) *Individual Therapy* Milton Keynes: Open University Press.

Fransella, F (2005) *Essential Handbook of Personal Construct Psychology*

Dilts, R., Hallbom, T and Smith, S. (1998) *Beliefs.* Metamorphous Press.

Kelly, G. (1955) *The Psychology of Personal Constructs* New York: W. W. Norton.

Kohut, H. (1971) *The Restoration of the Self* New York: International University Press.

Landfield, A. W. and Leitner, L. M. (eds) *Personal Construct Psychology: Psychotherapy and Personality.* New York: Wiley.

Marris, P. (1982) 'Attachment and Society' in Parkes, C. M. and Stevenson-Hinde, J. (eds) *The Place of Attachment in Human Behaviour* London: Tavistock Publications.

McGinn (1982) 'Thought and Language' in *The Character of Mind* Oxford: OUP.

Rock, I. (1975) *An Introduction to Perception* New York: Macmillan.

Rokeach, M. (1960) *The Open and Closed Mind* New York: Basic Books.

Smith, F. (1992) 'Patterns and stories' in *To think* London: Routledge.

Warren, N. and Jahoda, M. (1966) *Attitudes* London: Penguin Books.

Zajonc, R. B. (1960) 'Balance, Congruity and Dissonance' in Jahoda, M. and Warren, N. (eds) *Attitudes* London: Penguin, 1966.

INTEGRATIVE GROUP

Assagioli, R. (1965) *Psychosynthesis* London: Crucible, 1990.

Argyle, M. (2001) *The Psychology of Happiness* London: Rutledge.

Harmonisation

Binswanger, L. (1946) 'The existential analysis school of thought' in May, R., Angel, E. and Ellenberger, H. F. (eds) *Existence* New York: Basic Books, 1958.

Boss, M. (1963) *Psychoanalysis and Daseinsanalysis* New York: Basic Books.

Ferrucci, P. (1982) 'Synthesis' in *What We May Be* London: Mandala

Horney, K. (1945) *Our inner conflicts* NY: W.W. Norton, 1992.

Laing, R. D. (1960) *The Divided Self* New York: Tavistock.

Mulligan, J. (1988) 'Managing yourself effectively' in *The Personal Management Handbook* London: Sphere.

Perls, F., Hefferline, R., Goodman, P. (1951) 'Orienting the Self: experiment 3' in *Gestalt Therapy* NY: Julian Press.

Epstein, S. (1993) 'Emotion and Self-Theory' in Lewis, M and Havilland J. (eds) *Handbook of Emotions* New York; London: Guilford Press.

Luria, A. (1932) *The Nature of Human Conflicts* New York: Liveright, 1976.

Stability

Davis, M. (2000) *The Relaxation and Stress Reduction Workbook*. Oakland, CA: New Harbinger.

Elliott-Kemp, J. (1986) *The Management of Stress and Human Potential* Sheffield: PAVIC Publications.

Hewitt, J. (1982) *The Complete Relaxation Book* London: Rider

Mulligan, J. (1988) 'Managing Stress' in *The Personal Management Handbook* London: Sphere.

Watts, M. and Cooper, C. (1992) *Relax: Dealing with Stress* London: BBC books.

Weekes, C. (1962) *Self Help For Your Nerves* London: Angus & Robertson, 1991.

Self-Discipline

Assagioli, R. (1972) 'The Nature of the Will' in *The Act of Will.* Turstone Press, 1990.

Farber, L. H. (1966) *The Ways of the Will* London: Constable.

Goleman, D. (1995) 'The Master aptitude' *Emotional Intelligence* London: Bloomsbury

May, R. (1969) 'Part II: Will' in *Love and Will* London: Fontana, 1972.

Peck, S. (1978) 'Discipline' in *The Road Less Travelled* London: Arrow, 1990.

Development

Bee, H. L. (1987) *The Journey of adulthood* New York: Macmillan.

Bower, T. G. R. (1979) *Human Development.* San Francisco: W. H. Freeman

Haaften, W. van, Korthals, M., & Wren, T. (eds) (1997) *Philosophy of Development* Dondrecht: Kluwer Academic Publishers.

Hirst, P. H. and Peters, R. S. (1970) 'Development' in *The Logic of Education* London: Routledge & Kegan Paul.

Jung, C. G. (1930) 'The Stages of Life' in *Modern Man in Search of a Soul* London: Kegan Paul.

Lawin, K. (1951) 'Regression, retrogression and development' in Cartwright, D. (ed.) *Field Theory and social science.* New York: Harper and Row.

Magai, C. and Hunziker, J. (1993) 'Tolstoy and the Riddle of Developmental Transformation: A Lifespan analysis of the Role of Emotions in Personality Development' in Lewis, M and Havilland J. (eds) *Handbook of Emotions* New York; London: Guilford Press.

Mulligan, J. (1988) 'Developing your capabilities' in *The Personal Management Handbook* London: Sphere.

Pring, R. (1984) 'Personal Development' in *Personal and Social Education in the Curriculum* London: Hodder and Stoughton.

BEING CATEGORY

PRESERVATION GROUP

Foot, P. (1978) 'Virtues and Vices' in *Virtues and Vices and Other Essays in Moral Philosophy* Berkeley; London: University of California Press.

Plato 'Laches' In Hare, R. M. and Russell, D. A. (ed.) (1951) *The Dialogues of Plato* Vol. 2. London: Sphere books Limited.

Wright, G. H. von, (1963) *The Varieties of Goodness* London: Routledge & Kegan Paul.

Courage

Aristotle, 'Courage' in *The Nicomachean Ethics* Oxford: Oxford University Press, 1983

Boyd, T. and Levis, D. J. (1983) 'Exposure is a necessary condition for fear reduction: A reply to de Silva and Rachmann' in *Behaviour Research and Therapy,* Issue 21.

Fensterheim, H. and Bear, J. (1977) *Stop Running Scared* New York: Dell Publishing.

Gilling, D. and Brightwell, R. (1982) 'Fear' in *The Human Brain* London: Orbis.

Goleman, D. (1995) 'Appendix C: The Neural Circuitry of Fear' in *Emotional Intelligence* London: Bloomsbury.

Hunt, D. (1988) *No More Fears* London: Thorsons

Marks, I. M. (1978) *Living With Fear* New York; London: McGraw-Hill.

Oltmanns, T. F., Neale, J. M. and Davison, G. C. (1995) 'Psychopathy' in *Case Studies in Abnormal Psychology* New York: John Wiley & Sons.

Rachman, S. J. (1990). *Fear and courage* (2nd ed.). New York: W. H. Freeman & Co.

Rorty (1986) 'The Two Faces of Courage' *Philosophy*, Iss. 61.

Rowe, D. (1987) *Beyond Fear* London: Fontana/Collins.

Wallace, J. D. (1978) *Virtues and Vices* Ithaca and London: Cornell University Press.

276

Walton, D. N. (1986) *Courage* Berkeley; London: University of California Press.

White, P. (1996) 'Courage' in *Civic Virtues and Public Schooling* New York: Teachers College Press.

Confidence

Eccles, J. (1983) 'Expectancies, Values and Academic Behaviours' in Spence, J. (ed.) *Achievement and Achievement Motives* San Francisco: W. H. Freeman.

Hambly, K. (1987) *How to Improve Your Confidence.* London: Sheldon Press

Lindenfield, G. (1989) *Super Confidence* London: Thorsons.

Jeffers, S. (1987) *Feel the Fear and Do it Anyway* London: Century.

Goodhart, D. (1986) 'The effects of positive and negative thinking on performance in an achievement situation' *Journal of Personality and Social Psychology,* Issue 51.

Anticipatory Attitudes

Carnegie, D. (1948) *How to stop worrying and start living* London: Vermilion, 1996.

Folkman S. and Lazarus, R. (1990) 'Coping and Emotion' in Monat, A. and Lazarus, R. (eds) *Stress and Coping* New York: Columbia University Press.

Phillips, A. (1993) "Worrying and its discontents" in *On Kissing, Tickling and being Bored* London: Faber & Faber.

Roemer, L. & Borkovec, T (1993) 'Worry: Unwanted cognitive Activity That Controls Unwanted Somatic Experience' in Wegner, D. and Pennebaker, J. (ed.) *Handbook of Mental Control* Englewood Cliffs: Prentice Hall.

Sarnoff, I. (1962) 'Social attitudes and the Resolution of Motivational Conflict' in Jahoda, M. and Warren, N. (eds) *Attitudes* London: Penguin, 1966.

Security

Bourne, E. (2001) *The Anxiety and Phobia Workbook.* Oakland, CA: New Harbinger

Deurzen-Smith, E. van (1988) 'Facing the world alone' in *Existential Counselling in Practice* London: SAGE

Kierkegaard, S (1844) *The Concept of Dread* Princeton: Princeton University, 1944.

May, R. (1950) *The Meaning of Anxiety* New York, London: W. W. Norton, 1979.

Perls, F., Hefferline, R., Goodman, P. (1951) 'Orienting the Self: experiment 11' in *Gestalt Therapy* New York: Julian Press.

Popovic, N. (2002) 'Existential Anxiety and Existential Joy' *Practical Philosophy* Vol. 5 No.2

Tillich, P. (1952) *The Courage to Be* Glasgow: Penguin

ENGAGEMENT GROUP

Maslow, A. (1968) *Towards a Psychology of Being* New York: Van Nostrand Reinhold.

Lyons, J. (1973) *Experience* London: Harper & Row.

Experience

Csikszentmihalyi, M. (1982) 'Toward a psychology of optimal experience' *Review of Personality and Social Psychology,* Issue 3.

Csikszentmihalyi, M. and Csikszentmihalyi I. S. (1988) *Optimal Experience* Cambridge University Press.

Csikszentmihalyi, M. (1992) *Flow* London […]: Rider.

Krueger, F. (1928) 'The essence of feeling' in Arnold, M. B. (ed.) *The nature of emotion* London: Penguin, 1968.

Masschelein, J. (1998) 'World and Life or Education and the Question of Meaning (of Life)' *Conference papers,* Philosophy of Education Society of GB.

Montaigne, M. (1580) 'On experience' in *The Complete Essays* London: Penguin, 1991.

Privette, G. (1983) 'Peak experience, peak performance, and peak flow: a comparative analysis of positive human experiences' *Journal of Personality and Social Psychology*, Issue 45.

Openness

Rogers, C. (1954) 'Toward a Theory of Creativity' in Parnes, S. J. and Harding, H. F. (eds) *A Source Book for Creative Thinking* Charles Scribner's Sons, 1962.

Rogers, C. (1980) *A Way of Being* Boston, Mass: Houghton Mifflin.

Rosenbaum, M. (1998) 'Opening versus closing strategies in controlling one's responses to experience' in Kofta, M., Weary, G. and Sedek, G. (eds) *Personal Control in Action* New York; London: Plenum Press.

Interest

Berlyne, D. E. (1960) *Conflict, Arousal, and Curiosity* New York: McGraw-Hill.

Fromm, E. (1973) 'Chronic depression of boredom' in *The Anatomy of Human Destructiveness* London: Jonathan Cape.

Gergen, K. (1969) *The Psychology of behaviour exchange* Reading (Mass.); London: Addison-Wesley.

Phillips, A. (1993) 'On being bored' in *On Kissing, Tickling and being Bored* London: Faber and Faber.

Pintrich, P. R. and Schunk, D. H. (1996) 'The Role of Values, Interest and Affect' in *Motivation in Education* Englewood Cliffs: Prentice Hall.

Smith, R. P. (1981) 'Boredom: A review' *Human Factors,* Issue 23.

Winnicott, D. W. (1941) 'The observation on infants in a set situation' in *Collected Papers* London: Tavistock Publications, 1958.

Zuckerman, M. (1979) *Sensation Seeking: Beyond the Optimal Level of Arousal* Hillsdale, NJ: Lawrence Erlbaum Associates.

Pleasure

Aristotle, *The Nicomachean Ethics* (chapters I, VII and X) Oxford: OUP, 1983.

Eysenck, M. W. (1990) *Happiness* Hove: Erlbaum.

Fromm, E. (1948) 'Pleasure and Happiness' in *Man for himself* London: Routledge

Gaskin, J. (ed.) (1995) *The Epicurean Philosophers* Everyman.

Gosling, J. C. B. (1969) *Pleasure and Desire* Oxford: Clarendon Press.

Kenny, A. (1963) 'Pleasure' in *Action, Emotion and Will* London: Routledge & Kegan.

Perry, D. (1967) *The Concept of Pleasure* The Hague: Mouton.

PERSPECTIVE GROUP

Yalom, I. (1980) *Existential Psychotherapy* (part I) New York: Basic Books.

Relating To Death

Becker, E. (1973) *The Denial of Death* New York: Free Press.

Bryant-Mole, K. (1992) *Death* Hove: Wayland.

Eddy, J. and Alles, W. (1983) *Death Education* St Louis; London: Mosby.

Hanfling, O. (1987) *The Quest for Meaning* (chapter 4) Oxford: Blackwell.

Heidegger, M. (1926) 'Preparatory fundamental analysis of Dasein' and 'Dasein's Possibility of Being-a-Whole, and Being-towards-Death' in *Being and Time*8:39 PM Oxford: Basil Blackwell, 1973.

Kalish, R. A. (1981) *Death, Grief, and Caring Relationships* Belmont: Brooks/Cole.

Kübler-Ross, E. (ed.) (1975) *Death the Final Stage of Growth* Englewood Cliffs: Prentice-Hall.

Lepp, I. (1968) *Death and its mysteries* New York: Macmillan.

Macquarrie, J. (1972) 'Death' in *Existentialism* London: Penguin Books

Palmer, G. (1993) *Death: the trip of a lifetime* San Francisco: Harper.

Plato 'Phaedo' In Hare, R. M. and Russell, D.A. (ed.) (1951) *The Dialogues of Plato* Vol. 1, London: Sphere books.

Rainwater, J. (1979) 'Death (and the Possibility That You're in Charge Here, Too!)' in *You're in Charge* California: DeVorss & Company, 1989.

Sanders, P. (1990) *Death and Dying* London: Gloucester Press.

Shneidman, E. S. (1984) *Death: Current perspectives,* 3rd ed. Palo Alto: Maryfield.

Warren, W. G. (1989) *Death Education and Research* The Haworth Press.

Yalom, I. (1989) 'Love executioner' in *Love executioner* London: Penguin.

Importance

Lewis, H. (1991) *A Question of Values* New York: Harper Collins.

Carlson, R. (1997) *Don't Sweat the Small Stuff... and It's All Small Stuff* London: Jodder & Stoughton.

Attachment

Assagioli, R. (1988) 'Obstacles to spiritual development: Attachments' in *Transpersonal Development* London: Crucible, 1991.

Bee, H. and Mitchell, S. (1984) 'Attachments in Adulthood' in *The Developing Person* London: Harper & Row.

Bowlby, J. (1988) 'Lecture 2: The origins of attachment theory' in *A Secure Base: clinical applications of attachment theory* London: Routledge.

Nyanoponika, T. (1962) *The Heart of Buddhist Meditation* London [etc.]: Rider.

Parkes, C. M. and Stevenson-Hinde, J. (eds) (1982) *The Place of Attachment in Human Behaviour* London: Tavistock

Parkes, C. M., Stevenson-Hinde, J. and Morris, P. (eds) (1991) *Attachment Across the Life Cycle* London: Routledge.

Wegner, D. (1988) 'Stress and Mental Control' in Fisher, S. and Reason, J. (eds) *Handbook of Life Stress Cognition and Health* New York: John Wiley & Sons.

Tolerance

Ferrucci, P. (1982) 'The School of life' in *What We May Be* London: Mandala

Grotberg, E. (1995) *A Guide to Promoting Resilience in Children* The Hague: Bernard van Leer Fondation.

Kleinke, C. (1978) 'Learning to tolerate pain' in *Self-Perception: The Psychology of Personal Awareness* San Francisco: W. H. Freeman

Matthews, K. A., Carver, C. S. and Scheier, M. F. (1982) 'Focus of Attention and Awareness of Bodily Sensations' in Underwood, G. (ed.) *Aspects of Consciousness* New York; London: Academic Press.

Maultsby, Jr., M. C. and Ellis, A. (1974) *Technique for Using Rational-Emotive Imagery* New York: Albert Ellis Institute

Nussbaum, M. (1994) *The Therapy of Desire* (chapters 9-12) Princeton: Princeton University Press.

Ouellette, S.C. (1993) 'Inquiries into Hardiness' in Goldberger, L and Breznitz S. (eds) *Handbook of Stress* New York: The Free Press.

Reivich, K. and Shatte, A. (2002) *The Resilience Factor* New York: Broadway Books

THE CONTEXT GROUP
The Present

Ferrucci, P. (1982) 'Focus' in *What We May Be* London: Mandala

Kabat-Zinn, J. (1994) *Mindfulness Meditation for Everyday Life* New York: Hyperion.

McDonald, K. (1985) *How to Meditate* Wisdom Publications.

Naranjo, C. (1970) 'Present-centeredness in Gestalt Therapy' in Fagan, J. and Shepherd, L. (eds) *Gestalt Therapy Now* London: Penguin.

Perls, F., Hefferline, R., Goodman, P. (1951) 'Orienting the Self: experiments 1, 2 and 4' *Gestalt Therapy* New York: Julian Press.

Rainwater, J (1979) 'Awareness and the Art of Being in the

now' in *You're in charge*. California: Devorss & Co, 1989

Stevens, J (1971) *Awareness* Lafayette: Real People Press.

Stoyva, J. and Carlson, J. (1993) 'A Coping/Rest Model of Relaxation and Stress Management' in Goldberger, L. and Breznitz, S. (eds) *Handbook of Stress,* 2nd ed. New York: The Free Press.

The Past

Rainwater, J (1979) 'The Uses of Autobiography' in *You're in charge* California: Devorss & Company, 1989.

Perls, F., Hefferline, R. & Goodman, P. (1951) 'Orienting the Self: experiment 5'in *Gestalt Therapy* New York: Julian Press

Schiffman, M. (1971) *Gestalt Selftherapy* Berkeley: Bookpeople, 1990.

Goleman, D. (1995) 'Trauma and Emotional Relearning' in *Emotional Intelligence* London: Bloomsbury, 1996.

The Future

Hicks, D. (1991) *Exploring Alternative Futures* London: Institute of Education.

Hicks, D. and Holden, C. (1995) *Visions of the Future* Stoke-on-Trent: Trentham Books.

Tiger, L. (1979) *Optimism, The biology of Hope* New York: Kodansha, 1995.

White, P. (1996) 'Hope and Confidence' in *Civic Virtues and Public Shcooling* New York: Teachers College Press

Relating to the situation

Bastick, T. (1982) *Intuition: How we think and act* New York: John Wiley & Sons.

Deurzen-Smith, E. (1988) 'Coming to terms with life' in *Existential Counselling in Practice*. London: SAGE

Frankl, V. (1962) *Man's search for meaning*, Part I. London: Hodder and Stoughten, 1964.

Thomas, L. (1983) *The Youngest Science*. New York; London: Academic Press.

DOING CATEGORY

CHOICE GROUP

Deurzen-Smith, E. van (1988) 'Action and commitment' in *Existential Counselling in Practice* London: SAGE

Sartre, J. P. (1943) *Being and Nothingness* London: Methuen, 1958.

Meaning

Corey, G. and Corey, M. (1997) 'Meaning and values' in *I Never Knew I Had a Choice* Belmont: Brooks/Cole.

Deurzen-Smith, E. (1988) 'Discovering meaning' in *Existential Counselling in Practice*. London: SAGE

Farber, M. L. (1968) *Theory of Suicide* New York; London: Funk & Wagnalls.

Frankl, V. (1970) *The will to meaning* New York: New American Library.

Frankl, V. (1978) *The unheard cry for meaning* New York [etc.]: Bantam.

Hanfling, O. (1987) *The Quest for Meaning.* Basil Oxford: Blackwell.

Hanfling, O. (ed.) (1987) *Life and Meaning* Oxford: Blackwell.

Kiesler, C.A. (1971) *The psychology of commitment: Experiments linking behaviour to belief* New York; London: Academic Press.

Klinger, E. (1977) *Meaning and void: Inner experience and the incentives in people's lives* Minneapolis: University of Minnesota Press.

Trigg, R. (1973) 'Commitment' in *Reason and Commitment* Cambridge University Press.

Williams, B. (1976) 'Persons, Character and Morality' in Rorty, A.O. (ed.) *The Identities of Persons* Berkeley; London: University of California Press.

Freedom

Berlin, I. (1968) 'Two concepts of liberty' in *Four Essays on Liberty* Oxford: OUP.

Berne, E. (1974) 'Part II: Parental Programing' in *What Do You Say After You Say Hello?* London: Corgi Books.

Collinson, D. (1981) *Free Will* Milton Keynes: Open University Press.

Foot, F. (1987) 'Free Will as Involving Determinism' in *Virtues and Vices* Oxford: Basil Blackwell

Honderich, T. (ed.) (1995) 'Freedom and Determinsm' and 'Determinsm' in *The Oxford Companion to Philosophy* Oxford: Oxford University Press.

Peters, R. S. (1981) 'Freedom and the Development of the Free Man' in *Moral Development and Moral Education* London: Allen & Unwin.

Searle, J. (1984) 'The Freedom of the Will' in *Minds, Brains and Science.* London: BBC

Responsibility

Glover, J. (1970) *Responsibility* London: Routledge & Kegan Paul.

Peck, S. (1978) 'Responsibility' *The Road Less Travelled* London: Arrow, 1990.

Raz, J. (1986) *The Morality of Freedom* Oxford: Clarendon Press

Taylor, C. (1976) 'Responsibility for Self' in Rorty, A. O. (ed.) *The identities of Persons* Berkeley; London: California University Press.

Deciding

Assagioli, R. (1972) 'Deliberation, Choice, and Decision' in *The Act of Will* The Turstone Press, 1990.

Isen, A. (1993) 'Positive Affect and Decision Making' in Lewis, M and Havilland J. *Handbook of Emotions* New York; London: Guilford Press.

Juniper, P. (1976) *Decision-making for Schools and Colleges* Oxford [etc.]: Pergamon.

LeBon, T. and Arnaud, D. (2001) 'Towards Wise Decision-Making III: Critical and Creative Thinking' *Practical Philosophy* Vol. 4, No. 3.

Macquarrie, J. (1972) 'Decision and Choice in *Existentialism*, London: Penguin.

Nadel, L., Haims, J. and Stempson, R. (1990) *Sixth Sense* London: Prion.

Sloan, T. S. (1986) *Deciding* New York; London: MeHuen.

DIRECTIVE GROUP
Desires

Egan, G. (1994) 'Step II-A: A better future: What do you want?' in *The Skilled Helper* Belmont: Brooks/Cole.

Maslow, A. (1962) *Motivation and personality* London: Harper & Row.

May, R. (1969) 'Wish and Will' in *Love and Will* London: Fontana, 1972.

Thomson, G. (1987) *Needs* London: Routledge & Kegan Paul.

Aims

Egan, G. (1994) *The Skilled Helper* (chapter 13) Belmont: Brooks/Cole

Elliott, E. S. and Dweck, C. S. (1988) 'Goals: an approach to motivation and achievement' *Journal of Personality and Social Psychology,* Vol 54, Issue 1.

Festinger, L. (1957) *A Theory of cognitive dissonance* Row: Peterson.

King, L. (1998) 'Personal goals and personal agency' in Kofta, M., Weary, G. and Sedek, G. (ed.) *Personal Control in Action* New York; London: Plenum Press.

Winell, M. (1987) 'Personal Goals: The Key to Self-Direction in Adulthood' in Ford & Ford, D. (ed.) *Humans as Self Constructing Living Systems* Mahwah, NJ: Lawrence Erlbaum Associates.

286

Intention

Anscombe, G. E. M. (1957) *Intention* Oxford: Basil Blackwell.

Assagioli, R. (1972) 'From Intention to Realization' in *The Act of Will* London: Turstone

Davidson, D. (1978) 'Intending' in *Essays on Actions & Events* Oxford: Clarendon Press.

Farber, L. H. (1966) 'Intention' in *The Ways of the Will* London: Constable.

Ford, D. (1987) 'The Directive Function' in *Humans as Self-Constructing Living Systems.* Mahwah, NJ: Lawrence Erlbaum.

Honderich, T. (ed.) (1995) 'Intention' in *The Oxford Companion to Philosophy* Oxford: Oxford University Press.

May, R. (1969) *Love and Will* (chapters 9 and 10) London: Fontana, 1972.

Meiland, J. (1970) *The Nature of Intention* London: Methuen.

Searle, J. (1984) 'The Structure of the Action' in *Minds, Brains and Science.* London: BBC Books.

Gratification

Ainslie, G. (1986) 'Beyond microeconomics: Conflict among interests in a multiple self as a determinant of value' in Elster, J. (ed.) *The multiple self* Cambridge: CUP

Assagioli, R. (1972) 'The Direction and Execution' in *The Act of Will* London: Turstone.

Montaigne, M. (1580) 'On moderation' in *The Complete Essays* London: Pinguin, 1991.

PROBLEM GROUP
Strategy

Egan, G. (1986) *The Skilled Helper* (chapters 10 and 11) Belmont: Brooks/Cole.

Marzano, R. J., Brant, R. S., Hughes, C. S., Jones, B. F., Presseinsen, B. Z., Rankin, S. C. and Suhor, C. (1988) *Dimensions of Thinking* Alexandria, VA: ASCD

Mulligan, J. (1988) 'Problems, decisions and plans' in *The Personal Management Handbook* London: Sphere.

Siegler, R. and Jenkins, E. (1989) *How Children Discover New Strategies* Mahwah, NJ: Lawrence Erlbaum Associates.

Achievement

Egan, G. (1986) *The Skilled Helper* (chapters 2, 14 and 15) Belmont: Brooks/Cole.

Fisher, R. (1990) 'Problem solving' in *Teaching Children to Think* Oxford: Blackwell.

Ford, D. (1987) 'Control functions: Problem Solving and Behavioural Organisation' in *Humans as Self-Constructing Living Systems* Mahwah, NJ: Lawrence Erlbaum.

Leggett, T. (no info.) *The Dragon Mask* London: Ippon Books.

Rubinstein, M. and Pfeiffer, K. (1980) in *Concepts in Problem Solving* Englewood Cliffs, NJ: Prentice-Hall.

Coping

Cox, T. (1988) 'Psychobiological factors in stress and health' in Fisher, S. and Reason, J. (ed.) *Handbook of Life Stress Cognition and Health* New York: John Wiley & Sons.

Evans, P. (1991) 'Stress and coping' in Pitts, M. and Phillips, K. (eds) *The Psychology of Health* London: Routledge.

Haan, N. (1993) 'The Assessment of Coping, Defence, and Stress' in Goldberger, L. and Breznitz S. (eds) *Handbook of Stress* New York: The Free Press.

Lazarus, R. and Folkman, S. (1984) 'The Concept of Coping' in Lazarus, R. and Monat, A. (ed.) *Stress and Coping* New York: Columbia University Press, 1991.

Meichenbaum, D. and Fitzpatrick, D. (1993) 'A Constructivist Narrative Perspective on Stress and Coping: Stress Inoculation Applications' in Goldberger, L and Breznitz S. (eds) *Handbook of Stress* New York: The Free Press.

Monat, A. and Lazarus, R. S. (1991) *Stress and Coping* New York: Columbia University.

Mulligan, J. (1988) 'Support Systems' in *The Personal Management Handbook* London: Sphere.

Pennebaker, J. W. (1988) 'Confiding Traumatic Experiences and Health' in Fisher, S. and Reason, J. (eds) *Handbook of Life Stress Cognition and Health* New York: John Wiley & Sons.

Wortman, C. and Silver, R. (1989) 'The Myths of Coping with Loss' in Monat and Lazarus (ed.) *Stress and Coping* New York: Columbia University Press, 1991.

Control

Sternberg, R. J. and Spear-Swerling, L. (1998) 'Personal Navigation' in Ferrari, M. and Sternberg, R. J. (eds) *Self-awareness* New York; London: Guilford Press

Goleman, D. (1995) 'Managing with Heart' in *Emotional Intelligence* London: Bloomsbury, 1996.

ACTIVITY GROUP
Motivation

Assagioli, R. (1972) 'Purpose, Evaluation, Motivation, Intention' in *The Act of Will* London: Turstone Press, 1990.

Benjamin, L. T., Hopkins, J. R. and Nation, J. R. (1987) 'Motivation' in *Psychology* London: Macmillan.

Blundell, J. (1975) 'Neurophysiology of motivation' in *Physiological Psychology* London: Methuen

Deci, E. L. (1975) *Intrinsic Motivation* New York; London: Plenum Press.

Deci, E. L. (1996) *Why we do what we do* New York: Penguin

Eiser, J. R. (1986) 'Motivation, incentive and dissonance' in *Social Psychology* Cambridge: Cambridge University Press

Pintrich, P. R. and Schunk, D. H. (1996) 'The Role of Values, Interest and Affect' in *Motivation in Education* Englewood Cliffs: Prentice Hall.

Weiner, B. (1979) 'A theory of motivation for some classroom experiences.' *Journal of Educational Psychology,* Vol 71.

Wright, A. (1991) 'Motivation' in the set of booklets *Developing Self-Discipline* USL.

Energy

Blanche, C. (1997) *The Book of Energy* London: Time8:39 PM-Life.

Laban, R. and Lawrence, F. C. (1947) *Effort* Macdonald & Evans.

Organisation

Assagioli, R. (1972) 'Planning and Programing' in *The Act of Will* London: Turstone Press, 1990.

Atkinson, J. (1992) *Better time management* London: Thorsons.

Back K. & Back, K. (1982) 'Assertiveness and change' in *Assertiveness at Work.* New York, McGraw-Hill Book Company, 1991.

Hall, N. (ed.) (1992) *The NewScientist Guide to Chaos* London: Penguin.

Kemp, R. and Race, P. (1992) 'Developing students' time management skills' in *Promoting the Development of Personal and Professional Skills* Sheffield: CVCP.

Macquarrie, J. (1972) 'Space and Time8:39 PM' in *Existentialism* London: Penguin.

Marris, P. (1974) *Loss and Change* London: Routledge and Kegan Paul.

Smart, J. J. C. (1964) *Problems of Space and Time*8:39 PM London: Macmillan.

Performance

Arendt, H. (1958) *The Human Condition* Chicago: University of Chicago Press.

Macquarrie, J. (1972) 'Action' in *Existentialism* London: Penguin Books

Montaigne, M. (1580) 'On practice' *The Complete Essays*, London: Pinguin, 1991.

Spence, J. T. and Helmreich, R. L. (1983) 'Achievement-Related Motives and Behaviours' in Spence, J (ed.) *Achievement and Achievement Motives* San Francisco: W. H. Freeman

SOCIAL CATEGORY

IDENTITY GROUP

Eiser, J. R.(1986) 'Social identity and intergroup processes' in *Social Psychology* Cambridge: Cambridge University Press

Sherif, M. (1936) *The psychology of social norms* New York: Harper.

Dependence

Dowrick, S. (1991) 'Solitude: Knowing your self'' in *Intimacy & Solitude* New York; London: W. W. Norton.

Fromm, E. (1942) *Escape from Freedom* New York: Harper & Row.

Gewirtz, J. L. (1972) *Attachment and dependency* Washington: V. H. Winston.

Montaigne, M. (1580) 'On solitude' *The Complete Essays*, London: Pinguin, 1991.

Weiss, R. S. (1973) *Loneliness: The experience of emotional and social isolation* Cambridge, Mass.: M.I.T. Press.

Individuality

Bonnett, M. (1986) 'Personal authenticity and public standards: towards the transcendence of dualism' in Cooper, D. (ed.) *Education, Values and Mind* London; New York: Routledge & Kegan Paul.

Buss, A.H. (1980) *Self-consciousness and social anxiety* San Francisco: W. H. Freeman.

Emerson, R. 'Self-Reliance' in *Essays and Journals* Edited by Humford, L., New York: Doubleday, 1968.

Erickson, E. H. (1968) *Identity: Youth and crisis* New York, London: W. W. Norton.

Janis, I. L. (1972) *Victims of groupthink* Boston, Mass: Houghton Miflin.

Latane, B. and Darley, J. (1968) 'Group inhibition of bystander intervention in emergencies' *Journal of Personality and Social Psychology,* vol. 10.

May, R. (1953) *Man's Search for Himself* New York, London: W. W. Norton.

Moustakas, C. (1967) *Creativity and Conformity* New York: Van Nostrand Reinhold.

Tyler, L. E. (1978) *Individuality* San Francisco, London: Jossey-Bass Publishers.

Wilson, C. (1956) *Outsider* London: Indigo, 1997.

Influence

Back K. & Back, K. (1982) 'How others influence you' in *Assertiveness at Work* McGraw-Hill Book Company, 1991.

Carnegie, D. (1936) *How to win friends and influence people* London: Vermilion, 1996.

Eiser, J. R.(1986) 'Attitudes, attraction and influence' in *Social Psychology* Cambridge: Cambridge University Press

Hill, T. E. (1991) *Autonomy and Self-respect* Cambridge University Press.

Kelman, H. C. (1961) 'Three Processes of Social Influence' in Jahoda, M. and Warren, N. (ed.) *Attitudes* London: Penguin, 1966.

Leman, P. J. and Duveen, G. (1998) 'Representations of authority and children's moral reasoning' *Conference papers* Philosophy of Education Society of Great Britain.

Wheeler, L., Deci, E., Reis, H. and Zuckerman, M. (1978) *Interpersonal Influence,* 2nd ed. Boston, Mass.; London [etc.]: Allin and Bacon.

Zimbardo, P., Ebbesen, E. and Maslach, C. (1977) *Influencing attitudes and changing behaviour* Reading (Mass.); London: Addison-Wesley.

Belonging

Argyle, M. (1983) 'Groups, Organization and Culture' in *The Psychology of Interpersonal Behaviour* London: Penguin Books

Berne, E. (1963) *The Structure and Dynamics of Organizations and Groups* New York: Ballantine, 1973.

Deurzen-Smith, E. van (1988) 'The Public world' in *Existential Counselling in Practice* London: SAGE

Gaskell, G. and Sealy, P. (1976) *Groups* Milton Keynes: Open University Press.

Forsyth, D. (1998) *Group Dynamics* Wadswarth Publishing

Johnson, D. and Johnson, F. (1991) *Joining Together* Englewood Cliffs: Prentice Hill.

Macquarrie, J. (1972) 'Being-with-Others as Fundamentally Characterizing Existence' in *Existentialism* London: Penguin Books.

Mulligan, J. (1988) 'Managing Groups' in *The Personal Management Handbook* London: Sphere.

SOCIAL ATTITUDES GROUP

Warnock, G. J. (1967) *Contemporary Moral Philosophy* London: Macmillan.

Williams, B. (1985) *Ethics and the Limits of Philosophy* London: Fontana.

Wringe, C. (1999) 'Being Good and Living Well: Three Attempts to Resolve an Ambiguity' *Journal of Philosophy of Education,* Vol. 33, Issue 2.

Moral Sense

Aristotle, 'Moral Virtue' in *The Nicomachean Ethics* Oxford: OUP, 1983

Baron, J. (1988)'Moral Thinking' in *Thinking and deciding* Cambridge University Press

Blum, L. (1980) *Friendship, Altruism and Morality* London: Routledge & Kegan Paul.

Buber, M. (1952) *Images of Good and Evil* London: Routledge and Kegan Paul, 1980.

Crittenden, P. (1990) *Learning To Be Moral* Humanities Press International.

Dancy, J. (1991) 'Intuitionism' in Singer, P. *A* (ed.) *Companion to Ethics* Oxford: Blackwell, 1993.

Jennings, C. (1999) 'The neurobiology of morals' *Nature* London: Macmillan Publishers.

Kant, I. (1876) *Fundamental Principles of the Metaphysic of Ethics* London; New York; Bombay: Longmans, Green, and Co., 1923.

Kegan, J. and Lamb, S. (ed.) (1987) *The Emergence of Morality in Young Children* Chicago: University of Chicago Press.

Kohlberg, L. (1981) *The Philosophy of Moral Development* London: Harper & Row.

Lennhoff, F. G. and Lampen, J. (1974) *Thinking about Conscience* Shrewsbury: Shotton Hall Publication.

Nagel, T. (1986) *The View From Nowhere* Oxford: Oxford University Press.

Nietzsche, F. (1886) *Beyond Good and Evil* New York: Vintage Books, 1966.

Norman, R. (1983) *The Moral Philosophers* Oxford: Clarendon Press.

Nussbaum, M. (1986) *The fragility of Goodness* Cambridge: Cambridge University.

Piaget, J. (1967) *Six psychological studies* Vintage Books.

Ruse, M. (1991) 'The significance of evolution' in Singer, P. *A Companion to Ethics* Oxford: Blackwell, 1993.

Rustin, M. (1997) 'Innate Morality: A Psychoanalytic Approach to Moral Education' in Smith, R. and Standish, P. (eds) *Teaching Right and Wrong* Stoke-on-Trent: Trentham Books.

Slote, M. (1992) *From Morality to Virtue* Oxford: Oxford University Press.

Stocker, M, with Elizabeth, H. (1996) *Valuing Emotions* Cambridge: Cambridge UP.

Wilson, J. Q. (1993) *The Moral Sense* New York: The Free Press.

Protection

Asbell, B. & Wynn, K. (1991) 'Crime, Violence, and Aggression' in *Look Yourself Up.* London: Fourth Estate.

Bandura, A. (1977) 'Self-efficacy: Towards a unifying theory of behavioural change' *Psychological Review,* Issue 84.

Benjamin, L. T., Hopkins, J. R. & Nation, J.R. (1987) 'Aggression' in *Psychology* Macmillan Publishing Company

Elgin, S. (1980) *The Gentle Art of Verbal Self-Defence* Englewood Cliffs: Prentice-Hall.

Ferrucci, P. (1982) 'Tigers of Wrath' in *What We May Be* London: Mandala

Gregory, R. (1973) *Man's Aggression* London: Constable.

Mulligan, J. (1988) 'Difficult People' in *The Personal Management Handbook* London: Sphere.

Relating To Others

Downie, R. S. and Telfer, E. (1971) *Respect for Persons* London: Allen and Unwin.

Macquarrie, J. (1972) 'Interpersonal Relations' in *Existentialism* London: Pinguin

Relationship Symmetry

Adler, A. (1932) *What Life Could Mean To You* London: George Allen & Unwin.

Adler, A. (1964) *Superiority and Social Interest: A Collection of Later Writings* Ansbacher H. L. and Ansbacher R. R. (eds) New York; London: W. W. Norton.

Duveen, G. (1998) 'Symmetric and Asymmetric Relations as Contexts for Development' *Conference papers* Philosophy of Education Society of Great Britain.

Orgler, H. (1973) *Alfred Adler The Man and His Work* London: Sidgwich & Jackson.

Rawls, J. A. (1972) *Theory of Justice* Oxford: Claredon Press.

Tawney, R. H.(1938). *Equality* London: Allen and Unwin.

Wringe, C. (1988) 'Equality' in *Understanding Educational Aims* London: Allen & Unwin.

INTERACTION GROUP

Appearance

Argyle, M. (1983) 'Self-image and Self-presentation' in *The Psychology of Interpersonal Behaviour* London: Penguin Books

Asbell, B. & Wynn, K. (1991) 'Your Outer Self and What it Says About You' in *Look Yourself Up.* London: Fourth Estate.

Burns, R. (1982) 'Body Image and Appearance' in *Self-Concept Development and Education* London: Holt, Rinehart and Winston.

Goffman, E. (1959) *The Presentation of Self in Everyday Life* London: Penguin Books.

Osborne, H. (1952) *Theory of Beauty* London: Routledge & Kegan Paul.

Awareness Of Others

Argyle, M. (1983) 'Perception of others' in *The Psychology of Interpersonal Behaviour* London: Penguin Books

Bolton, R. (1979) 'Listening Skills' *People Skills* New York, London: Simon & Schuster

Cook, M. (1979) *Perceiving Others* London: Methuen.

Eisenberg, N. and Strayer, J. (ed.) (1987) *Empathy and its development* Cambridge: Cambridge University Press.

Goleman, D. (1995) 'The Roots of Empathy' in *Emotional Intelligence.* London: Bloomsbury, 1996.

Hochberg, J. (1978) 'Social Perception and Communication' in *Perception,* 2nd ed. Englewood Cliffs: Prentice Hall.

Morris, D. (1977) *Manwatching* London: Jonathan Cape Thirty Bedford Square.

Power, R. P., Hausfeld, S. and Gorta, A. (1981) 'Perception of language' and 'Social Perception' in *Workshops in Perception* London: Routledge & Kegan Paul.

Rogers, D. (1986) 'Listening skills' in *The Skilful Mind* Milton Keynes: Open University Press.

Staub, E. (1987) 'Commentary on Part I' in Eisenberg, N. and Strayer, J. (eds) *Empathy and its development* Cambridge: Cambridge University Press.

Whitaker, P. (1984) *Developing Empathy* (no info.): Personal Learning Associates.

Communicating

Bolton, R. (1986) *People Skills.* New York: Touchstone.

Deurzen-Smith, E. van (1988) 'Communicating and relating' in *Existential Counselling in Practice* London: SAGE

Egan, G. (1990) 'Basic communication skills' in *Exercises in Helping Skills.* Belmont: Brooks/Cole.

Ford, D. (1987) 'Transactional Functions: Communication' in *Humans as Self-Constructing Living Systems* Mahwah, NJ: Lawrence Erlbaum.

Macquarrie, J. (1972) 'Thought and language' in *Existentialism* London: Pinguin.

McKay, M., Davis, M. and Fanning, P. (1997) *How to Communicate: The Ultimate Guide to Improving Your Personal and Professional Relationships* New York: Fine.

Miller, G. (1981) 'Conversation' and 'Language and Thought' in *Language and Speech* San Francisco: Freeman.

Mulligan, J. (1988) 'Communication' in *The Personal Management Handbook* London: Sphere.

Rogers, D. (1986) 'The Skills of the Speaker' in *The Skilful* Milton Keynes: *Mind* Open University Press.

Tannen, D. (1986) *That's Not What I Meant* J. M. Dent & Sons.

Behaviour

Berne, E. (1964) *Games People Play* New York: Random House.

Buber, M. (1937) *I and thou* Edinburgh: Clark, 1959.

Goffman, E. (1961) *Encounters* Indianapolis: Bobbs-Merrill.

Goffman, E. (1967) *Interaction Ritual* London: Penguin Books.

Goleman, D. (1995) 'The Social Arts' in *Emotional Intelligence* London: Bloomsbury.

Macquarrie, J. (1972) 'Inauthentic and Authentic Being-with-Others' and 'Interpersonal Relations' in *Existentialism* London: Penguin

Rainwater, J. (1979) 'You're in Charge of Your Personal Relationships: Getting Along with Other People' in *You are in charge* California: DeVorss & Company, 1989.

Turiel, E. (1983) *The Development of Social Knowledge* Cambridge University Press.

White, P. (1996) 'Decency and Education for Citizenship' in *Civic Virtues and Public Shcooling* New York: Teachers College Press

Zimbardo, P. (1987) *Shyness* Reading, MA: Addison-Wesley.

RELATIONSHIP GROUP

Relationship Dynamics

Argyle, M. & Henderson, M. (1985) *The Anatomy of Relationship.* London: Heinemann

Bolton, R. (1979) 'Conflict Management Skills' in *People Skills* New York, London: Simon & Schuster

Duck, S. (1989) *Relating to others* Milton Keynes: Open University Press.

Grant, W. (1997) *Resolving Conflicts* Shaftesbury: Element.

Levinger, G. (1983) 'Development and change' in Kelley, H. H., *at al. Close relationships* New York: W. H. Freemen.

Sandole, D. J. D. and Sandole-Staroste I. (1987) *Conflict Management and Problem Solving, Interpersonal to International Applications* New York: New York University Press; London: Frances Pinter.

Scott, G. G. (1990) *Resolving Conflicts* Oakland, Calif.: New Harbinger Publications.

Tannen, D. (2001) *I Only Say This Because I Love You* New York: Random House.

Intrinsic Relationship

Aristotle, *The Nicomachean Ethics* (chapters VIII and IX) Oxford: OUP, 1983.

Boyatzis, R. E. (1973) 'Affiliation Motivation' in McClelland, D. C. and Steele, R. S. (eds) *Human Motivation* Morristown, NJ: General Learning Press.

Duck, S. (1991) *Friend for life* Harvester: Wheatsheat.

Fehr, B. (1996) *Friendship Process* London: Sage.

Howarth I. and Dussuyer, D. (1988) 'Helping People Cope with the Long-term Effects of Stress' in Fisher, S. and Reason, J. (eds) *Handbook of Life Stress Cognition and Health* New York: John Wiley & Sons.

Macmurray, J. (1949) *Conditions of Freedom* London: Faber and Faber.

Miller, S. (1983) *Men and Friendship* London: Gateway Books.

Montaigne, M. (1580) 'On friendship' in *The Compete Essays,* London: Pinguin, 1991.

Plato 'Symposium' In Hare, R. M. and Russell, D.A. (ed.) (1951) *The Dialogues of Plato* Vol. 2, London: Sphere books Limited.

Reisman, J. (1979) *Anatomy of Friendship* New York: Irvington Publishers.

White, P. (1996) 'Friendship' 'Trust' and 'Honesty' in *Civic Virtues and Public Shcooling* New York: Teachers College Press

Wilson, J. (1995) 'Intrinsic friendship' in *Love between Equals* London: Macmillan.

Instrumental Relationships

Alberti, R. & Emmons, M. (1995) *Your Perfect Right.* San Luis Obispo, CA: Impact/

Back K. & Back, K. (1982) 'Assertiveness and stress' in *Assertiveness at Work.* New York, McGraw-Hill Book Company, 1991.

Bolton, R. (1979) 'Assertion Skills' in *People Skills* New York, London: Simon & Schuster, 1986.

Cornelius, H. and Faire, S. (1989) *Everyone can Win* New York: Simon & Schuster.

Fisher & Ury (1991) *Getting to Yes* New York: Penguin

Lindenfield, G. (1986) *Assert Yourself* Wellingborough: Thorsons.

Mulligan, J. (1988) 'Getting things done' in *The Personal Management Handbook* London: Sphere.

Taylor, M. (1990) 'Transmission and compound skills' in *Effectiveness in Education and Training* Aldershot: Avebury.

Intimate Relationship

Asbell, B. & Wynn, K. (1991) 'Your Relationships' in *Look Yourself Up.* London: Fourth Estate.

Beck, A. T. (1988) *Love is Never Enough* London: Penguin.

Boon, S. D. and Holmes, J. G. (1991) 'The dynamics of interpersonal trust: resolving uncertainty in the face of risk' in Hinde, R. A. and Groebel, J. (eds) *Cooperation and Prosocial Behaviour* Cambridge: Cambridge University Press.

Byrne, D. and Murnen, S. (1988) 'Theories of Love and Relationship Maintenance' in Sternberg, R. and Barnes, M. (eds) *The psychology of love* New Haven; London: Yale University Press.

Ferrucci, P. (1982) 'What we live by' in *What We May Be* London: Mandala

Fisher, M. (1990) *Personal Love* London: Duckworth.

Fromm, E. (1957) *Art of loving* London: Thorsons, 1995.

Goleman, D. (1995) 'Intimate Enemies' *Emotional Intelligence* London: Bloomsbury.

Hatfield, E. (1988) 'Passionate and Companionate Love' in Sternberg, R. and Barnes, M. (eds) *The psychology of love* New Haven and London: Yale University Press.

Hatfield, E. and Rapson, R. (1993) 'Love and Attachment Processes' in Lewis, M and Havilland J. (eds) *Handbook of Emotions* New York; London: Guilford Press.

Lee, J. A. (1988) 'Love-Styles' in Sternberg, R. and Barnes, M. (ed.) *The psychology of love*. New Haven and London: Yale University Press.

Lund, M. (1991) 'Commitment old and new: social pressure and individual choice in making relationships last' in Hinde, R. A. and Groebel, J. (ed.) *Cooperation and Prosocial Behaviour* Cambridge University Press.

May, R. (1969) 'Part I: Love' in *Love and Will* London: Fontana, 1972.

Morris, D. (1971) *Intimate behaviour* London: Jonathan Cape Thirty Bedford Square.

Peck, S. (1978) 'Love' *The Road Less Travelled* London: Arrow, 1990.

Price, A. W. (1989) *Love and Friendship in Plato and Aristotle* Oxford University Press.

Stanley-Jones, D. (1970) 'The Biological Origin of Love and Hate' in Arnold, M. B. (ed.) *Feelings and Emotions* New York; London: Academic Press.

Sternberg, R. J. (1986) 'A triangular theory of love' *Psychological Review,* Vol 93, 2.

Sternberg, R. J. and Barnes, M. L. (1985) 'Real and ideal others in romantic relationships: Is four a crowd?' *Journal of Personality and Social Psychology,* Vol 49, Issue 6.

Sternberg, R. J. and Barnes, M. L. (ed.) (1988) *The psychology of love* New Haven; London: Yale University Press.

Sternberg, R. J. and Grajek, S. (1984) 'The Nature of Love' *Journal of Personality and Social Psychology,* Vol 2, Issue 47.

NOTES

[1] Braudel, F. (1980) *On History* London: Weidenfeld and Nicolson, p.215

[2] Ferri, E. *at al.* (2003) *Changing Britain, Changing Lives*, London, IoE.

[3] Deurzen-Smith, E. van (1994) *Can Counselling Help?* Durham: School of Education, University of Durham, p.19

[4] See Sprinthall, N. (1980) 'Psychology for secondary schools: the saber-tooth curriculum revisited' *American Psychologist* Issue 35, p.341-342

[5] The internal-external axis departs from the classic distinction between inner and outer in so far as the internal is not identified with the subjective, or the external with the objective. They only represent domains or directions of individual awareness and intent.

[6] The categories take positions that roughly correspond to the major areas of the brain (looking from left to right): our receptive abilities are mainly grouped in the anterior part of the cortex; the posterior part of the cortex is predominantly responsible for our agency; language, one of the central social aspects, is mainly situated in the left hemisphere, while the right hemisphere is believed to have a central role in the mental activities that are traditionally considered more subjective or personal (e.g. creativity, emotions). However, any further similarities or attempts to find parallels between the brain structure and this model would be strained.

[7] This is because our desires, aims and intentions (that comprise the Directive group) are first begotten in ourselves before we 'reach out'. On the other hand, problems come from the outside - we don't create them (even when we want them).

[8] This term, of course, does not have an evaluative meaning, it only reflects the position of the groups.

[9] Rogers, C. (1951) *Client-cantered therapy* Boston, Mass: Houghton Mifflin, p.136-137.

[10] Rogers was not concerned with the division between the self-concept and the world-concept, so some areas that he mentions are in this model situated within the world-concept. However, it is important that the four major components of the self-concept are recognised in both models.

[11] Which is, coincidentally, also the number of areas in this model.

[12] Shotter, J. (1982) 'Contemporary Psychological Theory - Human Being: Becoming Human' in Dufour, B. *New Movements in the Social Sciences and Humanities* London: Maurice Temple Smith, p.88.

[13] The fourth mode, intuitive learning, is addressed through included quotes and recommended literature.

[14] Taylor, M. (1990) 'Transmission and compound skills' in *Effectiveness in Education and Training* Aldershot: Avebury, p.135.

[15] The term *self-valuation* is used instead the more common term *self-evaluation* to indicate that the sense of self-value does not need always to be based on judgements.

[16] Other symbols and an evaluation of this method can be found in Assagioli, R. (1965) *Psychosynthesis* London: Crucible, 1990, 287-302

[17] See, for example, Parlett, M. and Page, F. (1990) 'Gestalt therapy' in Dryden, W. (ed.) *Individual Therapy* Milton Keynes: Open University Press, 1992, p.191 or Rainwater, J. (1979) *You are in charge* California: DeVorss & Company, 1989, p.118.

[18] See 'Self-deceit' in the area Self-awareness.

[19] Isenberg, A. (1980) 'Natural Pride and Natural Shame' in Rorty, A. (ed.) *Explaining Emotions* Berkeley; London: University of California Press, p.364.

[20] How to do this will be the main subject of the following area *Personal Change*.

[21] These attitudes are addressed in the preceding areas *Self-awareness* and *Relating to oneself,* respectively.

[22] This point relates to the area *Personal change*.

[23] Coopersmith, S. (1967) *The Antecedents of Self-esteem* San Francisco: W. H. Freeman p.19 and p.62.

[24] Of course, this should not be confused with a deliberate change of style deployed to convey the meaning better.

[25] This is partly based on etymology of these words (e-motion clearly refers to a movement). To minimize possible confusion when it is important to make a clear distinction between these two, the term *emotional reaction* will be used instead *emotion*.

[26] One psychologist for example writes: 'I might be angry without realising it... I might mistakenly think that I am in no emotional or affective state at all.' (Stocker, M, with Elizabeth, H. (1996) *Valuing Emotions* Cambridge: Cambridge UP, p.22-23)

[27] Greenberg, L. S. (1996) 'Allowing and Accepting of Emotional Experience' in Kavanaugh, R.D., Zimmerberg, B. and Fein, S. (eds) *Emotion, Interdisciplinary Perspectives* Mahwah, NJ: Lawrence Erlbaum Associates, p.323

[28] See, for example, Pennebaker, J. W. (1988) 'Confiding Traumatic Experiences and Health' in Fisher, S. and Reason, J. (eds) *Handbook of Life Stress Cognition and Health* New York: John Wiley & Sons, p.670-671.

[29] Goleman, D. (1995) *Emotional Intelligence* London: Bloomsbury, 1996, p.64

[30] Zillmann, D. (1993) 'Mental Control of Angry Aggression' in Wegner, D. and Pennebaker, J. (eds) *Handbook of Mental Control* Englewood Cliffs: Prentice Hall.

[31] Ford, D. (1987) 'The Directive Function' in *Humans as Self-Constructing Living Systems.* Mahwah, NJ: Lawrence Erlbaum, 519.

[32] Fromm, E. (1973) 'Excitation and Stimulation' in *The Anatomy of Human Destructiveness* London: Jonathan Cape.

[33] Stoyva, J. and Carlson, J. (1993) 'A Coping/Rest Model of Relaxation and Stress Management' in Goldberger, L. and Breznitz, S. (eds) *Handbook of Stress,* 2nd ed. New York: The Free Press, p.742-745.

[34] See Argyle, M. (1987) *The Psychology of Happiness* London: Methuen, p.138.

[35] Salovey, P., Hsee, C. K. and Mayer, J.D. (1993) 'Emotional Intelligence and the Self-regulation of Affect' in Wegner, D. and Pennebaker, J. (eds) *Handbook of Mental Control* Englewood Cliffs: Prentice Hall, p.264.

[36] Morris, W. (1989) *Moods, the Frame of Mind* New York: Springer-Verlag, p.2.

[37] First four chapters in Podvoll, E. M. (1990) *Seduction of Madness* London: Century, are moving examples of this point.

[38] Frijda, S. (1993) 'Moods, Emotion Episodes and Emotions' in Lewis, M and Haviland J. *Handbook of Emotions* New York; London: Guilford Press, p. 384.

[39] Empirical support for this exercise can be found in Morris, W. (1989) *Moods, the Frame of Mind* New York: Springer-Verlag, p.29.

[40] Philosopher Popper claims though that even conditioning requires an active element.

[41] Thomson, R. (1959) *The Psychology of Thinking* London: Penguin Books, p.185.

[42] *ibid.*

[43] see, for example, Matlin, M (1983) *Cognition* London: Holt, p.85.

[44] Beck, A. T. (1976) *Cognitive therapy and the Emotional Disorders* London: Penguin, p.243.

[45] Epstein, S. (1993) 'Emotion and Self-Theory' in Lewis, M and Havilland J. (eds) *Handbook of Emotions* New York; London: Guilford Press, p.323

[46] Barrow, R. (1990) *Understanding Skills* Ontario: Althouse, 1990 p.127.

[47] See Beck, A. T. (1976) *Cognitive therapy and the Emotional Disorders* London: Penguin.

[48] in Sloan, T. S. (1986) *Deciding* New York; London: MeHuen, 1986, p.45

[49] Bandura, A. (1977) 'Self-efficacy: Towards a unifying theory of behavioural change' *Psychological Review,* Issue 84, p.19)

[50] Kant, Buber, Winnicott, Kelly, Piaget and many others.

[51] Epstein, S. (1993) 'Emotion and Self-Theory' in Lewis, M and Havilland J. (eds) *Handbook of Emotions* New York; London: Guilford Press, p.322

[52] See, for example, Fransella, F. (1990) 'Personal construct therapy' in Dryden, W. (ed.) *Individual Therapy* Milton Keynes: Open University Press.

[53] More detailed description of this method can be found for example in Buzan, T. (1974) *Use Both Sides of Your Brain* E. P. Dutton.

[54] Fromm, E. (1973) *The Anatomy of Human Destructiveness* London: Jonathan Cape, p.240

[55] Adapting to some adverse circumstances (e.g. a compulsory army service or prison) may even require changes that are contrary to personal development. Similarly, switching from the habit of, for example, drinking coffee to drinking tea does not necessarily have an effect on one's development.

[56] See, for example, Horney, K. (1945) *Our inner conflicts* New York; London: W. W. Norton, 1992.

[57] Argyle, M. (1987) *The Psychology of Happiness* London: Methuen, p.116

[58] Barrow, R. (1990) *Understanding Skills* Ontario: Althouse, p.135

[59] Motivational conflicts are not included here, but in the area *Aims* (p.157).

[60] See James, W. (1890) 'The Consciousness of Self' in *Principles of Psychology,* Vol 1. New York: Dover Publications, 1950; Binswanger,

L. (1946) 'The existential analysis school of thought' in May, R., Angel, E. and Ellenberger, H. F. (eds) *Existence* New York: Basic Books, 1958; Boss, M. (1963) *Psychoanalysis and Daseinsanalysis* New York: Basic Books; Deurzen-Smith, E. van (1988) 'Clarification of personal worldview' in *Existential Counselling in Practice* London: SAGE

[61] These domains can also be related to Maslow's motivational levels (physiological and safety needs; belongingness and love needs; esteem needs; self-actualisation needs); Piaget's stages of cognitive development (sensory-motor period, preoperational thinking, concrete-operational thinking, formal-operational thinking); and Kohlberg's stages of moral development (pre-conventional, conventional, post-conventional, and universal).

[62] See the area *Harmonisation* (p.70).

[63] See Assagioli, R. (1965) *Psychosynthesis* London: Crucible, 1990, and Rainwater, J. (1979) *You are in charge* California: DeVorss & Company, 1989.

[64] Although it is closely related to the will, the term *will* is not used because of the ambiguity and controversy that surrounds it.

[65] Spence, J. T. and Helmreich, R. L. (1983) in Spence, J (ed.) *Achievement and Achievement Motives* San Francisco: W. H. Freeman, p.27.

[66] Assagioli, R. (1965) *Psychosynthesis* London: Crucible, 1990, p.131

[67] See, for example, Csikszentmihalyi, M. (1992) *Flow* London: Rider p.221 and p.278 and Bee, H.L. (1987) *The journey of adulthood* New York: Macmillan (ch. 10 and 13).

[68] See Haaften, W. van, Korthals, M., and Wren, T. (eds) (1997) *Philosophy of Development* Dondrecht: Kluwer Academic Publishers, p.77.

[69] See, for example, Oltmanns, T. F., Neale, J. M. and Davison, G. C. (1995) *Case Studies in Abnormal Psychology* New York: John Wiley & Sons, from p.306

[70] See the Practical level in the area *Stability* p.73.

[71] Eccles, J. (1983) 'Expectancies, Values and Academic Behaviours' in Spence, J. (ed.) *Achievement and Achievement Motives* San Francisco: W. H. Freeman, p.86)

[72] Folkman S. and Lazarus, R. (1990) 'Coping and Emotion' in Monat, A. and Lazarus, R. (eds) *Stress and Coping* New York: Columbia University Press, p.221

[73] *hubris* (that can be roughly translated as overconfidence) is a main theme of many Greek myths, often thought to be a cause of human tragedy.

[74] Isenberg, A. (1980) 'Natural Pride and Natural Shame' in Rorty, A. (ed.) *Explaining Emotions* Berkeley; London: University of California Press, p.365

[75] Weekes, C. (1962) *Self Help For Your Nerves* London: Angus & Robertson, p.145

[76] These terms do not have a value connotation, they refer to subjective perspectives.

[77] Goleman, D. (1995) *Emotional Intelligence* London: Bloomsbury, p.65

[78] *Ibid.*, p.67

[79] *Ibid.*

[80] *Ibid*, p.88

[81] Roemer, L. and Borkovec, T. (1993) 'Worry: Unwanted cognitive Activity That Controls Unwanted Somatic Experience' in Wegner, D. and Pennebaker, J. (ed.) *Handbook of Mental Control* Englewood Cliffs: Prentice Hall, from p.227

[82] Averill, J. (1980) 'Emotions and anxiety: sociocultural, biological, and psychological determinants' in Rorty, A. (ed.) *Explaining Emotions* Berkeley; London: University of California Press, p.68

[83] See, for example, May, R. (1950) *The Meaning of Anxiety* New York, London: W. W. Norton, 1979, p.197

[84] Argyle, M. (1987) *The Psychology of Happiness* London: Methuen, p.93-97.

[85] Wellek, A. (1970) 'Emotional Polarity in Personality Structure' in Arnold, M .B. (ed.) *Feelings and Emotions* New York; London: Academic Press, p.284

[86] Se Argyle, M. (1987) *The Psychology of Happiness* London: Methuen, p.128, and Privette, G. (1983) 'Peak experience, peak performance, and peak flow: a comparative analysis of positive human experiences' *Journal of Personality and Social Psychology*, Issue 45.

[87] Csikszentmihalyi, M. (1992) *Flow* London: Rider, p.67

[88] *Internal environment* refers to memories, thoughts, feeling, images, beliefs, desires, dreams and other mental events that constitute our inner world.

[89] Rogers, C. (1954) 'Toward a Theory of Creativity' in Parnes, S. J. and Harding, H. F. (eds) *A source Book for Creative Thinking* Charles Scribner's Sons, 1962, p.67

[90] See, for example, Berlyne, D. E. (1960) *Conflict, Arousal, and Curiosity* New York: McGraw-Hill.

[91] Gergen, K. (1969) *The Psychology of behaviour exchange* Reading (Mass.); London: Addison-Wesley, p.89

[92] Ford, D. (1987) *Humans as Self-Constructing Living Systems.* Mahwah, NJ: Lawrence Erlbaum, p. 534

[93] Fromm, E. (1973) *The Anatomy of Human Destructiveness* London: Jonathan Cape, p.241

[94] Eysenck, M. W. (1990) *Happiness* Hove: Erlbaum, p.120

[95] See area *Harmonisation* p.69.

[96] Fromm, E. (1973) *The Anatomy of Human Destructiveness* London: Jonathan Cape, p.240

[97] See Boss, M. (1977) *Existential foundations of Medicine and Psychology* New York; London: Aronson; or Yalom, I. (1980) *Existential Psychotherapy* (part I) New York: Basic Books.

[98] See the area *The present* (p.126).

[99] This one and the following point are addressed in the area *Meaning* (p.140)

[100] Lepp, I. (1968) *Death and its mysteries* New York: Macmillan; Kalish, R. A. (1981) *Death, Grief, and Caring Relationships* Belmont: Brooks/Cole.

[101] Baron, J. (1988) *Thinking and Deciding* Cambridge: CUP, p. 275

[102] See Assagioli, R. (1965) *Psychosynthesis* London: Crucible, 1990; Rainwater, J. (1979) *You are in charge* California: DeVorss & Company, 1989; Ferrucci, P. (1982) *What We May Be* London: Mandala

[103] Tolerance (and intolerance) can also refer to certain social attitudes. However, in this case it is not universal and irreducible, and therefore is not included here. Such attitudes will be addressed in the Social category within the area *Relating to others* (p.216).

[104] Matthews, K. A., Carver, C. S. and Scheier, M. F. (1982) 'Focus of Attention and Awareness of Bodily Sensations' in Underwood, G. (ed.) *Aspects of Consciousness* New York; London: Academic Press, p.191

[105] Argyle, M. (1987) *The Psychology of Happiness* London: Methuen, p.195

[106] Stoyva, J. and Carlson, J. (1993) 'A Coping/Rest Model of Relaxation and Stress Management' in Goldberger, L. and Breznitz, S. (eds) *Handbook of Stress,* 2nd ed. New York: The Free Press, p.732

[107] *Ibid.*, p.731-733.

[108] See Pennebaker, J. W. (1988) 'Confiding Traumatic Experiences and Health' in Fisher, S. and Reason, J. (eds) *Handbook of Life Stress Cognition and Health* New York: John Wiley & Sons, p.670

[109] *Ibid.*, p.672

[110] Empirical support for this method can be found, for example, in Goleman, D. (1995) 'Managing with Heart' in *Emotional Intelligence* London: Bloomsbury.

[111] Barrow, R. (1990) in *Understanding Skills* Ontario: Althouse, p.108.

[112] See Thomas, L. (1983) *The Youngest Science* New York; London: Academic Press.

[113] Victor Frankl have written several books on this subject: (1962) *Man's search for meaning* London: Hodder and Stoughten; (1970) *The will to meaning* New York: New American Library; (1978) *The unheard cry for meaning* New York [etc.]: Bantam. See also Yalom, I. (1980) *Existential Psychotherapy* New York: Basic Books.

[114] Bee, H. (1996) *The Journey of Adulthood* New Jersey: Prentice Hall, p. 329

[115] Argyle, M. (1987) *The Psychology of Happiness* London: Methuen, p.215

[116] In Norman, R. (1983) *The Moral Philosophers* Oxford: Clarendon Press, p.165).

[117] Klinger, E. (1977) Meaning and void: Inner experience and the incentives in people's lives Minneapolis: University of Minnesota Press.

[118] As defined in the introduction to this group, p.139.

[119] See Rainwater, J. (1979) *You are in charge* California: DeVorss & Company, p.202.

[120] There are also external limits to one's freedom that can be physical (e.g. gravitation force) or social (e.g. legal system), but they are only contingently related to autonomy. For example, learning to swim or fly an airplane may increase one's freedom but it does not, in itself, affect one's autonomy.

[121] Lazarus, R. (1975) 'The Self-Regulation of Emotion' in Levi, L. (ed.) *Emotions: Their Parameters and Measurement.* New York: Raven Press, p.62.

[122] Even if we accept a dubious claim that aggression, for example, is genetically predisposed, this still leaves room for a person to utilize it either in some competitive sports or jobs, or to waste it on street fights.

[123] This term is coined by psychologist Erick Berne, see, for example, his famous book *Games People Play* New York: Random House, 1964.

[124] In Sloan, T. S. (1986) *Deciding* New York; London: MeHuen, p.119

[125] Deurzen-Smith, E. van (1988) 'The Public world' in *Existential Counselling in Practice* London: SAGE, p.57

[126] Paraphrased in Sloan, T. S. (1986) *Deciding* New York; London: MeHuen, p.53

[127] Meiland, J. (1970) *The Nature of Intention* London: Methuen, p.78

[128] *Ibid.*, p.75

[129] Davidson, D. (1978) 'Intending' in *Essays on Actions & Events* Oxford: Clarendon Press, p.89)

[130] Taylor, G. (1985b) *Pride, Shame, and Guilt* Oxford: Claredon Press, p.124

[131] For example, one's need to change the environment can trigger a number of different desires: to go for a walk, to visit friends, to do some shopping, or even to watch a travel programme or read a book about an exotic place.

[132] Ford, M. E. and Ford, D. H. (ed.) (1987) *Humans as self-constructing living systems: putting the framework to work* Mahwah, NJ: Lawrence Erlbaum, p.292.

[133] Ford, D. (1987) *Humans as Self-Constructing Living Systems* Mahwah, NJ: Lawrence Erlbaum, p.412-413)

[134] King, L. (1998) 'Personal goals and personal agency' in Kofta, M., Weary, G. and Sedek, G. (ed.) *Personal Control in Action* New York; London: Plenum Press, p.124)

[135] Donaldson, M. *(1992) Human Minds* London: Penguin, p.110.

[136] See Goleman, D. (1995) *Emotional Intelligence* London: Bloomsbury, p.80-83.

[137] Cox, T. (1988) 'Psychobiological factors in stress and health' in Fisher, S. and Reason, J. (ed.) *Handbook of Life Stress Cognition and Health* New York: John Wiley & Sons, p.609.

[138] See Spence, J. T. and Helmreich, R. L. (1983) 'Achievement - Related Motives and Behaviours' in Spence, J (ed.) *Achievement and Achievement Motives* San Francisco: W. H. Freeman, p.25

[139] Csikszentmihalyi, M. (1992) *Flow* London: Rider, p.50.

[140] Unconstructive ones such as aggression, smoking or taking drugs are not included because they may bring, at best, only very short relief.

[141] See Wortman, C. and Silver, R. (1989) 'The Myths of Coping with Loss' in Monat and Lazarus (ed.) *Stress and Coping* New York: Columbia University Press, 1991.

[142] Gregory, R. (ed.) (1987) *The Oxford Companion to the Mind* Oxford, New York: Oxford University Press, p.749

[143] Stoyva, J. and Carlson, J. (1993) 'A Coping/Rest Model of Relaxation and Stress Management' in Goldberger, L. and Breznitz, S. (eds) *Handbook of Stress,* 2nd ed. New York: The Free Press, p.731

[144] Argyle, M. (1987) *The Psychology of Happiness* London: Methuen, p.116; and Pintrich, P. R. and Schunk, D. H. (1996) *Motivation in Education* Englewood Cliffs: Prentice Hall, p.266

[145] Pintrich, P. R. and Schunk, D. H. (1996) *Motivation in Education* Englewood Cliffs: Prentice Hall, p.285

[146] Marzano, R. J. *at al.*(1988) *Dimensions of Thinking* Alexandria, VA: ASCD, p.25

[147] *Ibid.*, p.284.

[148] Pintrich, P. R. and Schunk, D. H. (1996) *Motivation in Education* Englewood Cliffs: Prentice Hall, p.285

[149] Spence, J. T. and Helmreich, R. L. (1983) 'Achievement-Related Motives and Behaviours' in Spence, J (ed.) *Achievement and Achievement Motives* San Francisco: W. H. Freeman, p.25

[150] Pintrich, P. R. and Schunk, D. H. (1996) *Motivation in Education* Englewood Cliffs: Prentice Hall, p.277

[151] Stoyva, J. and Carlson, J. (1993) 'A Coping/Rest Model of Relaxation and Stress Management' in Goldberger, L. and Breznitz, S. (eds) *Handbook of Stress,* 2nd ed. New York: The Free Press, p.743-745

[152] One of the earliest observations came from the II World War. German war prisoners marching back from the East Front were more energetic than the soldiers escorting them, although they lived in worse conditions. It was stipulated that the reason for this was that they were going home, while the end of the journey for the soldiers meant going back to the front. A more familiar and common example is a different level of energy exhibited by winners and losers after a sport competition.

[153] For more detailed description of such exercises see Lawen, A. (1976) *Bioenergetics* London: Penguin.

[154] See Hall, N. (ed.) (1992) *The NewScientist Guide to Chaos* London: Penguin.

[155] Spence, J. T. and Helmreich, R. L. (1983) 'Achievement-Related Motives and Behaviours' in Spence, J (ed.) *Achievement and Achievement Motives* San Francisco: W. H. Freeman, p.24)

[156] Moustakis, C. (1967) *Creativity and Conformity* New York: Nostrand Reinhold, p.1

[157] For a more thorough account of this point, see Janis, I. L. (1972) *Victims of groupthink* Boston, Mass: Houghton Miflin.

[158] Kelman, H. C. (1961) 'Three Processes of Social Influence' in Jahoda, M. and Warren, N. (ed.) *Attitudes* London: Penguin, 1966.

[159] This last point is known as *group inertia* (or 'diffusion of responsibility'). For example, experimental evidence suggests that people are more likely to respond, and more quickly, to an emergency if they are alone, than with others (Latane, B. and Darley, J. (1968) 'Group inhibition of bystander intervention in emergencies' *Journal of Personality and Social Psychology,* vol. 10, p.215-221).

[160] Goleman, D. (1995) *Emotional Intelligence.* London: Bloomsbury, p.124.

[161] Note that moral sense relates to the perception and assessment of an action, rather than action itself (which is why it belongs to the *existence* mode). You can act morally without moral sense (because of benefits that it could bring, or because you are conditioned to do so). You can also act immorally despite your moral sense if other factors are sufficiently strong to override it.

[162] Moustakis, C. (1967) *Creativity and Conformity* New York: Nostrand Reinhold, p.94

[163] For bio-neurological support see Kegan, J. and Lamb, S. (ed.) (1987) *The Emergence of Morality in Young Children* Chicago: University of Chicago Press; Ruse, M. (1991) 'The significance of evolution' in Singer, P. *A Companion to Ethics* Oxford: Blackwell; Wilson, J. Q. (1993) *The Moral Sense* New York: The Free Press; Goleman, D. (1995) *Emotional Intelligence.* London: Bloomsbury; Jennings, C. (1999) 'The neurobiology of morals' *Nature* London: Macmillan Publishers. For psychological support see Assagioli, R. (1965) *Psychosynthesis* London: Crucible, p.233; Blum, L. (1980) *Friendship, Altruism and Morality* London: Routledge & Kegan Paul; and Turiel, E. (1983) *The Development of Social Knowledge* Cambridge University Press. Writings of Aristotle, Shaftsbury, Hutchinson, Heidegger, Nigel and McDowell provide philosophical support for this notion.

[164] Horney, K. (1945) *Our inner conflicts* New York: W. W. Norton, 1992, p.111

[165] Psychologists Piaget and Kohlberg were concerned with this type of development.

[166] Aristotle was one of the first thinkers who recognised the significance of developing morality in this direction.

[167] The importance of character for moral development was emphasised by Aristotle, and more recently by Philipa Foot ('Virtues and Vices' in *Virtues and Vices and Other Essays in Moral Philosophy* Berkeley; London: University of California Press, 1978), Blum, L. (*Friendship, Altruism and Morality* London: Routledge & Kegan Paul, 1980) and Slote, M. (*From Morality to Virtue* Oxford: Oxford University Press, 1992). Reason has a central role for philosopher Kant and psychologist Kohlberg (*The Philosophy of Moral Development* London: Harper & Row, 1981). For the role of affect see, for example, Nussbaum, M. (1986) *The fragility of Goodness* Cambridge: Cambridge University, and Stocker, M (1996) *Valuing Emotions* Cambridge: CUP.

[168] Apparently, there are some crooks who specialize in cheating their compatriots abroad who would rather trust them than 'foreigners'.

[169] Hochberg, J. (1978) 'Social Perception and Communication' in *Perception,* 2nd ed. Englewood Cliffs: Prentice Hall, p.224

[170] Downie, R. and Telfer, E. (1971) *Respect for Persons* London: Allen & Unwin, p.49.

[171] Goffman, E. (1967) *Interaction Ritual* London: Penguin Books, p.1

[172] Duck, S. (1991) *Friend for life* Harvester: Wheatsheat, p.45

[173] Goleman, D. (1995) *Emotional Intelligence* London: Bloomsbury, p.97

[174] Duck, S. (1991) *Friend for life* Harvester: Wheatsheat, p. 73

[175] Macquarrie, J. (1972) 'Feeling' in *Existentialism* London: Penguin Books, p.118

[176] Strictly speaking friendship and intrinsic relationship are not identical. As Wilson points out (*Love between Equals* London: Macmillan Press, p.45), friendship can be intrinsic, instrumental and contingent. This area includes only the first type.

[177] Ford, D. (1987) *Humans as Self-Constructing Living Systems* Mahwah, NJ: Lawrence Erlbaum, p.551

[178] See Duck, S. (1991) *Friend for life* Harvester: Wheatsheat, p.55

[179] *Ibid.,* p.128

[180] *Ibid.*

[181] *Ibid.*

[182] Sternberg, R. J. and Barnes, M. L. (1985) 'Real and ideal others in romantic relationships: Is four a crowd?' *Journal of Personality and Social Psychology,* Vol 49, Issue 6, p.134

[183] Bee, H. and Mitchell, S. (1984) *The Developing Person* London: Harper & Row p.572

[184] Jourard, cited in Duck, S. (1991) *Friend for life* Harvester: Wheatsheat, p.71

[185] Argyle, M. (1987) *The Psychology of Happiness* London: Methuen, p.199

[186] Assertiveness implies behaviour between permissiveness and aggressiveness. Overly 'assertive' behaviour that may cause some negative feelings is not considered to be assertiveness at all, because it usually covers insecurity.

[187] Goleman, D. (1995) 'The Master aptitude' *Emotional Intelligence* London: Bloomsbury, p.75)

[188] The empirical research that supports this point can be found in Howarth I. and Dussuyer, D. (1988) 'Helping People Cope with the Long-term Effects of Stress' in Fisher, S. and Reason, J. (eds) *Handbook of Life Stress Cognition and Health* New York: John Wiley & Sons, p.662.

[189] Hatfield, E. and Rapson, R. (1993) 'Love and Attachment Processes' in Lewis, M and Havilland J. (eds) *Handbook of Emotions* New York; London: Guilford Press, p. 598.

[190] *Ibid.,* p.600

[191] *Ibid.,* p.599-600

[192] Byrne, D. and Murnen, S. (1988) 'Theories of Love and Relationship Maintenance' in Sternberg, R. and Barnes, M. (eds) *The psychology of love* New Haven; London: Yale University Press, p.303

[193] See Gergen, K. (1969) *The Psychology of behaviour exchange* Reading (Mass.); London: Addison-Wesley, p.89; and Sternberg, R. J. (1986) 'A triangular theory of love' *Psychological Review,* Vol 93, 2, p.134

[194] Wilson, J. (1995) *Love between Equals* London: Macmillan Press, p.43

Personal Synthesis courses are available for individuals, educational institutions and professional organisations. Training and materials for those who would like to run the programme are also available. For further details, please, contact us on:

info@personalsynthesis.org